A NOTE ON THE AUTHOR

Zoë Howe's books include *Barbed Wire Kisses – The Jesus and Mary Chain Story, Stevie Nicks – Visions, Dreams and Rumours, Typical Girls? The Story of the Slits* and *'How's Your Dad?': Living in the Shadow of a Rock Star Parent.* She co-authored and collated Dr Feelgood guitarist Wilko Johnson's memoir *Looking Back at Me* (Cadiz Music, 2012) and was a contributing author to the Eel Pie Island book *British Beat Explosion: Rock'n'Roll Island* (Aurora Metro, 2013).

Zoë's journalism has appeared in The Quietus, *Company Magazine, Notion*, BBC Music, Holy Moly, Classic Rock and *NME*, and she has made music radio series for stations including Resonance FM. Zoë can be heard talking about rock'n'roll from time to time on BBC 6 Music, BBC London, Absolute Radio, E4 and Planet Rock. She lives in Leigh on Sea with her husband Dylan and cat Marzipan.

First published in Great Britain in 2015
by Polygon, an imprint of Birlinn Ltd.

Birlinn Ltd
West Newington House
10 Newington Road
Edinburgh EH9 1QS
www.polygonbooks.co.uk

ISBN 978 1 84697 335 2
eBook ISBN 978 0 85790 264 1

British Library Cataloguing-in-Publication Data
A catalogue record for this book is available on
request from the British Library.

Design and typesetting by Teresa Monachino
Printed by T J International Ltd, Padstow

ZOË HOWE

LEE BRILLEAUX

ROCK'N'ROLL GENTLEMAN

THE ADVENTURES OF DR FEELGOOD'S ICONIC FRONTMAN

Polygon

CONTENTS

Prolougue.

In this book we have included some of the stories that for one reason or another we have decided to exclude from the Crollie Art books. These stories are divided into two main categories — the Absurdist style and the crollie style. I hope that you do not find these stories funny as they are not meant to be humourous. (this applies to the crollie Art books) They are intended purely as stimulants of the imagination apart from being examples of absurdist writing.

Remember that some of these stories may sound stupid and silly at first sight, but dig deeper under this mask of absurdism and impossibility and you will find the true meaning of the story and its application to modern day life. In this book we attempt to destroy or at least break down the modern day faults of society ie. officiality, conformity to a ridiculous degree and petiness. This book also aims to destroy with obliterating vitality the answer that is a classic of our time "Oh its always done this way".

L Collinson.

A 'prologue' written by the teenage Lee Collinson in one of the school exercise books he transformed with his friends into a 'Crollie Art Book' (more on these later). It seemed oddly fitting for this book in that, unwittingly, Lee has somehow provided the prologue to his own biography.

PROLOGUE

What is a rock'n'roll gentleman, and how does one become one?

There aren't many bona fide examples to look to for inspiration. Some have tried to become one, only to fail. Some don't try at all, proudly going to the other extreme. Some wear the costume and assume this to be sufficient. It is not.

The true rock'n'roll gentleman is hard to find. The process of becoming one is equally challenging and time-consuming. He is one who takes pride in how he lives, works, plays and dresses; one who greets his days and nights with energy and commitment; listens rather than talks, buys a round (and expects you to as well), makes mistakes and owns them. A self-educated, self-made individual capable of doing, at times, utterly ungentlemanly things in an utterly gentlemanly manner. Most of the time anyway. It is worth remembering that this particular example is also someone who, as the poet Hugo Williams observed, had a remarkable flair for conjuring obscenity out of mundanity. If you were hoping to read the tale of a saint, now would be an excellent time to go elsewhere.

But in these dark times of the reality show, the middle-class pop monopoly, the auto-tuned monstrosity, the self-aggrandising Facebook addiction and the brash cruelty of tabloid culture, there remains a figure we can look to, a man whose combination of qualities, honed and cultivated throughout decades, endures beyond trends, beyond the machinations of the music business, beyond even music, and ultimately beyond death itself. Ladies and gentlemen, I give you Lee Brilleaux. No angel, but a rare and extraordinary cove, certainly. This vibrant, multi-faceted character, often left in the margins, lived by his wits, was addicted to 'the road' and survived show business by refusing to take it too seriously.

Ask anyone about Brilleaux and the word 'gentleman' will usually be uttered within the first sentence. That defining word had to be in the title of this book, arguably before even 'Dr Feelgood'. Brilleaux was, of course, the mercurial frontman of this underrated British rhythm & blues group, a band that roared out of the Thames Estuary in 1974, ripped into London's pub rock scene, booted the hippy past well out of the picture and kickstarted punk in turn, frightening, thrilling and motivating as they went.

There were, initially, two great frontmen in Dr Feelgood: Brilleaux was one half of an incendiary double act with guitarist Wilko Johnson; two great friends and mutual admirers who would eventually end up 'hating' each other. But there's a sense that some etheric version of Wilko and Lee will always exist in a way – in the belligerent rhythmic interplay between Lee's voice and Wilko's guitar, and the fearsome chemical reaction that seemed to occur whenever they interacted (or didn't) on stage. That energy was so intense it probably still hasn't dissipated.

Brilleaux, alongside Feelgood manager Chris 'Whitey' Fenwick, would take the band into the 1980s and 1990s after not just Wilko's departure, but that of original rhythm section Big Figure (drums, glowering) and Sparko (bass, pelvic thrusts) as well. Indeed, they propelled the group beyond even Brilleaux's own demise in 1994, at the age of just forty-one. Despite his erstwhile bandmates' initial reluctance, Lee Brilleaux insisted that 'no one is indispensable', insisted they carried on bringing good-time R&B to the faithful.

I've wanted to write about Lee since I first saw Julien Temple's Dr Feelgood film *Oil City Confidential*. Watching it with Wilko at London's ICA in 2010, this documentary, crammed with as much archive footage as Temple could find and edited (by Caroline Richards) in a choppy, high-octane style, absolutely befitted the Feelgoods. It's hard to convey the real magic and energy of a live performance on screen, but *Oil City* comes close – just seeing them on the screen like that gave me a physical rush.

Wilko and I knew each other, and were soon to start working on *Looking Back at Me*, the book that would become Wilko's 'memoir' of sorts, but in the back of my mind there was always the intention to write about Lee one day too – even if it was just a compendium of memories and anecdotes that would principally be for his family.

This book was originally to have 'Roadrunner' in the title, an early suggestion of Lee's wife Shirley, being as it was Lee's favourite song (the Junior Walker version). The song says a lot about him, not least because of his obsessive touring schedule and lifelong love of a good wander, the freewheeling life of the map, the suitcase, the tour bus, the next venue, the next town, the next country, and the next, and the next.

Even as a teenager, Lee Collinson (Brilleaux is, unsurprisingly, a pseudonym, the origins of which we will explore later) would go on epic treks, some of which would go on for days. Even as a youngster living in Ealing in the late 1950s, he would take himself off on the train, alone, to Canvey Island in Essex where his grandparents lived, a place infinitely more interesting and exotic to a little boy (mud, marshes, the beach, the boats, the shacks, the wildlife, the sunsets) than a built-up suburb of West London.[1] 'In the end it got so bad,' Lee's mother Joan lamented, 'we never saw the boy ... ' And so the Collinson family packed up and moved east to Canvey, where Lee's life would truly start. Lawless, eccentric, a little fierce, Canvey had its own thing going on. Rather like Lee. You can see how the two were magnetised to each other.

Even from an early age, the fast-moving, fast-talking Lee was a roadrunner to his very bones, thanks to his peripatetic parents; after the restriction of the war years, the Collinsons wanted to see the world, and they'd take a very young Lee to Egypt, Italy, Switzerland – 'he was so excited to see the snow for the first time,' said Joan.

And so, as appropriate as 'Roadrunner' would have been, eventually it was agreed something broader was needed for the title of this book, something that wouldn't only attract the attention of those who already know about Brilleaux and his travelling-man image. There seemed so much to put across simply on the cover that the title was getting longer and longer ... But the essence of 'Roadrunner' is still at its core. As well as being a celebration of a life, this book will explore different aspects of Lee: what was important to him, his interests, hidden gifts, quirks and flights of fancy. Sometimes the biography will turn into a handbook; sometimes the handbook will turn into a surreal trip into Lee's imagination, a place from which Edward Lear-esque poems, Heath Robinson-style illustrations and stories hilarious, dark and peculiar would often emerge. Amid the main text you'll find wisdom, asides, hangover cures and a few morsels of the unexpected.

There are many who knew and continue to love Lee who still ask themselves, 'what would Brilleaux do?' in times of conflict. His take (or presumed take) remains a benchmark of ethics, quality, style and class, whether cogitating over which record to buy or during a moment of indecision at the bar. So, to return to the original question, 'what is a rock'n'roll gentleman, and how does one become one?', your advised course of action is to read on and learn from the best.

Z.H.
November 2015

Family snaps from Lee's early years in Durban, South Africa, and the UK. Top right: Lee masters two wheels outside the family home in Ealing, West London, after moving back to the UK. Lee's mother Joan Collinson was adamant he would not be educated in apartheid-torn South Africa. Images are from Joan Collinson's private collection.

1. JOURNEY TO THE CENTRE OF CANVEY ISLAND

Even as a boy he had a fearlessness and sense of adventure.

Joan Collinson, Lee's mother.

Canvey Island, Essex, 1965. A regular Saturday night at the Collinsons' bungalow. TV on. A skinny, intense, preternaturally aware thirteen-year-old boy stares at the flickering screen. His father Arthur, known to all as 'Collie', equally intense, glances sharply between the black and white of the television and the black and white of his book. Joan, the boy's mother, is engrossed in needlework, only occasionally lifting her eyes to the television set, chuckling at the sarcastic commentary given by her only son. All there with the acid drops, that one.

Something is about to change.

'And here they are – The Rolling Stones …'

All eyes to the screen. Collie and Joan see five sneering, long-haired reprobates, they hear a god-awful racket. Lee sees, and hears, the future: his future. He sits up, he takes them in, he's hooked. The fact that his parents are purportedly 'horrified by them, their *hair*' – merely adds to their raw appeal. Beyond the defiant fringes, the scowls, the challenging eyes and general air of unpredictability, there is intelligence, frustration and subversion – qualities not alien to Lee's own character. There is also rhythm and blues. The Bo Diddley beat of 'Not Fade Away'. The neurotic, tremulous slide of 'Little Red Rooster', contrasting with Mick Jagger's lazy, insolent vocal. In a moment, the twee, chirpy pop of the 1960s falls away and exposes something dark, exciting, promising treasures Lee had hitherto been oblivious to.

'I thought they were great,' said Lee. 'I always liked pop music, but it wasn't until I heard blues via people like the Stones that I really started to become obsessive about it. There was something about that music which a thirteen-year-old schoolboy from Canvey Island just fell in love with. First time I saw Muddy Waters on TV, I just couldn't believe it.'

The television, above and beyond the record player at this stage, was the most powerful initial conduit of the music that would take over Lee's life. To suddenly be exposed to black American blues – and to be able to see the people who made it – was revelatory. Another equally vital connector was a charismatic older boy called John Wilkinson, later known as Wilko Johnson, who played skiffle and blues with his brother Malcolm and their friends around Canvey. We'll come to him later.

Lee might have been described frequently as a Canvey boy, but his background was a little more exotic than that. Lee's parents were 'bored', as Joan put it, after the long war. 'We just wanted to get away.' Arthur, a lathe operator (and an impressive flyweight boxer, which goes some way to explain Lee's ability with his fists), moved himself and Joan, a legal secretary, from Ealing to South Africa in response to a call-out for skilled contractors. Lee Collinson would be born in Durban on 10 May 1952. As a toddler, Lee would pick up a few words of Zulu from his nanny Rosie allegedly before he could even speak English, but Joan was adamant their son should not be educated in South Africa.

'The system was so bad,' she said. 'They'd just indoctrinate him with all these terrible [beliefs] … apartheid, shocking it was. I was always in trouble because I'd go in a shop and they served all the whites, no matter how long a poor black man stood there. When I could see it was his turn and they were going to serve me, I'd say, "No, he was here before me." I became very unpopular. I expect I'd have got thrown out of South Africa eventually.'

By the winter of 1955, the Collinsons had moved back to London, with Lee attending Oaklands Primary School in Hanwell, and eventually, after passing the 11-plus, Ealing Grammar.[2] Lee was clever, but he wasn't just book smart. He was perceptive and creative, a voracious reader, an observer and a questioner, hungry for discovery and fuel for his imagination. Luckily for him, holidays would be spent with his grandparents on Canvey. In comparison to smashed-up postwar London, this peculiar place in the Thames Estuary was a haven of wildlife, mystery and Huckleberry Finn possibilities. 'He liked it so much that on Fridays, I'd get home from work and there'd be a note on the table – "Dear Mum, gone to Nan's, see you Sunday." And that was it. He'd be gone for the weekend. It was easy from Ealing Broadway, you could pick up the Barking train.'

Lee was a sociable boy, and it didn't take long for him to build up a social circle on Canvey. There were always other children around, mudlarks beckoning Lee to join them. The most significant of these kids was Chris White (aka Chris Fenwick), who would introduce Lee to his own friends, including Geoff Shaw and John B ('Sparko') Sparkes. The boys would spend hours meandering about the Island and engaging in all manner of covert piratical shenanigans from their HQ 'The Hut' on the Long Horse Island sandbank in Benfleet Creek.

Chris Fenwick

Lee and I were friends since I was eleven years old. He was a great and colourful friend to have at that age. We did a lot of adventuring together when we were kids. We both had an interest in boats, and built a camp on Long Horse Island in the marshes off Canvey. We went on a barge trip to the Dutch canals when I was thirteen and then the next year we hitchhiked to the Rhine valley in Germany. Those were big things for such young guys.

Lee was a very clever and intelligent guy, and introduced me to literature, blues music and many other things. He was the main man in our earliest group, the Southside Jug Band, playing slide guitar and banjo. I was allowed to play the jug and the washboard, but the thing that I was best at was taking the hat around. I guess that's why I fell into management.

Initially, Lee Collinson was known to Chris's wider circle of friends simply as 'the boy from London', a title that radiated a certain intrigue in itself, but his growing enthusiasm for visiting Canvey independently of his parents meant that the Collinsons themselves would soon install themselves on the Island, building a house near the Whites' on Kellington Road, if only to guarantee they could actually spend some time with their roving son.

'We lived right on the sea wall facing Hadleigh Castle,' explained Joan. 'Lee and his friends would go out in the boat, and every hour I'd go upstairs with my binoculars to check they were [all right]. He and Chris would row, pick up people from the camp two at a time, charge them sixpence each, and take them out to Two Tree Island. Lee would make up all these stories about monsters and things ... They were such buddies. This boat, he called it *The Corsair*, he put up the skull and crossbones on a black flag and there he was, Pirate Lee! All summer was spent like that, it was a child's dream, really.'

'Canvey was a rural community in lots of ways,' Lee told the writer Christopher Somerville. 'We knew about tides, about birds and shellfish, alongside the bookies and the boozers.'

There would be plenty of *Boy's Own*-style adventures on the mudflats, including one in which the intrepid and ever curious Lee took himself off in his little dinghy and tried to row against the cross-currents over the shipping channel to North Kent, a trip that culminated in him having to be rescued by the lifeboat. 'They'd put him in a boiler suit,' remembers Joan. 'He was in big trouble when he got back.'

'It was all boyhood stuff,' remembers Geoff Shaw. 'Climbing up things, being horrible. Chris and Lee were special. Most of the kids at school were just regular guys, everybody wanted to be like everybody else, but Chris was sparkly, confident and bright. Lee was probably even brighter. As a personality, Lee was really powerful.' Lee and Chris would keep the other boys entertained with constant mimicry and role playing. 'They were both really good at accents,' adds Geoff. 'I don't remember them ever speaking in a normal way for more than ten minutes.'

Lee would attend Rayleigh Sweyne grammar school on the mainland, and here he instantly connected with another kindred spirit: Phil 'Harry' Ashcroft. So began an epoch of deep, sometimes surreal conversations, swapped books, long walks and, it must be said, a bit of a reign of terror over the younger or duller students. 'We weren't always very nice,' admits Ashcroft. Even at this age Lee was testy, nervy; he'd pace and expound, sometimes plotting, sometimes ranting, sometimes just using his authoritative persona to keep the people around him on their toes. (In later years at Sweyne, he'd steal a prefect's badge and stride about intimidating younger pupils – he wasn't a prefect at all but he had the swagger and the confidence, and they believed it.)[3] There was a sense of Lee, even at this age, being fully formed.

'Third year, Rayleigh Sweyne, September 1965,' remembers Phil Ashcroft. 'We were in the same class, 3b. We just happened to be sitting next to each other.' Like Phil, Lee was a 'thinking kind of person. The other kids were hitting each other with rulers[4] and talking about football. Lee had this laser-like consciousness that used to take things in.'

'He was precocious when it came to his understanding of personality,' continues Phil. 'We'd have endless conversations during private study about meaning, death, history, art, the characters of Canvey Island...' Lee's tales of Canvey were, to be fair, as much of an education as anything else. Sex, alcohol, violence: Oil City delivered it all. The fact that the community lived with the threat of devastating floods, fires and the possibility of gas explosions from the nearby refineries seemed to engender something of a seize-the-day attitude.

Canvey Island was like 'another world over the water', Phil observes, remembering Lee getting on a bus that looked more like a cattle truck to take him and the other Canvey kids back through the mists and marshes to that strange place below sea level, in the shadow of Coryton's blazing tower, fascinating and frightening in equal measure.

'There'd always be weird stuff happening over there,' says Phil, who lived in Hadleigh, where little seemed to happen in comparison. 'There were still strange old people living with chickens on bits of scrubland and people with odd religious beliefs. It was a Deep South feeling. There'd be lots of people who were just kind of ... odd.' Come Monday morning, Lee would be back at school, tantalising his friends with wild but believable stories of 'gangster activity, so-and-so getting his legs broken ... he had a vivid imagination'.

Another vital and enduring element of Lee's magnetic character was that he was older in his way and his look than his contemporaries. At fourteen, many boys are monosyllabic, awkward and hormonally conflicted, but Lee was articulate, capable and apparently confident, and this unlocked a door into other worlds – specifically, at this stage, the world of girls. His friends were, like him, surrounded by girls every day – Sweyne being a mixed school – but talking to them was another matter. Lee was 'at least two or three years ahead of the rest of us', said Phil, and his tales of conquests on Canvey (admittedly not necessarily all his own) were thrillingly lurid, possibly embellished and always involving activities 'of an unmentionable nature. I would blush to repeat them. *Things* happening in the park. He did a lot of reporting. It was fairly animal at times on Canvey.' Lee was an avid storyteller, and in the drab, pylon-studded plains of Rayleigh, having him around certainly made school life more colourful for the people in his orbit – teachers included, not that they necessarily appreciated it in the same way.

Lee viewed school, teachers in particular, through narrowed eyes of mistrust. He was mature enough to realise this was not all there was, that school wasn't to be taken entirely seriously, that impressing teachers was not a satisfactory ambition, and that said teachers were rarely the admirable figures they purported to be. Lee took an autonomous stance to learning; a dedicated self-educator, he inhaled adventure stories and biographies, and he would also absorb classics such as *The Grapes of Wrath*, *Robinson Crusoe*, *Great Expectations* and Joseph Heller's *Catch-22*, the last becoming 'like a bible for us, a template'. Lee was Yossarian, naturally, and he and Phil would liken various people they knew to the characters in the book, immersing themselves in the satire.

Surrealism was an important survival mechanism for Lee, Phil and their friends (including the marvellously named John 'Crusher'

Wardropper), often providing the mental escape they required in order to avoid becoming beaten down by the system or the futility of school rules. No one could say they weren't productive; together they put exercise books to good use by filling them with bizarre and brilliant sketches, witty couplets and doom-mongering stories, riddles and maybe a bit of free association. The books that contained these very art-school doodlings would be titled 'Crollie Art Books'. (Phil Ashcroft has retained a number of them.) Think Lewis Carroll, Spike Milligan and John Lennon in *A Spaniard in the Works* mode.

'Lee had started vandalising desks by doing pseudo-abstract art in biro, big eyeballs and jagged bits, like a *Punch* version of modern art,' says Phil. 'Then he started pinching exercise books. Lee did this thing with little stick figures and called it "The Pillock's Progress", long stories about "beasties". I was enthralled. It was like performance art.

'Then we drew a Map of the World, with Canvey Island right in the middle, and I just enjoyed that so much, taking reality and mixing it all up.' (As for Canvey's very symbolic position bang in the centre, 'we all knew that it wasn't, but we liked to think that it was,' said Lee. 'Bit like the British Empire.')

Another way to escape would be to skive off, something Lee and Phil did quite a lot. They'd use their time to wander and talk about books ('We decided James Joyce was cool'), drifting for miles over the fields of Hullbridge and Rawreth, and at one point attempting to walk from Chelmsford to Colchester, armed with Knorr packet soup, after hitching a ride to the county town. It was a blazingly hot day, but Lee was determined to continue wearing the deerstalker hat he'd come out with. With the combination of heat, fatigue and car fumes, 'we were half demented by the time we got there'.

If the weather wasn't conducive to exploring, another favourite activity during periods of truancy would be to visit an unlovely destination Lee and Phil dubbed the 'Armpit Café' at nearby Rayleigh Station. 'A horrible little place with windows that would steam up,' remembers Phil. 'Lee would smoke Player's Number 6 and we'd drink rancid tea and eat Penguin or Blue Riband biscuits. The place would be full of sweat and smoke and all these down-at-heel characters. It was a place to hang out. We were trying to create a colourful life for ourselves.'

Lee was a leader, the kind of commanding character who would automatically be viewed as a mentor by the kids around him, his presence sparking or nurturing an open enthusiasm for literature, music, even architecture. But apart from his wise, witty parents, who was Lee's mentor? And did he even need one? Not necessarily, but a character was about to come into the frame who would, inadvertently, shove him in the direction he was already starting to move towards, give him something to aspire to, and, ultimately, be a figure that would be associated with him, whether he liked it or not, for the rest of his life. Enter the force of nature that is Wilko Johnson, then a nineteen-year-old going by his given name of John Wilkinson, and his brother Malcolm. They were both accomplished, off-the-wall guitarists, artists, blues obsessives. For once, Lee himself would be in awe.

One of their chief diversions on the tough Canvey Island (considering they weren't particularly into drinking or fighting) was busking with the jug band they'd formed, which went by the name of 'The Northside Jug Band'. 'I used to play violin and harmonica,' recalls Wilko, 'and my brother used to play banjo and guitar. There was another guy with a tea-chest bass, and we used to play on the seafront.'

'We did a performance at the Casino Ballroom,' adds Malcolm. 'The thing I remember is these younger kids coming up and asking about the music.' These 'younger kids' were Chris White, John B Sparkes and Lee Collinson. 'The one who turned out to be Lee seemed to ask the most questions.' The vaudevillian aspect of these hip beatnik-type characters, bashing out ancient country blues stompers, was irresistible to Lee. He wanted a piece of it.

Wilko continues. 'Lee, even then, seemed so self-possessed and intense, and obviously *clever*. There was something about him. He was asking about this skiffle group of ours, and we were talking about blues music. Now, these boys were about fourteen – big age gap at that point – they were like kids. The one I remembered was Lee. I remember walking home with my brother, and we were like, "Fucking hell, that kid's a bit sharp, isn't he?" He *radiated*.'

For Lee's part, 'something clicked' when he saw The Northside Jug Band. 'I thought, this is better than The Rolling Stones. Not better played, just meaner. I was really knocked out by it.'

Neither party could have known yet quite what this meeting had set in motion, although Wilko was struck by Lee's vivid personality and Lee was duly inspired to plunge further into his nascent fascination with the blues. Wilko would subsequently go up to Newcastle to read English at university, but he never forgot the eager, charismatic young boy he had met back home, and they would encounter each other from time to time when Wilko and Malcolm came back from their respective studies during the holidays. On one of these occasions, Malcolm found

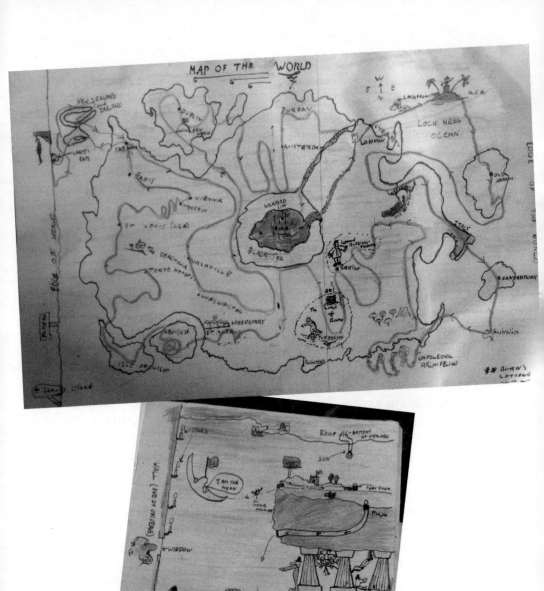

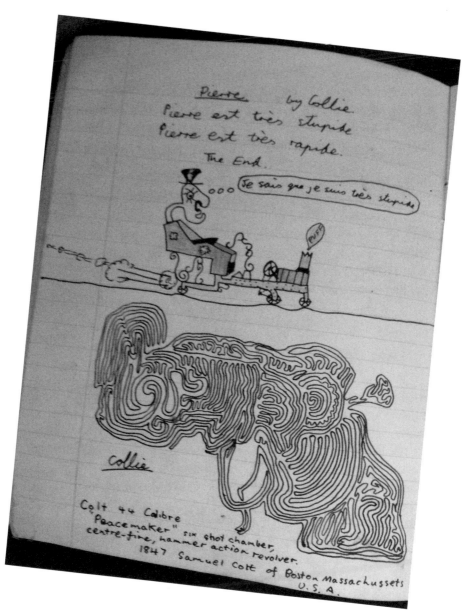

From the 'Crollie Art Books' of Lee's schooldays at Rayleigh Sweyne. The famous 'Map of the World', as seen in Julien Temple's film Oil City Confidential, was created with Phil 'Harry' Ashcroft, and naturally has Canvey Island right at the centre. Access to these precious books was kindly provided by Phil Ashcroft.

that Lee had been doing some studying of his own. '[He] seemed to have developed a much wider range of knowledge about obscure blues singers than either of us. It took some careful conversational skills to cover up my relative ignorance.'

Wilko might not have realised it fully at the time, but Lee was just as intrigued by him as he was by Lee – more so, in fact. Because of Wilko's relative life experience, Lee looked up to him as a figurehead, even doing a school project on the Icelandic sagas after learning about them from Wilko, who had been studying them at university. Lee and Wilko's relationship might have broken down irrevocably just a decade later ('the old feet of clay,' muses Wilko), but at this stage Lee was in Wilko's thrall.

'I remember getting reports of this John Wilkinson,' said Phil. 'This guy really impressed Lee. He read literary books and knew about politics and Karl Marx … he was in the background as this revered figure who was seen as cool and amazing. We'd get reports about Wilko having taken LSD and having out-of-body experiences above Canvey Island, stuff like that. "John Wilkinson did this, John Wilkinson did that."'

When it came to R&B, what grabbed Lee and appealed to his inner detective was the 'wealth of untapped talent' that was out there to discover, glimpsed thanks to bands such as The Stones, The Animals and The Who. There was a plethora of black American artists who just should have been better known – the likes of Little Walter, John Lee Hooker, Muddy Waters and, of course, Howlin' Wolf. Known to his mother as Chester Burnett, this outwardly intimidating purveyor of Chicago blues possessed the kind of voice – rich, emotive and charged with overwhelming life force – that could pull the shutters down on daylight, raise the dead and shake the foundations of your weather-boarded Canvey shack. 'I do everything the old way,' the singer once said. It's a quote that could easily have come from the lips of Lee Brilleaux.

Once the fuse had been lit, Lee's father's prized jazz collection provided another route to the blues for Lee, who was tracing the music back to its roots via every group, combo and artist he could find. 'I was listening to a real hotchpotch. Some people specialise in Chicago, or Mississippi, the Delta … I liked all of it.' Catholic tastes within the blues remit, maybe, but while many of his contemporaries were avidly paying attention to the pop currently bothering the hit parade or whimpering its way out of the wireless speaker, Lee's taste was becoming all the more focused (with occasional deviations, often in the name of surrealism – the Bonzo Dog Doo Dah Band, featuring fellow Southend native Vivian Stanshall, were a favourite).

This wiry, blue-eyed white kid wanted to understand the music, the lifestyle and the people at the heart of the blues on an intellectual as well as a visceral level. He wanted to collect the records, subscribe to magazines such as *Blues Unlimited* (he had a bit of money to spend on such things as he did odd gardening jobs on Canvey), and immerse himself in the biographies of bluesmen such as Big Bill Broonzy, allowing the louche, evocative stories to conjure images of the Deep South in his mind. Lee would later look back and wonder whether he bored his friends with this fevered obsession, but it seems this was not the case. (Although as far as his mother was concerned, the constant record playing 'nearly drove me mad. It never let up.')

'Lee played me records the like of which I'd never heard before,' remembers Geoff Shaw. 'Jesse Fuller, Leadbelly, spirituals … stuff I had no other way of hearing. The local record shop would have nothing in it other than what was in the charts. He turned me on to music. He opened up a world to me that was completely new.'

But ultimately, Lee Collinson didn't want to just read about bluesmen or even listen to them. He wanted to be one. Whether he was musically gifted or not was almost neither here nor there (a brief attempt at learning to play the violin bore no fruit – 'was never very good at it, hated it,' he grumbled). Rather it was about attitude and passion, *wanting* to do it from the very depths of your soul. And acknowledging what you want – even if you're not sure how to go about it yet – is when the stars begin to align.

Picking up a banjo and twanging out a bit of skiffle was a good place to start; it was easy to learn a few chords, and starting a jug band of his own with a flexible line-up of friends, or at least the ones he'd infected with his enthusiasm for blues, seemed simple enough. All they needed was that DIY skiffle mentality, some songs to cover and a bunch of instruments, some of which would be customised household items. Joan supplied the thimbles for the washboard, and Crusher specialised in playing the garden shears. 'He'd loosen the bolt in them so they made a really good noise,' says Sparko.

'It was completely Lee,' adds Geoff. 'We just followed. Lee had a handle on the music so he taught us how to use the instruments. Lew

Lewis was there, he was very talented, Phil Ashcroft, Rico Burt – crazy guy who would dress up as a Red Indian and run around the woods with spears – and Lee, who could do everything. He'd come round my house and basically he was in charge. "Right, here's what we're going to do." He'd get on the kitchen table and do crazy dances, Mick Jagger-style, we were there strumming away on out-of-tune guitars.'

Lee would sing as well as play banjo, the dexterous John Sparkes played 12-string guitar, and 'Chris Fenwick was playing jug, but very wisely took up managerial duties,' remembered Lee. 'Various other people drifted in and out. We used to play at the Canvey Club, busk outside the Monico, the Haystack, the Oysterfleet [which would later play host to the 'Dr Feelgood Music Bar'], and we won a talent competition at our local holiday camp. It was real good fun.'

The immediacy of being able to just turn up and play was appealing, as was the fact that they could make a few quid if they played the right songs outside the pub at closing time. It wasn't surprising that, when Wilko and Malcolm came home one summer and hung out in the High Street during Canvey Carnival, they saw that kid ('that *kid*') – the one who had impressed Wilko so much when they'd met at the Casino Ballroom – deftly strumming his banjo and looking moody in a jug band of his own. As moody as one could look on a carnival float anyway.

Chris was 'doing a kind of medicine show,' remembers Phil. 'He had bottles of coloured water and he was shouting away, Lee was playing his three chords.' They would be awarded an impromptu fourth prize for their efforts – the unusual sight and sound of this spirited gang of kids bashing away like a bunch of good ol' boys had obviously delighted people.

'When I saw them playing in the carnival,' says Wilko, 'I thought, wow, there's that guy! They've followed the jug band thing. And so it went on.'

Joan Collinson
Canvey Island was uniquely scruffy. There was no planning permission – you could put up anything you like. The roads didn't go anywhere. Even now on Canvey you can go down a road and it comes to a dead end for no reason.

The Frisco Bay Jug Band was awarded an impromptu fourth prize in Class
by Judge Mr. Bernard Braine, M.P.

Lee's jug band rocked Canvey Carnival and
various talent shows to boot. In true rock'n'roll
style, they are the only ones not smiling in the
bottom picture. One should always stay cool,
even when surrounded by grinning grown-ups
in party hats and (shudder) a black-and-white
minstrel.

Shirley Brilleaux

A postcard from Canvey, and Joan and Arthur
Collinson, Lee's parents.

2. THE ODYSSEY (TO NORTH KENT) – AND A BIG BAD WOLF

There's nothing white that I draw off at all. Everything's black. The things that inspire me to do what I do are black things. There isn't any white rock 'n' roll singer, with the exception, perhaps, of Jerry Lee Lewis, that I can take 100% seriously.

Lee Brilleaux in later years to Jonh Ingham, *Sounds*

The jug band went by many names: the Razzamatazz Washboard Band was one; at another stage it was Chrissy White and his Mad Mates (my personal favourite); then there was the Frisco Bay Jug Band, the Southside Jug Band … When it came to equipment, resourcefulness and imagination was key, and John Sparkes and Lee would tinker away in Collie's garage, with Collie himself occasionally peering in to make sure they weren't using up all of his paint.

One such creation would be Lee's own invention of an 'eight-string guitar, tuned like a banjo', as Sparko remembers. They would also customise paint pots and fix candles inside, ready to hang on the end of the guitar and warm the fingers when the weather started to bite. Equipment was wheeled about in an old pram, and once they'd worked up a set, Canvey, Pitsea and the surrounding areas were at their mercy. 'You should see how they were dressed,' adds Joan. 'It was *awful*.'

Rehearsals would take place in various halls and front rooms, including that of friend and promoter Maggie Newman, who would also fix up gigs for the band locally. Maggie remembered Lee was always friendly to her little girl, teaching her how to play cards. 'They often played poker when he was round,' said Maggie, 'until she started beating him.'

The set they were developing included numbers such as Jesse Fuller's 'San Francisco Bay Blues', plus 'a few Lovin' Spoonful and Chuck Berry covers … not really strict jug band music,' admitted Lee. 'We used to put in old rock'n'roll songs as well, because we were playing in pubs and we wanted to please our audience. To attract their attention for at least half of the time, we'd be playing Buddy Holly songs.' Even at this stage, Lee knew what his priority was: entertaining other people, giving the crowd what they wanted.

Before long it became clear that just playing around Canvey and Pitsea wasn't enough. It was time for the jug band to broaden their horizons. And so, during the summer holidays of 1967, they planned 'The Grand Perambulation of North Kent', also known as 'The First World Tour of Kent' – a 'very Lee adventure', as Sparko puts it, free-wheeling, Tom Sawyer-esque and involving a bit of camping in the woods. They may have been restricted to performing relatively locally, but Lee's mindset was global and he wanted to get out there and see as much as he possibly could. 'They'd go to a place where Chris's dad had some land,' said Joan. 'There was a dreadful old caravan on there, and dozens of them would go. The mind boggles how they all managed to get into it.'

'It was part of our fantasy,' explains Phil. 'We'd done the Map of the World, and we'd created illustrations of ridiculous machines for travelling the world. We were all very excited, and I remember meeting up at Pitsea station where we would go down to Gravesend. On the first visit to Kent, we were near some place mentioned in Dickens: "Ooh, that's in *Pickwick Papers*." I mean, you wouldn't associate Lee and *Pickwick Papers*.'

The boys located said 'dreadful caravan' and set up camp after having 'walked for miles in the dark, compulsively exploring,' Phil says. 'It was all a bit crazy.' At least they'd planned ahead when it came to their evening meal. The intrepid gang of troubadours (think Mark Twain meets *The Inbetweeners*) had bought a chicken from a farm earlier that day. 'This bloke killed it, and we cooked it on a spit and all got food poisoning,' recalls Phil, although in true adventure story-style, 'we all agreed it was "the best chicken we'd ever had".'

As the rest of the boys retreated, exhausted and ill, to the caravan, the embers of the fire providing the only discernible light, Lee and Phil walked off their stomach cramps before returning to the camp. 'Lee said, "Let's frighten them",' says Phil. 'I was going to make a *wooooo* noise, but Lee said, "No, just break twigs." So we snapped twigs and crept around carefully. They were really scared.' Ghost noises were too obvious. Planting the subtle idea that a murderer was homing in? That's another nightmarish level altogether, and not implausible. It's hard to imagine how these fifteen-year-olds – with the exception of Lee – kept these slightly risky adventures under wraps from their families. But, as we know, what goes on tour, stays on tour.

September swung around all too soon, inevitably ushering in the beginning of another school term. Lee's now infamous stage persona might not have been in evidence outside the pubs, as he hollered out 'Tiger Rag' to the clack and scrape of Rico's washboard and ceramic one-note *toot* of the jug, but combine these musical forays with being back at school – with all of the simmering frustration and barely contained personal anarchy that this brought out in him – then you have the first electrifying glimmers of the figure we would come to know as Lee Brilleaux.

Because of their morbid fascination with 'weird religious sects', the jug band had recently had a photograph taken outside the Assemblies of God building on Canvey to give a certain swampy, God-fearing appeal. While one of Lee's acts of theological mockery on school grounds didn't go down especially well (demonically painting a huge cross in white paint with a broom on the side of the school building), Sweyne's religious studies teacher Mr Little was naively heartened when Lee and Phil told him they wanted to 'do a play,' says Phil. 'He didn't know what he was letting himself in for … We wrote this thing, and I was the Scottish Calvinist minister who tells the story, all these people are in hell suffering, and there's God on his throne. As the people go down through the hatch into hell, they shout, "Oh God, we dinnae ken!" And he goes, "Well, you ken noo!" and slams the trapdoor shut.

'I ranted on with this sermon, and then we had this thing we culled from *The Grapes of Wrath* – early in the book there's somebody singing "Yes, sir, that's my saviour" to the tune of "Yes, Sir, That's My Baby" – so we constructed a few words for that, and then Lee suddenly burst into this frenzied banjo solo. It was the same quality he showed years later, uncanny. He'd go bright red with the effort and sheer intensity. The class were just gawping with wonder at this energetic outburst of banjo chords.'

The Grapes of Wrath was a favourite book of Lee's, and his leather schoolbag always contained at least a couple of volumes of Steinbeck or Dickens or Heller, maybe a copy of the satirical *The Good Soldier Švejk* by Jaroslav Hašek, and *Tom Brown's School Days* by Thomas Hughes. He would become consumed by the detail and atmosphere of the stories, allowing them to seep into his own world, taking the elements he liked and working them into his character, his speech or his clothes. Before long, and together with Phil and Crusher, he would form the dandyish Utterly Club, harking back to another time altogether.

They started turning up at school in waistcoats, attempting to wear their ties as cravats, sporting watch chains and even homemade monocles (made from National Health glasses they'd snapped apart).

Bass player Dave Bronze, who would work with Lee in the latter days of Dr Feelgood, remembers Lee telling him about his school gang: 'a bit like Lord Snooty and his pals,' he said. 'They'd wear monocles so they could then pop them out in dismay. His favourite thing was popping his monocle if a teacher spoke to him. I think the "gentleman" thing was nestling in the background just waiting to get out. He was a closet toff.'

Lee would also start a Canvey-based society along the same lines under the name of the Lovely Club, as Geoff Shaw recalls. 'We had to have waistcoats and canes, maybe hats, a watch chain – he got us all doing this. Also, you had to pass tests, one of which was on the railway bridge near Canvey. We'd have to walk over the outside of the bridge, risk our lives. Maybe we'd roast each other on a fire.' It's hard to imagine how the sight of the various Lovely Club inductees would have gone down on Canvey Island. These boys were brave.

Members of the Lovely Club would also form a short-lived and unpromising band called The Dandies, with Lee at the helm. 'It was awful,' admits Geoff. 'Hideous, terrible noise.' Lee (or 'Lee Collinson Esquire' as he sometimes referred to himself, even in schoolbooks) was never off duty when it came to being Utterly or indeed Lovely – Phil Ashcroft recalls 'hitch-hiking to the Isle of Wight' with Lee, and as they set up camp for the night, Ashcroft noticed that Lee had ironed his pyjamas and had fallen asleep with that Utterly Club badge of honour, his prized watch chain, coiled neatly by his side.

Together the Utterly Club flooded their monochrome school days with colour, whimsy, pranks and constant attempts to outwit those in charge, in particular Lee's arch-enemy: Sweyne headteacher Mr Bowman. On one occasion, after presumably being, in his opinion, unreasonably punished, Lee elected to urinate on Bowman's door handle. Sometimes monocle popping just wasn't enough. But this wasn't merely an impulsive act of fury. 'He did it on the Friday afternoon,' explains Phil, 'so that by Monday, it would be dry. It was vindictive but focused.'

These acts of vengeance weren't solely saved for authority figures. On yet another of Phil and Lee's lengthy walks, a passing cyclist gave them a two-finger salute as they trudged along in the rain. Immediately incensed, Lee sprinted after the culprit, pulled him off his bicycle, tore off his hat, and beat the boy around the head with it. The full stop to this swift and spellbinding performance was nothing short of inspired. Lee flung the cap into the front garden of a nearby house, so that the sheepish cyclist would have to undergo the humiliation not only of being pounded over the head with his own hat, but having to enter someone else's garden to retrieve it.

Lee could be mischievous, but his behaviour was, as we have seen, often inspired by serious indignation. On a good day, he would laugh at the rules and subvert them. On a bad day, he'd explode. At home he was treated more or less as an equal, or at least with the kind of honesty his parents believed he could handle as a mature young man,[5] which made the imposition of school life all the more disagreeable. From a distance, the cultural backdrop of the late 1960s might have seemed alive with psychedelia and freedom, but the predominant atmosphere as far as Lee was concerned was one of suburban mediocrity and postwar restriction, a Britain buttoned up tight. Lee and his friends weren't waiting for someone else to give them the answer or guide them through life by the hand. They didn't have time for that. It was a case of constructing your own world, or getting swallowed up by this one. It's no wonder that Lee, and Wilko, in the context of the Feelgoods, would be instrumental figures in encouraging so-called 'punk' attitude just a few years later.

'We had the Bonzo Dog influence, John Smith and the New Sound, "Winchester Cathedral, You're Bringing Me Down", we used to like that,' says Phil. 'If we found something different, we'd bring it into school to celebrate the weirdness. Lee bought a really colourful jacket in 1967, he wore that for a while, but there was always a hint of irony. At one point he had braces like a skinhead, then he bleached his hair with hydrogen peroxide. He'd gone from his normal mousey brown to blond, you could see him from the other side of the school field. At one point we all cut our hair really short at the front like Dave Higgs [from the Hot Rods]. It was about breaking out of this stifling lower middle-class world. We wanted to be personalities rather than just pupils.'

There were three pivotal moments in Lee Collinson's teenage life that would steer him firmly onto the right course. The first was, of course, the moment he first heard the Stones transmuting black American music from the South. The second was meeting John Wilkinson and being lit up by the music he was playing, not to mention the possibility that he could do it too. And the third must surely be the moment Lee and Chris went to see Howlin' Wolf play the King's Head in Romford after school. As hard as it may be to imagine Howlin' Wolf emerging to play the back room of a dingy East London pub on a summer's evening, he did, and it was a night Lee would never forget.

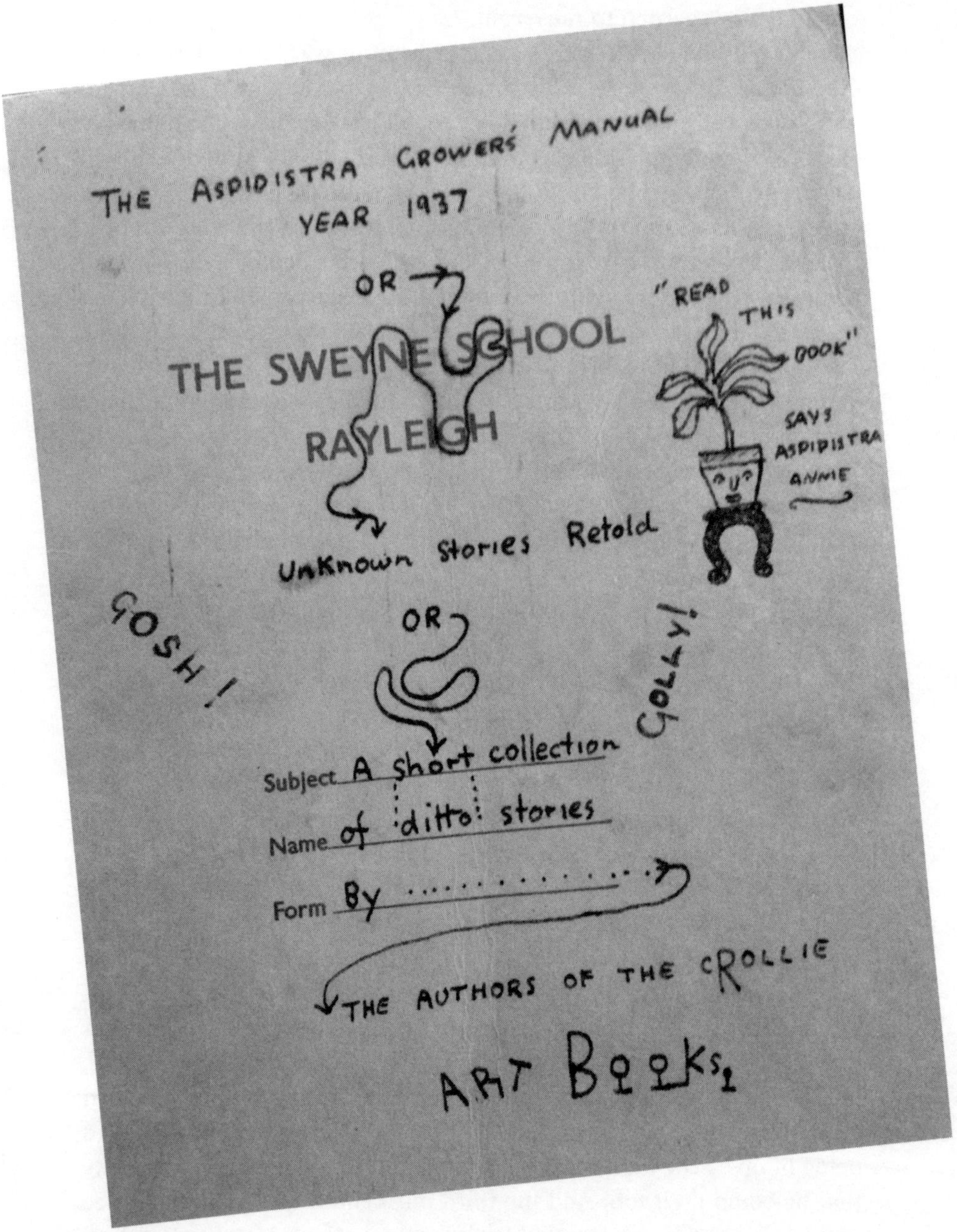

THE ASPIDISTRA GROWERS' MANUAL

YEAR 1937

OR

THE SWEYNE SCHOOL
RAYLEIGH

" READ THIS BOOK"

SAYS ASPIDISTRA ANNIE

Unknown Stories Retold

OR

GOSH!

GOLLY!

Subject A short collection

Name of ditto stories

Form By ....

THE AUTHORS OF THE CROLLIE

ART Books.

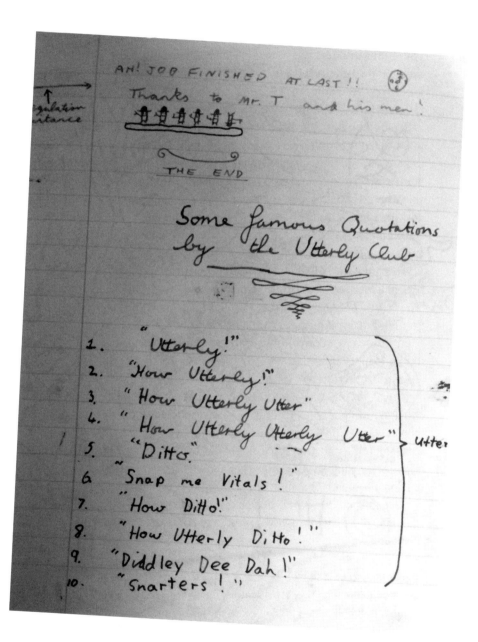

AH! JOB FINISHED AT LAST !!

Thanks to MR. T and his men!

THE END

Some famous Quotations
by the Utterly Club

1.   "Utterly!"
2.   "How Utterly!"
3.   "How Utterly Utter"
4.   "How Utterly Utterly Utter" ⎫ Utter
5.   "Ditto."
6   "Snap me Vitals!"
7.   "How Ditto!"
8.   "How Utterly Ditto!"
9.   "Diddley Dee Dah!"
10. "Snarters!"

regulation
distance

More 'Crollie Art Book' madness, plus some
Utterly Club maxims. Courtesy of Phil Ashcroft.

'Lee said Howlin' Wolf rolled on the floor and was crazy, just crazy,' adds Geoff Shaw. 'He'd never seen anything like it, eyes sticking out, writhing, wanking the microphone – he was an old guy – it made a massive impression. I think that's what influenced Lee's persona, scary on stage. It was all about the sexual edge, and there was an aggression, you didn't know where it was going. One minute he'd be on all fours, the next he'd shake a bottle up and put it in his flies and open the bottle and spray the audience. He came up from juke joints and brothels, it's raunchy. Lee saw how powerful that was.'

Seeing Howlin' Wolf changed everything for Lee. 'I thought, I don't want to sing "Won't You Come Home, Bill Bailey" any more. I wanted to sing serious blues. That was the way it had to go.' The jug band was jaunty, diverting, cheeky. What Lee had witnessed in Howlin' Wolf's show had depth, danger, sexuality, even offering a stolen glimpse into a darkly supernatural sphere. From the way Lee himself later stalked and stared onstage to the overtly provocative movements he made, much of Lee's own stagecraft can be traced back to this.

Lee spoke to BBC Radio 2's Paul Jones (of Manfreds fame) about this seminal moment, his voice strengthening as the memory sharpened. 'That really did seal it for me. I thought, that is what I want to do, what that big black man up on that stage is doing. That enormous guy with a harmonica just controlling a thousand punters in this sweaty room at the back of a pub – that was the most exciting thing.'

A thousand people? In the back room of a pub in Romford?

'It was a big old room,' protests Lee, before conceding with a chuckle, 'I might be exaggerating. But it seemed like a thousand people to me.' Given how important this night was to Lee, it's no surprise some elements of the story might have become magnified. It's also no surprise that, shortly after this show, Lee went out and bought his first harmonica. 'The first day I bought it, I was playing it. I never consciously sat down and played any instrument to become a virtuoso, I just used to play for my own pleasure.' No lessons required, just spirit. And spit.

Lew Lewis

When I first met Lee, I was walking down the street playing the harmonica. It was quite a rare thing to be into the blues then. He taught me a few little tricks, and he ended up learning a few bits off me. Next time I met him, I was saying, 'I'm getting on all right with the harmonica, but it keeps drying out.' 'Just dip it in some liquid,' he said. Then he just took it off me and dipped it right in the pond. This pond had leaves in it, old fag ends. 'Oh, thanks, mate, that's much better ...' I'd rather dip it in whisky.

By 1969, Lee was in sixth form and Chris 'Whitey' Fenwick[6] had gone to drama school. In the wake of the Howlin' Wolf show, Lee and John Sparkes decided that what was left of the jug band should move forward and go electric, and they spent a brief time in an amplified blues band called The Fix, a group they frequently used to watch live. The Fix featured the late Dave Higgs on guitar and, previously, Wilko Johnson in its personnel. The Thames Delta was ablaze with rock'n'roll and R&B, and The Fix was one of the early groups to foster this scene. Sparkes also explains that it was Dave Higgs who can be held responsible for what would come later, practically casting them in their future roles.

'Dave used to play in soul bands. He was one of the first people we knew with long hair and a moustache and round glasses – we thought that was really cool. He said, "You can join our band if you like." He turned to Lee and said, "We don't need a banjo but you can be the singer." I used to play 12-string then and he said, "Well, I'm the guitar player, you can be the bass player." I said, "I don't know how." "Oh, I'll show ya." That was the big change. Very underrated bloke, Dave Higgs. He was instrumental. I'd say he taught us our craft.'

Post-Fix, Sparko and Lee used their newly honed chops to form a new group called The Wild Bunch, aka The Pigboy Charlie Band, with a guitarist called Billy and the young Kevin Morris, who would later become Dr Feelgood's longest-serving drummer.

'We got a pianist and it was more like a rock'n'roll band,' said Lee, although it all collapsed when the pianist quit and the van, an out-of-commission ambulance with a flashing 'Pigboy' sign[7] courtesy of Sparko, 'blew up' on the M1. As for the variable nature of the band's name, the general rule was that if they were going out as a four-piece, they were The Wild Bunch, (no doubt a nod to the 1969 Sam Peckinpah spaghetti western of the same name, which would have been brand new at the time) and if they had their pianist with them, they were The Pigboy Charlie Band – 'Pigboy Charlie' himself being the pianist. (His real name was Vivian, which caused great hilarity. Lee took it upon himself to give Vivian a moniker worthy of an old-time bluesman instead.)

Kevin Morris, on the other hand, was at Rayleigh Sweyne, and while he was a few years younger, he was 'allowed' to hang out with Lee and his mates because he played the drums. 'I got special dispensation to smoke round the back of the swimming pool with them. It was like, "He's only a kid but he's all right." I was thirteen, fourteen. Lee seemed very grown-up. I was aware of him at school because he always had a bit of a gang.' Kevin also remembers Lee's prefect pretence quite clearly: 'He'd come up and ask to see your homework diary, then take it off you and tear it up.'

Current Dr Feelgood bass player Phil Mitchell, who initially joined the band in 1983, also remembers Lee at school. Phil was in a band called Daily Male at the time, but during an early gig at Hadleigh Public Hall, they were so terrified, they played their set at double speed and finished in record time. Leaving the stage was not an option – they still had a great chasm of time to fill and the audience was getting restless.

Lee, who had been watching from out front, wandered backstage and after a quick chat to see what the state of play was, assembled a scratch band from the audience, broke the neck off a beer bottle, put it on his finger and started playing slide guitar on a succession of standards, 'Dust My Broom' being one of them. One of the musicians to hit the stage with Lee was Southend guitarist Pete Zear. 'That was the first time I really interacted with him. We had a good old time.' And as for Daily Male? 'Without Lee, we would have been lynched,' admitted Phil, who humbly offered him the money they'd raised from the door. He refused it, of course.

Lee invited Kevin into the line-up on the recommendation of their mutual friend Alan Catton, who assured him he could play, and not to let his comparative youth put them off. There would be no rehearsals – they were mostly playing standards anyway – and off they went, playing rock'n'roll and a bit of Chicago blues to the good people of South Essex. Regular venues would include the roller-skating rink on Pier Hill, The Gun and the notorious Railway in Pitsea, also known as 'The Flying Bottle'. 'Quite a rough house,' confirms Kevin.

Sometimes the only way Lee, as frontman, could control the situation would be to unsettle the crowd, and his tactic of acting like a complete maniac went down extremely well. In terms of cultivating a stage identity, Lee was learning what worked as he went. 'He'd jump out of the window and play harmonica out there, singing in the car park,' remembers Sparko. 'We realised then that whenever you do stuff like that, the crowd love it.'

Sadly the Pigboy Charlie Band were doomed to fall apart (literally, in the case of the van), which disappointed Lee to say the least; he believed the group could go somewhere – they even had rather professional-looking cards printed, proclaiming their credentials for functions and the like – and he loved performing live. There were already whisperings wherever they played that the group had 'a star on their hands' in Lee.

But, perhaps with a little help from his family, Lee had to face facts: this wasn't a realistic dream. The blues boom of the 1960s was waning, it was now 1970, and prog and heavy metal had taken up where psychedelia and R&B had left off. The now clichéd 'twenty-minute guitar solos' and lofty rock explorations that were increasingly in favour were not the kind of thing Lee had in mind.

Lee Brilleaux on his First Hangover

It was after drinking eight pints of Guinness and four double rums. That was on Southend seafront when I'd just finished my A-levels. I remember waking up on Southend beach with the chap I'd been drinking with. It was a really hot day, and this was about four o'clock in the afternoon, and the beach was packed but within a twenty-yard radius of us there was just puke and all these families keeping well back. That was when I realised one has to be a little careful.

School was out, and Lee's mother Joan had fixed him up with a job at a local law firm as a solicitor's clerk. 'He'd said, "I know I've got to find work, but for the life of me I haven't got a clue what to do." I said, "I know what you think of solicitors, but if you go as an outdoor clerk, it's quite a nice job for a lad. You go to the court in a car, go up London." He said, "That sounds all right." I said, "You even get to go to the prisons." That seemed to clinch it,' said Joan.

Lee was sanguine about his supposed future 'serving writs'. He enjoyed the work, the compulsory suit-wearing and the fact that he could drive the company car – a 1960s Ford Consul – on a daily basis. It also appealed to his fondness for crime novels. He later claimed to have done a spot of moonlighting as an assistant to a private detective. Whether this was true or not, it certainly fitted his image.

Lee Brilleaux, Legal Eagle

I was serving writs on people. I haven't had any writs served on me. That's one thing about being a travelling man, you keep one jump ahead of your creditors. Only joking.

'I was filing divorce petitions, which, in a way, I liked,' he mused. 'I didn't really think about it that much. As long as I'm having a good time I don't really care what's happening.' It was hardly a vocation, but it was, at least, surprisingly 'free and easy,' Lee noted. 'Like everything else on Canvey.'

Had he ever put pen to paper himself and written a novel, the opportunities for character study were rich. Lee would often find himself utilising his sharp writing skills working up 'cagily conciliatory letters from one spouse to another' on behalf of his Canvey clients, many of whom, he told Hugo Williams, 'had trouble reading and writing'.

In the main, though, Lee admitted the bulk of his duties consisted of 'driving my guv'nor to and from Newmarket racecourse. He'd indulge in large quantities of alcohol and it would be my job to drive him back. In between interviewing clients for prospective matrimonial proceedings, I'd be driving up and down Canvey High Street with five hundred quid in my pocket to put on the horses.'

Not every day was 'free and easy', of course. On one occasion Lee was ordered to Chinatown to serve a writ on a Chinese gangster who'd been involved in smuggling heroin. Lee arrived in Soho with Chris White by his side as his 'heavy', their childhood roles reprised (when playing pirates in Benfleet Creek, Chris would row the boat and take care of the more physical side of things while Lee would do the talking). Thankfully business would be taken care of in a perfectly civilised manner over a cup of tea in a Chinese restaurant.

In terms of the band, or what was left of it, Lee and John Sparkes still wanted to play together, but Kevin was still at school and their guitarist had moved on. There was no way Lee wanted to stop performing, but he decided the next venture would just be a bit of fun to raise some beer money, a diversion which would temporarily release him from the frustration of 'the real world'. With every other band he'd been in up to now, he'd hoped for something more to happen, and it hadn't. Little did he realise that the situation was about to reverse.

Opposite: One of Lee's many satirical poems and his sardonic 'Regulations for Schoolboys'. It's hard to pick a favourite, but the loaded 'pupils with imaginations must NOT bring them to school' is a good one, and rather telling of Lee's frustration. Courtesy of Phil Ashcroft.

Regulations for Schoolboys.
by Collie

1) Each schoolboy must be exactly 5ft 2 inches tall.

2) There must be more than five and less than seven lace holes on each of his shoes.

3) Each schoolboy must have a head. (this must not exceed 20" diameter).

4) Caps must be firmly nailed on the head.

5) Talking at registration, assembly, lessons, break, dinner and games is strictly forbidden. (At other times normal conversation may be carried out)

6) Pupils with imaginations must NOT bring them to school.

7) School uniform must be worn at all times both in and out school. This includes cap and scarf. Special plastic bags can be purchased to save excessive damage to uniform when pupil bathes and washes.

8) Breathing in the lessons must be kept in time — every pupil taking their breath every six seconds.

9) Bullying is encouraged at all times.

10) Pupils must bring all their arms, legs etc with them to school.

11) Bullying is punishable by caning.

* how the hell do you spell it

The Alarm Clock   by Collie.

When a lie in my bed
I always listen to what
My alarm clock says.

The alarm clock which is very old
Sit and does,
Just what its told.

As I cant think of another verse
Please will you
Repeat the first.

The end

Here be men. And flares. Early 1970s promo shot of a denim-clad Dr Feelgood on Canvey Island, or 'Canvey Isle', as it is rather more exotically referred to in the top right of the picture. Left to right: a moustachioed Lee Collinson, Wilko Johnson, The Big Figure and Sparko.

3. TALES OF MYSTERY, IMAGINATION AND HEINZ BURT

I remember saying, 'Even if he can sing only slightly, he's a star. He's a star, even as a solicitor's clerk!'

Wilko Johnson

Early 1971. John Wilkinson had recently returned from a mind-expanding trail across India and was back on Canvey, family life underway, his guitar tucked safely under the bed under a thickening film of dust. Wilkinson was twenty-four to Collinson's nineteen, but both of them had had simultaneous, if misleading, epiphanies that it was now 'own-up time', as Wilko puts it. Lee was ensconced at the law firm, while Wilko, complete with hippy tresses and flares, was about to start teaching English at King John's School in Benfleet; one of the most unusual candidates to take on a class of unruly kids you could imagine.

Wilkinson hadn't played guitar since university; at this stage, he was more interested in poetry and painting, although this would soon change. 'I'm walking down the road in the council estate and who should be coming towards me but Lee? "'Allo, mate!" Fuck, he looked sharp. Pinstripe suit, sideburns … man, he looked good. I was wearing paisley-patterned denims or something.' While the pair caught up, they talked about their respective jug bands of yore. Lee filled him in on how his band had evolved into a rock'n'roll group, but that they were lacking a guitarist. Hint hint.

'I'm thinking, I've still got my guitar … Lee didn't have the nerve to just ask me to join. We were standing there talking for about twenty minutes and then I just walked home and thought, that was bloody mad.'

Part of the problem was that Lee was a little inhibited about presuming Wilko would *want* to join his band. 'Sparko was a shocking bass player, and I was a terrible singer,' he admitted, although this was hardly the general consensus and, as far as Wilko was concerned, hardly the point. Lee just 'had something about him'. But Wilko was waiting to be asked. Both walked away from each other with a distinct feeling of dissatisfaction.

Later that day, Lee caught up with Sparkes, who, after a quick chat with Dave Higgs, then staying *chez* Wilkinson, took matters into his own hands. 'Sparko came round,' remembers Wilko. 'He said, "Look, do you wanna join our band?" I said, "YES."

'I asked Dave Higgs, "That Lee, can he sing at all?" And he said, "Yeah, he's a pretty good singer." And I remember thinking, well, that's it, man. Because he just is a star. If he can half hold a tune, then I'm his man! And the fact was, he had a great voice. Very edgy guy but capable of being very, very funny, obscene and witty. In those early days [we'd have] a lot of laughs. He looked up to me … he probably never knew that I had absolute respect for him.'

The name of the new band was Dr Feelgood, which sparked mental images of a decadent and unscrupulous member of the medical profession, over-prescribing drugs for nefarious thrill-seekers. The name was also a nod to Willie Lee Perryman, aka Piano Red, a barrelhouse blues pianist who released the song 'Dr Feelgood' (later covered by The Pirates, Wilko's favourite band, in 1964). Piano Red was often referred to as Dr Feelgood himself, but this lot weren't bothered about that – they were convinced no one would hear of them beyond Canvey anyway. Roll on rehearsals, and many an evening getting stoned on some of Wilko's strong black hash, playing records from their respective collections – Lee's in particular having become so monstrous it was soon to force him out of his family home at the request of his increasingly desperate parents.

After pasting up an advert for a drummer, Terry 'Bandsman' Howarth, fresh from the army and living in Benfleet, spotted the notice and briefly joined before signing back up to army life to play in the 'tank band' instead. But a run of dates in Holland had been secured, thanks to Chris Fenwick, and a drummer was required quickly, so Wilko brought in his old friend and fellow Canvey-dweller John 'The Big Figure' Martin. Martin had been playing drums with pop bands around the country, including a group called Finian's Rainbow, or 'Flanagan's Flamethrower' as Lee preferred to call them. John shared their absurd sense of humour ('Sorry I'm late, I was cutting the kitchen in half') and was more than happy to use his downtime playing something other than chart music. 'Wilko dragged them over to my caravan where we proceeded to negotiate,' said Figure. The definitive Dr Feelgood line-up was complete.

'As soon as we had a rehearsal, it was just magic,' remembers Figure. 'Lee seemed fairly shy at the beginning. But as we got to know each other, he came out of his shell. He showed me how to drink properly and appreciate real ale. But how he often appears on stage, like a menacing growler, that wasn't him at all. He was a very nice guy, he had time for everybody.'

Musically, Wilko introduced a choppy, beat group sound, while Lee brought a pure blues influence to the table, and the combination was fresh and exhilarating rather than retro and staid. They still practised rock'n'roll and pop covers in an attempt to keep the punters happy, but something special happened when they simply played the music they loved. Singing 'Heartbeat' ('Can you imagine Lee singing that?' asks Wilko, still incredulous more than forty years on) to an indifferent audience on a Sunday afternoon in Pitsea was starting to pall. 'We were having a rehearsal and Lee put a Little Walter record on,' remembers Wilko. 'I said, "Oh, fuck all this pop music, let's just do this stuff." Which is what we did.'

Lee needed no persuading. As far as he was concerned, even playing rock'n'roll was a compromise. He'd only conceded to playing 'rock music' to secure the band some gigs. R&B was everything, and Lee was a purist. 'I was snobbish,' Lee admitted to *Sounds*' Jonh [sic] Ingham in 1975. 'To me, [rock'n'roll] was the stuff the generation before me were into. I used to half send it up. My uncle was into Elvis, he had a silly haircut and you know … fucking rubbish. But after a while I started to get into it, and [it was] fucking great. Then I started to feel really guilty.'

One afternoon while strolling on Canvey, Lee spotted a face from the not too distant past – that of his childhood friend Geoff Shaw. He'd recently come out of Borstal – 'I just decided to be a bit bad for a while,' he says airily. 'Lee *loved* that I'd been to Borstal. He was fascinated by the bad-boy thing. He wanted to know about the hierarchy, the language of the badass people: what do they do? What's it about?

'When you think about it, blues came out of a primitive environment. Most musicians would carry guns and knives, and in the South, at most of the dances, someone would get killed. The women would poison the men,[8] this is what they did. Lee was fascinated by that. He wanted to know everything. He wouldn't just take things on face value.'

While the pair caught up, Lee told Geoff about the new band he was in with Sparko, and invited him to come and see them play. 'I'd come out of this environment where even the tough guys in prison were listening to Gentle Giant, Yes, Gong, Rod Stewart … Dr Feelgood were weird and really shouty. It was hard-arse, my ear wasn't attuned to it, but it was definitely interesting. This was before punk; everyone else was singing about oak trees and swans.'

After the gig, the band took a stunned Geoff back to Wilko's house where they put on Chuck Berry and Little Richard albums, turned up the volume as far as it would go, and smoked 'ridiculous amounts of weed,' says Shaw. 'I mean, I smoked a bit of weed, but they were just off the Richter scale. I was sitting there witnessing this craziness, and they'd be playing this raunchy R&B really loud and just getting out of their minds. It almost scared me, but I liked it. Some of the records they played, I thought they were being ironic. Gimmicky R&B songs, 'Riot In Cell Block Number 9'. After a few more gigs, I started to get the hang of it, and it was fantastic. Fierce, bit sinister. It was a spectacle. The alternative was to go to a disco – so boring.'

Dr Feelgood spent quite a lot of time 'grubbing around the pubs', as Lee put it, even sending out circulars offering to play 'anywhere for nothing or, at the most, expenses' to increase their following, but that golden opportunity to play abroad for the first time was looming ever closer. Chris had recently attended the wedding of a fellow drama student over in Holland, where he met a small-time entrepreneur who had just set up a music agency. Chris proclaimed himself to be an in-demand DJ, bigged up the Feelgoods and blagged them some gigs that May, well and truly securing his own position as manager in the process. What followed was a short tour in Chris's ramshackle van, which attracted no small amount of attention from the Dutch police, and it was often Lee at the wheel, himself and Figure being the best drivers.[9]

They played a tight run of dates, drank, smoked, were decidedly merry, and the whole shebang was, as Chris put it, 'fun with a capital F'. This was their first tour together as Dr Feelgood, and the band's proficiency and stage presence suddenly ramped up several gears as a result of this intense stint of playing live. 'Now we were playing twice a day for a week,' said Sparko. 'And as they say, one gig's worth a hundred rehearsals.'

It was a shame, therefore, that just as Dr Feelgood was turning from, in Sparko's words, a 'crap amateur local band' into something that could be a going concern, Lee announced on the boat back that he was planning to quit and turn his attentions solely to a legal career. Not that there was any way Wilko would let Lee throw away his future with a 'proper job'.

'I remember us talking about this,' said Wilko. 'He had his legal exams coming up and I was saying, "Come on, man, *I* wanna go for it – I'm twenty-four, but you're nineteen, for God's sake."'

'Lee was being torn in half,' remembers Joan. 'Something had to give. He came to us, my husband and me, and explained it all, and he felt guilty because we'd supported him [while he studied for his exams]. He said, "I've got to make a decision – go on with the law or Dr Feelgood. It looks as if it's taking off." We said, "Which makes you the happiest?" He said, "Dr Feelgood." So I said, "Well, there's your decision made." The boss didn't take it quite so well.'[10]

'I quite enjoyed my days as a lawyer's clerk,' said Lee, 'but the idea of being in a rock'n'roll band sounded better.' Damn right it did. After all, what young man in his right mind, as Lee later expressed with a twinkle, 'would turn down foreign travel and crumpet?'

Further foreign travel would have to wait (crumpet, on the other hand ...), but before long the Feelgoods would be keeping their skills sharp on the Southend pub circuit and with a residency at the Cloud 9 (later known as Bardot's) on 'Canvey's Golden 100 Yards', as guitarist Pete Zear describes it – the short strip by the amusements, just up from the Monico pub.

Local Feelgood aficionado Hugh Cumberland remembers hearing from 'some of the cooler kids at school about this great band that they went to see at the Cloud 9. My sister came home one night raving about them – apparently Lee had slipped the mic down his strides in the middle eight and couldn't get it back out in time for the next verse so he sang it cross-legged on the floor with the lead sticking out of his trouser leg.'

Another new live outlet for Dr Feelgood would be the Esplanade on Southend seafront. A regular gig night had been set up by future Kursaal Flyers Paul Shuttleworth and Will Birch, who had also played drums in local 1960s band The Flowerpots with Wilko Johnson. The pair had been looking for gigs for their own band, then a country rock group called Cow Pie, and had finally decided to take matters into their own hands.

Birch takes up the story: 'This would be the spring of 1972. We put a gig on once a week, free entry. We played there, Mickey Jupp [played there],[11] and then Wilko got in touch and asked if the Feelgoods could play there. That was when I first met Lee, Chris and Sparko.' Will would play with the Feelgoods at their Esplanade debut as Figure was playing with 'Flanagan's Flamethrower' for the first part of the evening.

'I got quite pally with Lee, Chris and Sparko,' remembers Will. 'Wilko was out on his own, and Figure to a certain extent, maybe because they were both married. But the single guys, they were up for the match, up for the drink and everything and anything.

Top left and centre: Doctor Feelgood fixing the Transit (some members working a little harder than others, you will note). Bottom left: Chris 'Whitey' Fenwick DJ-ing in Holland, having blagged the Feelgoods a run of shows there – the band's first foreign tour. His fate as the band's manager was sealed from then on.

Above: the boys in Holland, Wilko still in hippy mode. Images from Wilko Johnson's personal archive.

'I was an aspiring songwriter then and I used to write lyrics. It was that post-progressive era and I used to write … well, crap really, but I remember sitting with Lee at the Castle Hotel near Thorpe Bay one night having a beer – this was just before Wilko started writing songs – and I said, "Have you thought about writing your own songs yet?" And he said, "Oh no, I can't write songs." And I said, "Well, I've got some lyrics."

'This lyric was about dinosaurs or something. I was trying to work prehistoric characters into this love lyric, and Lee was like, "This is great! This is great!" He was egging me on but nothing came of it.' At this point in their story, the Feelgoods stuck to mostly covers anyway. What *was* fast developing was Lee's compelling stage persona and use of props.

'I depped with them at the Haystack on Canvey,' said Will Birch. 'About nine people and a dog in the audience. We played "Blue Suede Shoes". Lee was actually wearing suede boots. I don't think they were blue but anyway, halfway through the song he took the boot off and held it in his right hand and held the microphone up to the boot, like the boot was singing. He got off the stage with the long lead and he'd go up to people with the boot, "Blue suede, blue suede shoes …" He was brilliant at improvising, which stood him in good stead.' Similarly, during a later show, Lee was observed taking a swig from his beer bottle only for the lager to froth up into his face. After giving the bottle a quick sniff, he then sprayed it theatrically under both arms for good measure, to the great amusement of those in the audience.

Wilko's brother Malcolm was in the audience at one of the Haystack shows on Canvey. He was primarily there to gee up the audience – what there was of an audience anyway. 'I went into the street trying to charm people into coming in with no luck at all,' he remembers. Did that matter to the band? Did it hell. Most groups would either can the gig or view it as a (not very well) paid rehearsal. Not the Feelgoods. 'God, they were good. In such an unpromising place I felt those shivers going up my back, like you know you've heard something extraordinary.'

Lee's opinion of what was happening at that time was that they were playing great music – people just didn't want to hear it. 'It's all played out,' he said. 'But [then] we did a few colleges, and people started dancing.'

Lee Brilleaux

Black music is corrupting and it's corruptible. That's what makes it so interesting. When I had my straight job working in an office, that was my outlet.

The Feelgoods might not have been widely appreciated on home turf just yet, but they were soon playing to new audiences thanks to former Joe Meek *protégé* and Tornados frontman Heinz Burt, an unusual character with an intriguing past; not only was the producer Joe Meek in love with him, but the shotgun with which Meek famously killed his landlady had actually belonged to Heinz. The bleach-blond rock'n'roller was now living in Southend and selling advertising space for local newspapers, but the early 1970s greaser revival had lured him back into playing live for nostalgia-niks, bikers and a new generation of Teddy Boys. He just needed the right backing band to go out on the road with.

Because Dr Feelgood were known to play a hard-hitting set of classic rock'n'roll covers, the band's local music shop put the band in touch with Heinz. There were plenty of Teddy Boy bands in Southend but, after a phone call and a brief jam in the garden, the Feelgoods got the job, even if it was given somewhat grudgingly. Heinz's first impression of Dr Feelgood was that they were a touch rough around the edges. Collectively they looked like a scruffy bunch of troublemakers who knew how to have a good time, were quick with their fists and probably drove too fast. Most of these concerns were superseded when Heinz heard them play, of course. 'We were good, excellent,' says Wilko. 'But he didn't like it.'

'We went to Heinzy's house and knocked on the door,' remembers the laconic Sparko. 'And he went, "OK, come round the back." Another one who wouldn't let us in the house.[12] He took us into this little summerhouse in the garden and we rehearsed in there. We just played about twenty seconds of "Great Balls Of Fire" and he was like, "Oh yeah, you obviously know that one then." And that was it.'

A few short, chaotic UK tours ensued, crucial for keeping up the post-Holland momentum, and the Feelgoods revelled in the opportunity to play 'proper gigs', as Lee remembers. 'Universities and clubs, it gave us a bit of an eye-opener on how to conduct ourselves in business at a later stage. Very useful experience working with him.'

'We didn't always have hotels,' adds Sparko. 'We'd sleep on people's floors, and one time we camped up on Portland Bill. Lee went fishing with Heinz and they came back with these fish and wanted to sell them to a fish and chip shop. They were all on the floor in the van, sliding about, people treading on them.'

Night after night, the still relatively long-haired Feelgoods would play a short set to crowds of ducktail-sporting hard nuts before Lee ceremoniously announced Heinz to the stage. Heinz would then stride on to deafening cheers, Lee taking up backing vocal duties with Chris Fenwick.

Lee and Chris were an unstoppable double act. Once they were together, the skits they came up with would leave everyone present laughing to the point of actually being in pain, so letting these two loose as 'backing singers' was a recipe for cheeky behaviour and ad-libs. Wilko remembers them chirpily singing 'Heinz bakes the meanest beans!' from the classic baked beans adverts. Had to be done, and, to be fair, Heinz was usually drunk and oblivious. In fact, during a show in Sheffield supporting Mungo Jerry, Lee announced Heinz as usual, but the singer was so pickled on barley wine he simply crashed straight through the curtain, knocking over a cymbal stand and causing the cymbal to slice through a power cable, plunging the stage into instant darkness. Quite the entrance.

On another occasion Wilko recalls Heinz telling him to sprint up to him suddenly during the show, as if about to attack. 'I did, and he did a sort of mock kung fu kick at me, and his foot hit my guitar and all the strings went out of tune.' Heinz would also regularly ignore the set list and start singing a completely different song than the one the rest of the group were expecting. 'He'd suddenly launch in and go, "One for the money!" and we'd all inevitably come in late.'

Every night was certainly an event, but the high point of the Feelgoods' summer with Heinz was undoubtedly the London Rock'n'Roll Show at Wembley Stadium on 5 August 1972, the first pop concert ever to be held at the stadium.

The night before the show, the Feelgoods convened at Wilko's house, sitting up late and trying to work through their jitters. One idea was to write a song about the festival itself – they were the first band of the day, it would kick things off nicely and, Wilko posited, their song might end up in the credits in the proposed concert film. 'So we're writing this song,' remembers Wilko. 'But Lee's kind of slumping, he's half asleep. At one point somebody just said the word "Wembley", and

Lee suddenly jumped up and shouted, "WEMBLEY?! WEMBLEY?!" Just panicked.'

Nerves were understandable. Not only would Dr Feelgood suddenly be playing on a vast stage to an audience of thousands, they would be rubbing shoulders backstage with their heroes. The monster bill featured Little Richard, Chuck Berry (whom Lee recalls as being rather unfriendly), Jerry Lee Lewis and Bo Diddley among others.[13] Also on the line-up was Teddy Boy band The Houseshakers, who apparently rather looked down upon the Feelgoods, possibly feeling that they themselves would have been a more appropriate band to back Heinz. Wires can get crossed and manners misread, but all the same, Lee took a dim view of The Houseshakers, and one of his 'party pieces' was an impersonation of the band's frontman pontificating about Heinz's importance to rock'n'roll, much to the rest of the Feelgoods' hilarity. (Reportedly Malcolm McLaren and Vivienne Westwood were also there, using the opportunity to sell Teddy Boy clothes to cash-rich rockers.)

Heinz, who might well have had a few ales before hitting the stage for his broad daylight slot, swayed, slurred and spat out the words to 'C'mon Everybody' as punters flooded the echoing stadium and the Feelgoods paced and grooved behind him. 'We all just look like scared little kids,' laughs Sparko. 'The gig before we'd probably played to about 150 people, then suddenly it was 80,000.' Wilko observed that hitting the stage at Wembley made them feel like 'gladiators going into the Colosseum. Just so frightening.'

The Feelgoods' set with Heinz seemed to flash past in a heartbeat, but they'd had a taste of what was to come. Despite the Teddy Boys' suspicion of this comparatively hippified band, no one could deny that Dr Feelgood rocked. Heinz, the man who was initially repelled by the band, even suggested they change their name to The Tornados – he insisted the original Tornados wouldn't mind – and back him permanently, an offer which was graciously declined.

It was time to go home, rejig their own set and think about the future. Southend's Esplanade was waiting, and it would welcome back a rather different Dr Feelgood; the edges had been knocked off, the nerves dissolved, and, within months, they would have a sharp new look that would better reflect their clean, hard R&B sound. This band was no longer 'just a bit of fun' – it was going somewhere. No one was quite sure where or how far, but, as Lee observed, if it allowed them to quit their day jobs, that was good enough for them.

Top: the longest legs in rock. Brilleaux looking
dangerous in double denim. Bottom: sweating
it out on the pub rock scene. Images from
Wilko Johnson's personal archive.

4. RED HOT IN (THE) ALEX

Asked as to whether [Lee] would soon be turning professional, he replied that he had always been 'professional', but would no doubt be working with the band full time after Christmas.

South East Essex News (a zine, penned in biro, by one of Lee's childhood friends), November 1973

The level of the Feelgoods' musicianship and stagecraft had been dialled up considerably since their summer with Heinz and, inevitably, people were noticing the difference. Audiences no longer had to be dragged in off the street to watch them play, and they were less likely to talk through their set once they were in. Will Birch noted in his diary on 10 September 1972 that Dr Feelgood had played the Esplanade that night and were 'very mean. Good bunce.'

Will was living at the time at his parents' home in the sedate area of Thorpe Bay, just east of the not so sedate Southend, and Lee, Sparko and Chris would often take the opportunity, while on the 'mainland', to pop in for a late-night coffee after a drinking session before roaring back to Canvey, maybe watch *The Old Grey Whistle Test* together, or just hang out before a Sunday evening show at the Esplanade. Many a Heinz anecdote would be shared, the fishing story being a particular favourite. (They may have sniggered about the idiosyncratic Heinz, but, as Hugo Williams observed in his essay 'The Breeding of Dr Feelgood', Lee owed almost as much to Heinz's warped Elvis impersonations as he did to Howlin' Wolf.)

Lee was partial to watching *Hawaii Five-0* with Will and the boys before a show at the Esplanade. Missing it was not an option. Lee was amused by the lingo and especially loved the central character of Steve McGarrett. An intriguing element of Lee's personality was his penchant for taking on characters from books, films or television programmes that appealed to him and melding them into his own persona for comedy effect, sartorial purposes or otherwise. Subversive offbeats such as Yossarian, Patrick McGoohan in *The Prisoner*, *Brighton Rock*'s menacing Pinkie Brown, enigmatic mavericks from pulp novels or Raymond Chandler stories … and now Detective Captain Steve McGarrett. They were all in there somewhere.

'Lee was taken with the dialogue, it became part of [his parlance],' continues Will. 'You know, "Book 'em, Danno. Murder one, two counts. Put out an APB." All this stuff, it all fed into it. "Put out an APB on my pint of beer."' Arguably, the suited-up, short-haired McGarrett played a part in informing the ultimate Brilleaux image. Up to this point, Lee would often hit the stage in denim, but it wouldn't be long until the spivvy moustache would go, the hair would get hacked off and the visual concept gradually became more defined. Malcolm Wilkinson recalls, however, that the alteration of the collective Feelgood barnets was actually sparked by something closer to home.

'As I remember it, Chris White had a part in a film of some sort that involved him filming on a Royal Naval vessel. He had to get his hair cut for the part. When the others saw it, they all thought it looked great, so all their hair was cut short too.'

The Feelgoods started playing at the Top Alex pub on Alexandra Street, Southend, in 1973, and that, as Will Birch remembers it, 'was when they got really hot'. The Top Alex was a haunt of the local bikers, Hell's Angels and hippies. You couldn't move for Afghan coats, and it was possibly the hairiest nightspot in Southend, so it was an interesting place for another key shift in Lee's image to come into play.

Will Birch continues: 'My brother Howard had a cream three-button Italian jacket. He traded it with Lee upstairs at the Alex. The minute Lee put that jacket on, that was when his persona was born. Eventually he got the famous white one. But that cream jacket was the start.'

Pete Zear also attended their shows at the Alex, and noticed the change, not just because of the attire, but because, after the best part of a year on the road, they had attitude, confidence, and musically they were so drilled they could concentrate more on working the crowd.

'They were like a different band. They were tight, and there was an aggression there; there was no "Oh, I've got my mojo working." No, it was "I've got my mojo working, you wanna argue about it?"[14] The whole thing was coming, and there was that tension between the two of them [Wilko and Lee].'

Rock'n'roll needs a sense of threat to truly excite. There arguably wasn't much on the scene that really had that quality at the time – there were groups who could entertain, yes, but were you worried about bumping into the singer on a dark night? Did you fear that if you met the guitarist's gaze you might inadvertently enter into some Faustian contract? Possibly not. But something dangerous had been unleashed in the Feelgoods, and it was as captivating as it was disorientating. When Lee wasn't barking out lyrics, fist pounding the air, he was launching frenzied attacks on the gob-iron, or staring, juddering obscenely, altogether ignoring Wilko as he careered across the stage, his guitar apparently having been possessed by a malevolent spirit that was somehow steering him around.

Rock'n'roll, of course, also needs style; it needs an image, a look. Will Birch recalls Ian Dury and the Blockheads publicist Kosmo Vinyl explaining that 'you can have a band that looks good and plays good, a band that looks good and plays bad, but you can't have a band that plays good and looks bad'. Admittedly, there was quite a number of bands who 'played good and looked bad' in the early 1970s, but Dr Feelgood were not one of them. What the Feelgoods were doing was evolving their own unique style, and the foundation of that style was the cheap suit.

The band would walk onstage apparently wearing what they'd come from work in (bricklayer Sparko was generally in jeans, shirt and a waistcoat before adopting what he refers to as his 'bastard suit', a frilly-shirted wedding whistle in hospital blue). The suits-and-sunglasses look (mirror-lensed, Aviator-style) also tied in with the Feelgoods' sleazy appeal, that of the suave baddie, the modern highwayman, Flash Harry, *The Ladykillers*, good guy turned bad with a top note of white-collar-worker-gone-insane. Lee often had the crazed, undone look of a corrupt, pill-popping DI who'd been up all night on a case, grubby shirt pulled open at the neck, tie yanked loose, sweat rapidly wiped from his brow as he snarled, swaggered and pointed an accusatory finger at no one in particular.

As the Feelgood buzz began to intensify, rumours circulated about their collective background, and excitable suspicions fizzed along the lines that, as Mick Farren salaciously noted, it was 'possible to believe they might have come together in jail'. (They weren't about to point out that they'd met as youngsters and had once been the pride of Canvey Carnival.) One former Canvey dweller told me that, whenever an act of vandalism was spotted on the Island, it was speculated by fevered teens that 'the Feelgoods had done it'.

'It was like *The Blues Brothers* before that film even came out,' says Wilko. 'We anticipated that. Lee looked like a very angry man indeed, and people loved it.'

Lee was always at pains to point out that the 'image' was unconscious, however. 'These are the only trousers I've got,' he'd protest, adding that the jacket had been nicked 'from a streaker in Durham [who'd] left his clothes on the stage'. But of course.

'We never sat down and said, "Right, we're going to go on looking like deranged bank clerks" or whatever,' Lee explained (and he's saying it like it's a bad thing). 'Since I was at school, I've dressed like this and had my hair cut this way.' Another essential part of Lee's stage look was the omnipresent Piccadilly or Rothmans cigarette. He'd chain-smoke through the show – it added to his hard-bitten image and coated his vocal cords in tar, ensuring that the lupine growl was always primed.

'As for the suits,' says Sparko. 'That was probably just before we went to London, and it was a thing we discussed, you know, to look professional. There was a book about The Hollies about their younger days; they talked about how it was important to dress up for the occasion. We didn't want to be "gangstery", we didn't idolise the Kray twins – to me it was a bit of a surprise, in a way, that the *Oil City* film played up the gangster thing – I can see the connection now, but at the time that wasn't where we were coming from.'

'I looked to old blues guys that Lee had played me the records of,' said Figure. 'I watched these guys wearing mirror shades and being cool and just tried to emulate that. The playing came first for me but Lee kicked my bum a bit and said, "Come on, let's try and present ourselves in a manner," and I followed suit as best I could.'

As well as the visual changes that were taking place, the Feelgoods would also play around with stage names, partly because when it came to getting paid for pub gigs, they had to give a name to the landlord to prove they had taken receipt of the funds, and if they gave fake names, they wouldn't have to declare the cash to the taxman. As a result, ever more ludicrous handles were given every time they were asked to sign the paperwork.

Giving people new and humorous names (again, reflecting characters from *St Trinian's*, the short stories of Damon Runyon, PG Wodehouse novels and the pages of the *Beano*) had long been a favoured pastime of Lee's, but another reason for these name-changing antics was that it helped avoid confusion – there were three Johns in the band (Lee's middle name was also John). The inscrutable John Martin had long been known as 'The Big Figure' anyway ('Figure' for short) on account of his formidable stature, but it also had the requisite air of mystery. John B Sparkes became Sparko, John Wilkinson was referred to as Wilko, which led him to swap his first and second name around, making it Wilko Johnson and Lee took on the surname 'Brillo' initially as a bit of a joke. Lee was convinced that, after an especially sweaty show, his hair matted up in the heat to the extent that it looked like the wire wool of a Brillo pad. Wilko remembers: 'Lee was talking about Brillo pads and then he went [in a cod American accent], "Lee Brill-O." And we went, "YES!"'

After deciding to adopt the name for good, Lee soon decided it would be better if he 'frogged it up a bit', changing the spelling to 'Brilleaux'. It was still rather droll but the new spelling had a sheen of glamour, putting one in mind of a New Orleans bluesman rather than the kind of thing one might find under the kitchen sink. Malcolm Wilkinson remembers that 'in a fit of paralytic laughter and free association, Lee posited the idea of Wilkeaux, Sparkeaux as well as Brilleaux'. The name 'Brilleaux' was soon etched onto the dashboard of the Feelgood Transit van (alongside 'Brillo Pads' – one must always remember one's roots). It was also changed by deed poll. This new moniker was not just a handy stage name, it was necessary because, thanks to Lee's work as a legal clerk, 'once you're articled to a solicitor and come under the Law Society,' Joan explains, 'you're not allowed to have another job.

'I typed him out the change-of-name deed in my lunch hour,' continues Joan, still working as a legal secretary at the time. 'I got it witnessed and he had it stamped the next time he went to London.'

Will Birch, in the meantime, had been working in an office, playing drums (probably not while in the office), and trying to get a gig on the now thriving London pub rock scene. Pub rock was a Petri dish for a diverse range of acts to build a following at a grass-roots level, and the movement, as it were, served as something of a reaction to the popular stadium bands of the time. Groups such as Ducks Deluxe, Brinsley Schwarz (featuring Nick Lowe), Eggs over Easy, Joe Strummer's pre-Clash band The 101ers, Bees Make Honey and Kilburn and the High Roads all took the opportunity to pack out drinking holes like the Kensington, the Lord Nelson, the Newlands Tavern, the Hope and Anchor and many other Victorian pubs across town. Will knew just the band that would blow the scene wide open.

'By a complete stroke of luck, I had a friend called Kevin Pursey who worked with Dai Davies, who used to book a couple of the venues. I pestered Dai for months saying, "There's this band on Canvey, you've got to see them, they are *made* for the pub rock circuit."'

Lee remembered Will as being 'very keen on reading about the next big thing in the music business, the latest buzz', but when he urged them to get up to London, Lee was flattered, if unconvinced. 'The idea of it was tremendous, but our reaction was that Will was being over-enthusiastic,' he said. 'But we checked it out, and thought, well, these bands are not a million miles away from what we're doing. No reason we can't muscle in here.'

What appealed was the immediacy of the scene – set up, plug in, play – a refreshing contrast to the overblown pomp rock currently ruling the charts. 'Everyone was expecting twenty-minute guitar solos and indulgence, and an arrogance which went with being a pop star in those days,' Lee told BBC Suffolk's Stephen Foster. 'The fact that it took all this equipment … [so] the pub rock thing wasn't a type of music, it was an attitude. It was: let's get back to what it's all about.' It would take time for a booking to open up for the Feelgoods, however.

'The months seemed to go by,' says Will. 'I remember standing in the Alex with Wilko one night. We were fantasising about what it was going to be like when we were rock stars, talking about limousines and groupies and cocaine … Then Wilko said, "I'm still waiting to get a gig on the pub circuit, it's not going to happen," and I said, "Yeah, it's going to happen."'

And it did. Will Birch finally got the call from Dai Davies, offering Dr Feelgood a show at the Tally-Ho. It was a last-minute booking, stepping in for Ducks Deluxe. Friday, 13 July 1973. Half of Southend was in the audience.

'They weren't fully formed yet, they were still playing "Johnny B Goode",' said Will. 'But they were probably the only band at that time doing that, and they had something about them. I remember watching Dai and thinking, is he enjoying it? Does he get it? He liked it. Two weeks later he got them a gig at the Lord Nelson and that was it, they were off.'

'People started hooking onto them,' adds Geoff Shaw. 'They always were a bit crazy, but in London they really cranked it up. The persona was, here was a bunch of guys who would not be very nice to go out with for an evening. They might even hurt you. Lee would be throwing bottles, lying on the floor, shagging the bass drum, Wilko was like a zomboid on rails, but quite beautiful in his movements. Sparko was punching all the time. Figure, you never saw his eyes, greased-back hair, he looked like a horrible mafioso. It was killer. I've never seen anything before or since as bad as that onstage. It didn't translate to a big stage – it was still good, but in the pubs it was incredible.'

Lee Brilleaux Talks Blues

Blues songs aren't really protest songs. I think the word 'lament' is better than 'protest'. They were about basic things – love, money, lack of it, boozing and what have you. They were very down to earth. If I was going to sing it convincingly, I was going to have to be in accord with the sentiment. If white people feel comfortable singing it, let them sing it.

I think most blues singers have their tongue very firmly placed in their cheek, they're almost saying, 'Well, all right, this is a lousy deal, but it'll be all right at the end of the day, and let's have a good time anyway.' We're not supposed to get people crying into their beer, we're supposed to have been enjoying themselves and having a good time.

A windswept Dr Feelgood pose on Canvey Island. Images from Wilko Johnson's personal archive.

Postcard to the Feelgoods and a road map
from Wilko Johnson's 1974 diary. Below: Dr
Feelgood shake the foundations of yet another
Victorian London pub, Brilleaux channelling
their old mentor Heinz Burt. Wilko Johnson's
personal archive.

5. THEY LIVED BY NIGHT

You gotta go up there and be a bit of a chauvinist bastard, a wild, violent nutcase, which is something I really enjoy. I do it in supermarkets all the time.

Lee Brilleaux to *NME*'s Neil Spencer, June 1975

Bookings were rolling in, and it was time to expand the team to get the whole operation working as efficiently as possible. While some of the pub rock acts shambled along, blowing wherever the wind took them, the Feelgoods, with Chris Fenwick at the helm, were organised. Geoff Shaw, then nineteen, would be employed to help with the gear and the live sound, and he would soon bring Fred Barker ('cool guy, good dresser, good laugh, could fight and didn't take any shit') into the mix as a roadie and also to take care of transport. Lee was often at the wheel of the van but he was not the most relaxed driver on the roads.

'We had to stop him from driving the mini-bus in town in the end because he'd get too stressed,' explains Sparko. 'He actually broke the hooter. Once, there was some old geezer driving like an idiot in front of us, and we got to the traffic lights and Lee jumped out to have a go at him, waving a baseball bat at him. He wasn't going to hit him, he just wanted to show his anger. I must stress he wasn't a violent person. It would just be people being stupid, in the way, maybe not buying a round ...'

And so, deeming it advisable to delegate driving where possible, Chris Fenwick took control. 'Chris was the main man,' stipulates Barker. 'Without Chris, it wouldn't have been a band. Proper driving force.' Despite the group being wooed by increasingly prestigious outside influences who were keen to take over the management reins (reportedly including Bob Harris, who would give the group their first radio session on *Sounds of the Seventies*) the Feelgoods closed ranks and together, the band, Chris Fenwick and roadies Fred and Geoff were 'the magnificent seven'.

'We were tearing the pubs apart,' says Fred. 'It was just awesome, exhausting. Best years of my life. Lee was a total gentleman. Two sides of him: onstage, street Herbert; offstage, gentleman scholar.

'At the time there was a lot of long hair, groovy guys, it was all "man", post-hippy … Even the road crew would be going, "You're over there, man." "Don't call me 'man'." It was a different attitude: "We're not hippies, we're not groovy, get your fucking shit out of the way, because our stuff's coming in." And that's how it was. Otherwise we were a bunch of idiots from Essex who were going to be lowest on the pecking order. Well, we're coming up and we're pushing you out of the way. Maybe we were the first punks, the rebels coming through.'

The savagery of the Feelgood stage show was largely based on make-believe, but if any genuine trouble kicked off in the crowd, Lee had the confidence to take control. He had a natural air of commander-in-chief at the best of times. Put him on a stage and his power, apparently, had no bounds. Thankfully he used that power for good.

'I remember playing at the Lord Nelson,' said Wilko. 'Suddenly this fight has broken out, there are these guys on the floor slugging it out. Then a knife appears. Lee just steps off the stage, takes the knife, and carries on singing. This was serious, one of these guys had his ear nearly cut off and Lee just took the knife off him.'

Fred Barker would be in charge of Lee's harmonicas – although, as he insisted to me, 'they're not harmonicas – they're gob-irons. You know he had a waistcoat? Kept a gob-iron in there. He used to have a bandana with all of the gob-irons in, in all of the keys. I'd have back-ups on the side of the stage, but you had to keep them in order, and keep them wet otherwise they'd dry out. He'd have a C, D, E and an F but if he dropped one or it broke, you'd have to have replacements in glasses of water on the side just in case. He had to have one ready to go – there was no stopping the show.

'I used to love when he played slide guitar. Not technically brilliant, don't have to be. I used to put his guitar over his shoulder, get him set up. It was down to timing, and there were no rules, it was just: "It's now!" Everybody had to be completely on the ball.'

Wilko's brother Malcolm would also accompany the Feelgoods to London as a mate and general helping hand. 'At first I would walk around the pubs cheering and clapping from different places to drum up support, but after a few weeks that was no longer needed,' he remembers. 'They were pretty sensational [and] Lee was the most amazing character. He ended up hanging upside down from this crude lighting frame over the stage at the Kensington. He announced, "Ladies and gentlemen, our last number, 'Bony Fucking Moronie'." In front of me this rather posh voice said, "Bony who?"'

During one of the Kensington shows, he also barked out the whole of 'Route 66' with a towel over his face, like an eerie mask. 'He would just do the strangest, most unexpected things,' said Will Birch. 'People just could not take their eyes off the guy.'

'Lee told me that when he was on stage he could work off all his suppressed anger at everything wrong in his life, the world and society in general,' continues Malcolm. 'That threatening power was him letting off steam against the slings and arrows of outrageous fortune. Wilko is the same in his way. They both played the part so well because it came to them naturally.' (Admittedly, the cathartic nature of the live show wouldn't always be sufficient in purging pent-up frustration. The writer Hugo Williams wandered backstage after a show at the Paddocks on Canvey to find Brilleaux standing next to a blackboard, a stick of chalk in his hand and the word 'LIAR' scrawled on the dusty black surface. Lee was 'pointing an accusing finger at Figure, who was already on the floor'.)

It is amusing to imagine the Feelgoods steaming in to 'posh' areas of West London, kicking Canvey sand in everyone's eyes. Rumours that the future Princess of Wales, Lady Diana Spencer, attended their shows are viewed with scepticism by then *NME* writer and rock biographer Chris Salewicz, however.

'She wasn't old enough!' he scoffs. 'I don't think it's true.' To be fair, speculation that Lady Di sneaked in and bobbed about awkwardly to the Feelgoods is one of the least interesting things about them at this time. They were startling, they were self-sufficient, and in an era of proto-stoner, prog, folk and space rock, they were clearly on a different drug to everybody else, literally and metaphorically.

Britain in the 1970s could be a dark, uncertain place. Many understandably wanted to escape altogether by entering into communion with shed-loads of psychedelics. Others wanted to stay in touch with a grittier side of life and just charge on through. For the Feelgoods, those Sunday lunchtime shows at the Kensington were fuelled by beer and black bombers. They weren't escaping; they were engaged, fiercely present – no frills or indulgence, just pure entertainment and hard work, sweat flying off Lee in great arcs, to the extent that he had to take salt tablets after the show lest he suffer agonising muscle cramps.

Hard as it may be to believe, Lee insisted to *Sounds*' Jonh Ingham that he'd 'never been that keen on physical exertion'. Even Wilko, a veritable pub rock Nijinsky, would protest that 'none of us is particularly athletic. We're the kids who used to hide in the bogs when there was sports at school.' But on stage, when it came to communicating a song, that was where Lee expended his energy. 'I think it's necessary,' he said. 'If you just stood there and sang "Route 66", I don't think it'd mean anything. There've been times when I've been feeling ill and I've said, "OK, I'm going to take it easy and not jump about tonight," but I find I just have to.' Brilleaux's shouty blues style was, he would later claim, at least partly down to the fact that during this period of the band's career, the PA systems were generally ropey and he'd *have* to yell out the vocals to be heard. 'I could sing better if I laid back a bit, but I can't do it,' he said. 'I like shouting. It's fun.'

Every show was conducted with one hundred per cent commitment, and there would be no exceptions – even when, during these early years, they were so skint they played two shows a night, like the hard-grafting music hall entertainers who had graced the same stages seventy years before them. 'We'd say, "Let's hold back on the first," but after five minutes you couldn't. "Fuck it, I don't care if I die in the taxi on my way to the next gig, this is where we are. This one."'

This was an attitude Lee would retain throughout his entire career – even when they weren't 'greedy for bread. It's always make-or-break time, however big you are,' he'd insist. 'I don't think there's ever a time when you can rest on your laurels.' It was rare to find a band with such vehement dedication, with not one but two wildly kinetic frontmen. As many have observed, as with Daltrey and Townshend, Jagger and Richards, you didn't really know who to watch. The press – 'bored', as Lee observed, with the current state of play – were paying attention.

'We were working two or three nights a week in London, I mean, for fifteen pounds a [show], and that was for the whole band, not each,' Lee Brilleaux told the BBC's Stephen Foster. 'All of a sudden one day this fella, who we later found out worked for the *NME*, I think it was the editor, came up to us and said, "I think you're wonderful. I want to do a thing in my newspaper." We said, "Oh yeah?" We'd heard this one before. "What paper do you work for?" and he said, "The *New Musical Express*."'

The man in question was Tony Tyler, and before long ever more key writers were transfixed by the earthy allure of the Feelgoods: Chris Salewicz thought they were 'tremendous. Like nothing I'd ever seen. They were distinctive, and much better than any of the other pub rock groups. They also behaved like grown-ups. There was a certain life experience there, even though they were young. Both Wilko and Brilleaux seemed like old souls.

'They were intimidating – Brilleaux looked like someone you'd meet in a betting shop, which of course he was. Wilko's doing his psychedelic tramlines, Figure looks threatening, Sparko looks like one of those Irish navvies you'd see later that afternoon in the Shepherd's Bush Odeon watching a film, pissed, flared trousers and stack heel boots … but not hip ones. Then there was the short hair, the way they moved, the choice of material, it was just fantastic.'

Writers Mick Farren (of Pink Fairies infamy) and Charles Shaar Murray were also early champions of the group, Farren seeing a stunning three-encore performance by the band at Dingwalls in Camden Town. Farren hailed their 'compelling, sinister weirdness … Lee Brilleaux is a tall hoodlum figure … and the kind of harmonica player who's not afraid to trade off with the guitarist.' The fact that the band had recently raised merry hell with a gig for the prisoners languishing in Wandsworth nick only added to their general ne'er-do-well chic.

The publication of Farren's *NME* review was delayed thanks to the printing strikes, but when it finally came out, while it was cause for celebration, Malcolm 'saw trouble ahead'. It was a lengthy, positive article clearly written by someone who was fascinated by them, but … 'The main focus was Wilko,' remembers Malcolm. 'He was a star, et cetera, et cetera … The fact was: Wilko played off Lee and Lee played off Wilko. They were much more together than they were apart. I could see that the unbalanced attention was in a way downplaying the role of Lee, and he was a great performer.'

As far as Wilko was concerned, 'Lee was the leader. When we were onstage, I'm looking at him. He would gesticulate and send me off on a guitar solo, and then I'm back and looking at Lee. I was kind of an adjunct to what he was doing. The focus came from Lee, he was the star, it doesn't matter what people say. People used to say when things went bad that it was something to do with this who's-the-leader? thing, but for my part, and I do believe for Lee's as well, that was never an issue. I'd say, "Lee's the frontman and I'm like the lieutenant, and that's why it works."'

Both characters were hypnotic for very different reasons, and it didn't go unnoticed to the sharp-eyed Fred Barker that there'd be a bit of 'playing up' onstage if Brilleaux seemed to be attracting more attention during the show than Johnson, or vice versa – basically you had two peacocks on full magnificent display, pulling focus in divergent directions.

'It was my job to keep everything that they were breaking fixed, and if one of them was getting a bit of attention, the other one would break something so I would have to attend to him. I've got Wilko playing up and Lee giving it plenty – for the stage, they'd be interacting terribly aggressively. Then they'd come off and were wired up like mad. You're going to get a bit of a hierarchy at the back end of it … I can't knock Wilko for it. If you get that much adulation, you get head trips. Lee was the same but not so bad.'

Rivalry would often rear up between the pair when it came to women; Wilko on one occasion hooking up with a girl who Lee had apparently been planning to unleash his own charms on at an opportune moment. Wilko wrote in his diary that Lee appeared to be in something of a black mood on the way home from a show, the real reason dawning somewhat later.

Purported feather ruffling aside, these were the days when favourable reviews in the *NME* had the power to change things, and change they did. Lee had been cautious of allowing himself to become too excited about what was happening – he was nonchalant about the reality of trying to 'make it', admitting he initially didn't think they would even transcend the local pubs. Within six months of their first foray in town, Dr Feelgood would not only have an increasingly full diary, but their London shows would be teeming with journalists, record executives and tastemakers.

'Those pub gigs,' remembers Fred Barker. 'Sod the fire total, there'd be hundreds of people going absolutely mental, to the point that it was getting scary. Fortunately there weren't any arseholes trying to get on stage, because Lee was up there, threatening them in this show that they didn't want to get too involved in, but they were loving it.'

Of course, thanks to their menacing stage act, no one in the audience could have imagined what really went on behind the scenes. Malcolm remembers going for a walk with Lee before a show, lamenting a romance that was now over. Lee was listening and advising, every bit the sensitive confidant. As soon as they got back to the band room, however, they were greeted by Figure, who immediately demanded Lee show Malcolm his impression of 'a Suffolk Punch lawnmower escaping from a shed', much to Wilkinson the younger's bafflement.

'I really had no idea what to expect. Lee instantly transformed from a consoling friend into this hyper-performing, loose-limbed, eye-rolling person who appeared to be having some kind of fit. Figure was rolling on the floor with laughter. I, meanwhile, was just looking in shock at this transformation into something I'd never seen a hint of before.' (Another memorable and inventive interpretation in the Brilleaux canon of characters would be 'Larry the Self-Wanking Penis'. Your mental image of how this one plays out is probably correct.)

Haring back down the A13 to Canvey, still towelling sweat from their hair, the Feelgoods would generally be wheezing with laughter, and not just because of the presence of those soothing jazz cigarettes or lawnmower impersonations, but because they were incredulous at just how popular they had become. They knew they put on a strong show but they didn't feel particularly entitled to their new status as the darlings of London's live music scene. It was akin to charging into a bank, turning it over, smashing the place up, and striding back out, leaving any survivors stunned, changed, even grateful. 'We thought it was all bollocks and we used to laugh ourselves sick about it on the way home,' Lee said to Charles Shaar Murray some years later. 'We're still laughing. You can't take yourself too seriously. Muddy Waters don't take himself seriously.'

On paper, none of this should actually have worked at all. They were playing 1960s R&B in the 1970s, it wasn't trendy (not enough time had really elapsed for this music to even be ready for a revival), but Dr Feelgood didn't care about what was 'current'. They were just doing what they wanted to do, and in turn, they were waking everybody up with violent immediacy. Rock'n'roll had been emasculated, the Feelgoods had just handed it its balls back, and now it appeared that everyone who encountered them had a hard-on.

Before long, the Feelgoods would be inviting smitten journalists from the major music papers over to Canvey Island, smoking weed with them, playing pool and getting drunk. Canvey, and the Feelgoods, had a certain alien appeal to the big-haired champions of the counterculture who were writing for the rock press at that time. So why did it take a comparatively long time for them to get a record deal? The Feelgoods wanted to cut a disc, Wilko was starting to write original material, and they were all keen to 'go pro', but few A&R executives were prepared to take a chance on them. Record companies were 'rather conservative', said Lee, one excuse being the so-called 'vinyl crisis'.

'That was the big excuse for not signing us up: shortage of vinyl apparently – they're always coming up with something. We had lots of media attention, everything looked good, all the big companies expressed an interest but none of them made a concrete offer.'

It would take a maverick to take them on, someone with a bit of courage and foresight. The planets were aligning, and Nick Lowe, then vocalist/bassist in laid-back pub band Brinsley Schwarz (and veritable lucky charm for the Feelgoods throughout the coming years), would be the connection to that coveted recording contract.

One spring afternoon in 1974, the spindly, shock-haired Lowe headed into the West End, took the rackety lift up to the United Artists office, wandered in and sat down by A&R man Andrew Lauder's desk. Unlike some of the larger record labels, the UA office was known as a place that signings, cool members of the press and various mates could hang out, check out the records on offer, smoke a joint …

Over coffee, Lauder told Lowe he was currently working on the release of a beat group compilation that would feature The Pirates, Johnny Kidd's band, the group so beloved by Wilko Johnson. 'Nick said, "Funny you should mention that. I just saw this group who reminded me of the Pirates. They're called Dr Feelgood. You should go and see them, you'll love them." I went to see them as soon as I could, because any group that reminds Nick of Johnny Kidd and the Pirates has got to be worth a visit,' said Lauder. To the Kensington he went, and promptly 'fell in love. The Feelgoods made perfect sense to me. It was so totally against what was going on.'

For that reason, he knew he had to sign them, although that, in turn, was probably the very reason no one else would. But Lauder was prepared to take that chance, and a shared passion for blues and R&B only strengthened his intention. Lee's reaction was that Andrew was 'brave. [He stuck] his neck out and gave us a chance. You couldn't ask for a better A&R man. He gave us free rein, much more so than we'd ever be allowed now, and [so we were] allowed henceforth to make our own mistakes. Best way to learn, isn't it?'

United Artists might have been a relatively small label, but they were approachable and, most importantly, they were regarded as cool. This was largely thanks to Lauder, who had signed, among others, cosmic rock pioneers Hawkwind and, on the other and perhaps more relevant end of the scale, Brinsley Schwarz and the Flamin' Groovies. German 'Krautrock' outfit Can were also on United Artists. 'Basically all the hip groups who took all the drugs,' explains Chris Salewicz.

Lee, Chris and the rest of the group could see that Lauder 'got' them, and wasn't going to try and change them. United Artists had a good deal with the Feelgoods too – a Dr Feelgood album was never going to be a drawn-out, high-budget affair. The contract was signed 'within a matter of days', an excuse, not that the boys needed one, to have one of their infamous 'jolly-ups', no doubt kicking off at their beloved Admiral Jellicoe pub and culminating at 4 a.m. with a lawnmower[15] race outside 'Feelgood House', a communal dwelling on Central Wall Road where the band and their cronies – Lew Lewis, Dave Higgs, Dean and Warren

Kennedy to name a few – could hang out. You could say the place was known to the local constabulary.

On the subject of the then very young Dean Kennedy, he was on the scene at the tender age of fourteen because Lee and Chris, living at Feelgood House at that time, took him in after he left home. Found 'sitting on the doorstep', Chris took pity on the lad and 'he and Lee became like my parents,' Dean explains. 'I was living at Feelgood House.' Soon the teenager was not only partying with the Feelgoods and bunking off school to go to their gigs, he was roadie-ing for the band, learning the trade – and plenty besides – as he went.

'Lee was funny,' he remembers. 'Your best mate. I learned more off him than I did at school. Lee always had these *National Geographic* magazines. He noticed I'd started reading them, so he got me a year's subscription for my birthday. Generous person. I was looked after. And how many kids had a studio, a cellar full of drink, a bar, two Range Rovers, an E-Type Jag? Later, when I got married, Lee bought me a 1940s Austin Princess as a wedding present, like from *The Ant Hill Mob*. Massive, Rolls-Royce engine, like a gangster car. I was thinking, what?'

Lee and Figure in particular were, as you may have gathered, great car enthusiasts. In addition to the Jaguar, Lee would buy a Jeep, while Figure bought himself a big American Dodge Challenger. 'Lee was really, really pleased to see that,' said Figure. 'Couldn't wait to have his photograph taken up against it. He had an interest in cars himself. Together we would invent quite aggressive names for cars, like the "Datsun Destroyer", things like that. It was just constant fun. Lee was a great guy to talk to, vicious sense of humour, very strong, how much more can I lay at his feet? He was fantastic.'

Meanwhile, back on the mainland, the ink on the Feelgoods' contract was dry, and everyone in the United Artists office was now just as wild about the band as Andrew Lauder. 'We went to as many gigs as possible because [we] just enjoyed it so much,' said Lauder. 'You wanted to take people and go, "You've got to see this group!" They were just unlike anything else.' *NME* star writer Nick Kent recalls seeing them in 1974, noting that 'the singer had all the physical grace of a homicidal plumber', and he celebrated the fact the 'spivs' were finally here to boot aside the 'fops' – even though Kent was one of said fops himself, as he was quite happy to admit.

UA arranged for the Feelgoods to support Hawkwind on a short run of key shows, including the Glasgow Apollo and Manchester. The idea was to get the group used to playing on bigger stages and to bigger crowds, but putting Dr Feelgood alongside their acid-drenched hippy stablemates was an incongruous mix. In Manchester, Hawkwind's fans conveyed their hostility towards the support by heckling and throwing coins onto the stage. Peace and love, man.

'Thing is, we knew we were on our way,' says Wilko. 'We were just thinking, plebs. At one point this coin landed near Lee. He picked up this coin, bit it and threw it aside in contempt. I tell you what, it felt great. We just rose above everything after that.'

The deal with UA might have changed things on a fiscal level – new cars, for example (Lee's Jaguar soon became a common sight around Southend), new duds and many celebratory rounds being bought at the Jellicoe – but the Feelgoods remained true to their working-class Canvey roots. They also continued to support their contemporaries and friends in up-and-coming Southend bands. Thanks to the phenomenal energy injected into the London 'scene' by Dr Feelgood – 'hell's own dance band', as Mick Farren described them – the associated spotlight had lit up the grimy Thames Delta and, for a short time, Southend rock was in focus, and we're not talking about the stripy stuff that rots your teeth.

In turn, the groups who were being discovered thanks to the Feelgoods' growing success tipped their hat to them – soulful Southend icon Mickey Jupp, for example, would perform the song 'Dr Feelgood' in tribute to his mates from Canvey who were present that evening. This was a great compliment; Brilleaux always held 'Juppy' in very high regard. Southend gig-goer Hugh Cumberland attended this very show, and on spotting Lee, Sparko and Figure leaving the Cricketers music pub in Westcliff that evening, boldly decided to extend the Feelgood homage (possibly while in an advanced state of refreshment) in the middle of the road for them.

'I treated them to my best Lee Brilleaux impersonation,' recalls Hugh. 'I was standing on the Zebra crossing, arm pumping, the works. Lee stood and watched, applauded at the end, and, as I made it back to the pavement, ruffled my hair and pressed a bunch of loose change into my hand, adding, "Don't give up the day job". He got in the Jag with the boys and roared off, totally pissed, I suspect.'

Another Southend nightspot was the Blue Boar on Victoria Avenue, and Lee would often be seen at the bar if Will Birch was playing with his soon-to-be hit band the Kursaal Flyers. As kind as he knew Lee was, Will was never sure whether his support was wholly altruistic. 'Although we were no threat – we were good but we were playing completely different music – I always felt Lee was keeping an eye on us. Actually he wanted to help us. He and Chris got us our first show in London at the Kensington in July 1974. It was a reciprocal thing. This Southend scene was developing, with us, the Feelgoods, Eddie and the Hot Rods, Mickey Jupp, the *NME* would talk about the Thames Delta … There was a scene going on, and you need a scene. There *was* a bit of Lee keeping an eye on us though,' Will adds wryly. 'You know, "Don't go *too* far …"'

Wilko Johnson

We had some defective loud speakers and they needed to go back to the factory in Ipswich. At that time, Sparko was doing Artex, wall-covering and all that. So our transport was 'the Artex van' – an A35 covered in Artex with all different swatches – so that's what we were going to drive to Ipswich. Before we set off, we smoked this black Afghan dope, and we were smashed, man. Really smashed. We got to Ipswich OK and did what we did with the speakers, and as we were driving back, we see a sign for Flatford Mill. So we said, 'Ooh, let's go to Flatford Mill and see where Constable painted his painting.' When we got there, there was a big van, kitted out like a caravan. Standing in the back door with a mug of cocoa was basically Tony Hancock in *The Rebel*. It was this artist and he was fucking painting Flatford Mill.

We were watching him and we started getting the giggles. We were saying, 'Shall we ask him if he wants to come and have a smoke with us?' And then we were saying, 'We can't, because once we get there we'll start laughing, and he'll think we're yobbos taking the piss.'
We were looking at him, and he looked so tragic with his double-coat and his boots and his mug. We decided we'd better just go, we were pretty stoned. So we're driving along behind this car, and there's this little dog in the back, a Chihuahua or something, and he's running up the back seat, running onto the back left of the car, down onto the back seat, over the driver's shoulder and just going round and round in circles. We were *pissing* ourselves laughing at this dog.

Then the Artex van broke down. Our expert on cars was Figure, so we phoned him and said, 'What are we going to do?' Because it had stopped

... I don't know ... something or other. Anyway, Figure told us we could get the thing to Canvey if we got it going one time and *did not stop*. We were *not* allowed to stop.

We were still up near Flatford Mill, and we were driving away. 'Fuck, it's a traffic light!' And we'd swerve off down another road, go around the block and get back on. 'Ah! A green light!' And we did it, we got to Canvey Island without stopping.

And that's the kind of guys we were.

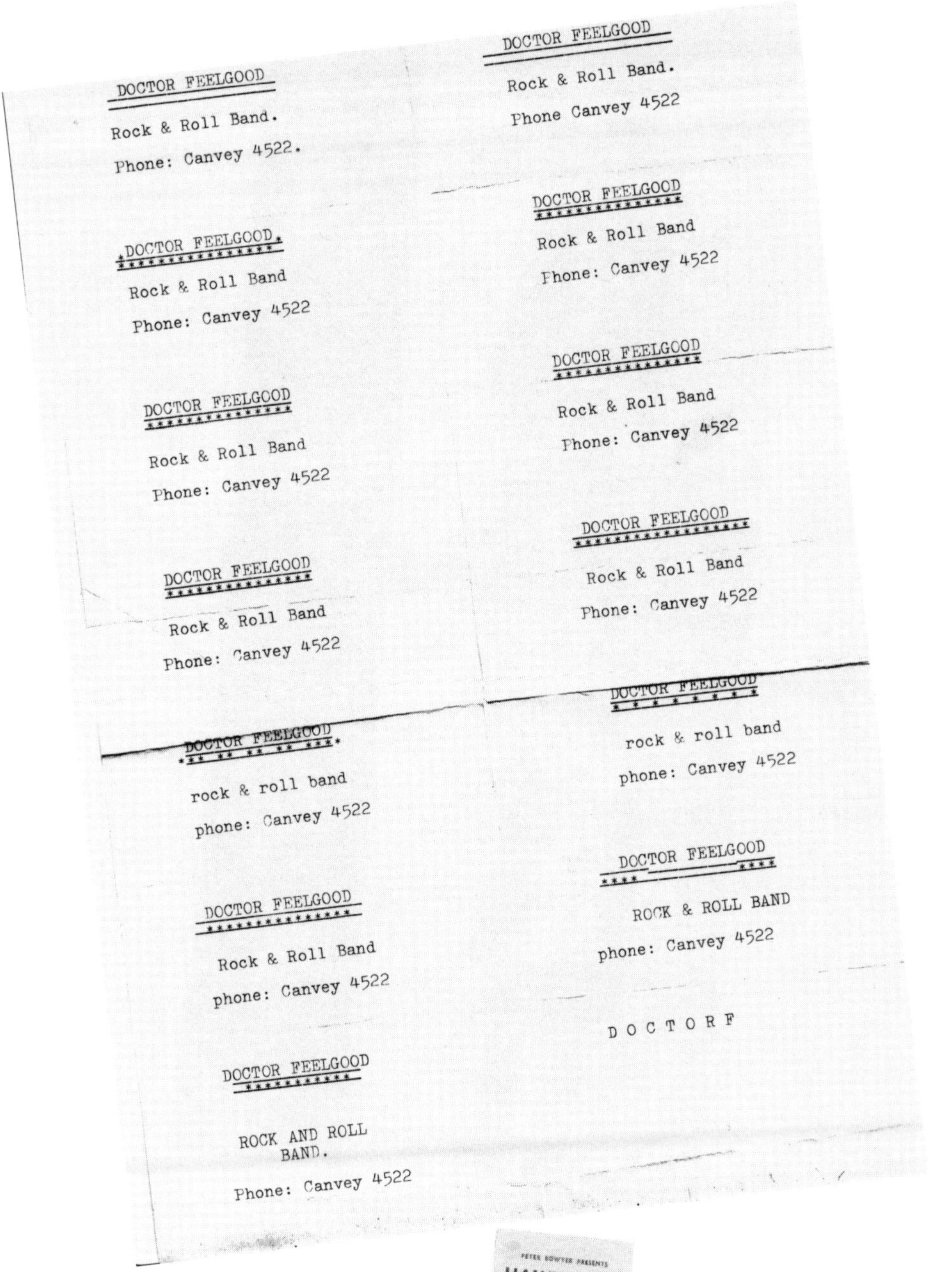

DOCTOR FEELGOOD

Rock & Roll Band.

Phone: Canvey 4522.

DOCTOR FEELGOOD.
****
Rock & Roll Band

Phone: Canvey 4522

DOCTOR FEELGOOD
****
Rock & Roll Band

Phone: Canvey 4522

DOCTOR FEELGOOD
****
Rock & Roll Band

Phone: Canvey 4522

DOCTOR FEELGOOD

Rock & Roll Band.

Phone Canvey 4522

DOCTOR FEELGOOD
****
Rock & Roll Band

Phone: Canvey 4522

DOCTOR FEELGOOD
****
Rock & Roll Band

Phone: Canvey 4522

DOCTOR FEELGOOD
****
Rock & Roll Band

Phone: Canvey 4522

DOCTOR FEELGOOD
****
rock & roll band

phone: Canvey 4522

DOCTOR FEELGOOD
****
rock & roll band

phone: Canvey 4522

DOCTOR FEELGOOD
****
Rock & Roll Band

phone: Canvey 4522

DOCTOR FEELGOOD
**** ****
ROCK & ROLL BAND

phone: Canvey 4522

DOCTOR FEELGOOD
****
ROCK AND ROLL
BAND.

Phone: Canvey 4522

D O C T O R F

Home-made, hand-typed business cards still waiting to be chopped up and distributed.

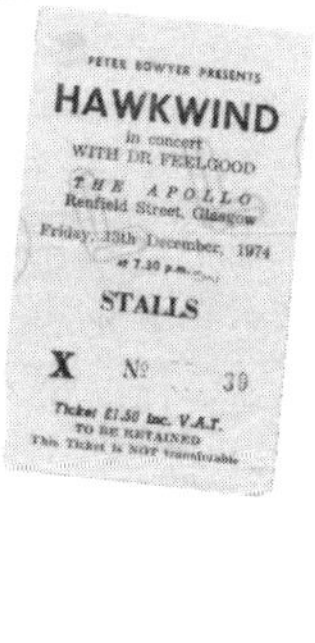

PETER BOWYER PRESENTS
HAWKWIND
in concert
WITH DR. FEELGOOD
THE APOLLO
Renfield Street, Glasgow
Friday, 13th December, 1974
at 7.30 p.m.

STALLS

X   Nº   30

Ticket £1.50 inc. V.A.T.
TO BE RETAINED
This Ticket is NOT transferable.

Wilko Johnson's personal archive

*The denim had been ditched and Lee
Brilleaux was now in suit-jacket-and-skinny-tie
mode. Simultaneously sharp and scruffy, this
was a somewhat radical look for the time. He
was turning a conservative look on its head
and taking it rather further than the Mods had
done before him.*

6. THE CASE OF THE ROCKFIELD STUDIO IRREGULARS

I'm not a fucking artist. These suckers in the record companies don't understand. 'Oh, you're a real musician ...' I can't even play guitar properly. Rock is an expression of what you feel in the moment. There is room for everyone, there is no real competition.

Lee Brilleaux to *Rock and Folk*

Aware as the Feelgoods were that they couldn't play a cover-heavy set for ever and maintain their momentum, Wilko Johnson had taken on the mantle of songwriter and was writing original material at a prodigious rate. Lee, on the other hand, was reluctant to write at all. This must partly have been because there was one member of the band who was more than happy to take on that task, and he was doing it with apparent ease and an impressive strike rate, but Lee admitted later that he was intimidated by Wilko. Lee was passionate in his continued self-education but Wilko had a degree, plus his credentials as an English teacher. Then there were the witty diatribes of free association, the spontaneous poetry recitation ... words were, to Lee's mind, *Wilko's* job. Lee too had the imagination, the gift for wordplay, 'he had everything, everything, everything,' protested Wilko, 'but he wouldn't do it.'

'Lee was well read; if I wanted to indulge in some quotation, or refer to some literature, I knew Lee would know what I was talking about. We used to just talk about nonsense, very funny. Stupid surreal things. Once he came round and we got stoned and started talking about circuses, circus horses running around in a circle, and there'd be a guy in the middle and he'd crack the whip and then they'd all run in the other direction. That was enough to set us off.'

Still, Lee would not feel relaxed enough to write with Wilko. He would occasionally contribute ideas, a line or a riff, but he would write and work in a more collaborative way after Wilko's departure from the band in 1977. During the Wilko years, however, as Lee's future wife Shirley 'Suds' Brilleaux recalls him saying, 'I sing 'em. I don't write 'em. I ain't fucking Shakespeare.' This was, to be fair, possibly a barb directed at Wilko who wrote poetry and would frequently quote the Bard. If it wasn't, then Lee was rather over-estimating the skills required to write an R&B song.

The themes were universal and basic: love, loss, money, sex, the Delta (Thames, natch – Canvey is often a backdrop in Feelgood songs). The words weren't always one hundred per cent discernible anyway; judging by Lee's performances almost all the way through his Feelgood career, he largely seemed to use lyrics as more of a rhythmic device through which he could express his own visceral musicality, barking and spitting percussively over the music, vocally performing complex, mesmerising interactions with Wilko's chopping chords – therein lay his 'art' (a term he would smart at, I know). Still, somehow he felt blocked. Even his mum Joan had a bash at writing some lyrics. 'Lee always sneered at them,' she shrugged. 'But I'd been listening to all these records anyway, and they're not brilliant are they, the words? They're so silly.'[16] But Lee was resolute.

'I really felt he stood above me in so many ways, and yet he had feelings like that,' says Wilko. 'I think there was a thing about this university business. I don't go on about it, but I remember him occasionally passing comment, getting a bit sarcastic about university, which suggested that he felt intimidated by that because he wanted to put it down. He was clever. He could easily have gone to university, but he didn't. So there were all these inhibitions.

'As for all the creative work he did [as a teenager], the poems and drawings, well, he would have kept that right from me. Oh wow, when you think about it, what was going on there? There were all these hurt and misunderstood feelings. Man, we got each other so wrong in so many ways.'

Wilko wrote with Lee's voice very much in his head, as if he was writing the script for a pre-formed character already on the set, awaiting his lines. The songs would have Lee's personality, or at least the one he would 'move into' onstage, writ large throughout – sharp, jabbing, stripped-back little songs about sexual jealousy, driving through the night, squinting at the dawn on Canvey's sea wall, wreaking revenge on hard-hearted women … One thing was for sure, the Milton-obsessed Wilko didn't feel 'poetry' would be necessary for the Feelgoods. Admittedly, Lee would probably have agreed, saying at the time that 'you're not exactly inspired by [Canvey] to sing about beauty, are you?'

The band had worked Wilko's new songs into their live set, pounding them out to ever more euphoric crowds around the country; the venues were getting bigger and the bookings more numerous. On one occasion, Lee was back behind the wheel of the van on the way back from a show in Glasgow – no road rage incidents were reported, but so much speed had been consumed that even an arduous overnight journey back down from Scotland seemed to go alarmingly quickly. It was an occasion Wilko remembers fondly, because, while the rest of the band were snoring in the back of the van, Wilko and Lee bonded as the hours flew by and the cat's eyes whizzed past, Toots and the Maytals' *Funky Kingston*[17] – one of Lee's favourite albums – booming from the speakers as they went.

'It was late,' explains Wilko. 'We were tired, so I gave Lee one of these black bombers and said, "You drive, I'll talk." Lee was driving down the A1, really intense, and I'm talking about Shakespeare and everything in the universe, I felt great. Lee was so tense at the wheel, everyone else had crashed out, and I'm talking away and thinking, I love amphetamine. Everything just seemed very, very groovy. We were getting quite close, Lee and I, we were saying things to each other we wouldn't otherwise have said.'

Lee to Jonh Ingham, *Sounds*
The first album was approached in that we were asked to go down to Rockfield Studios and lay down *anything.*

Sessions had been booked at Rockfield in Monmouth, Wales, from 26 August 1974 for the recording of the Feelgoods' debut album *Down By The Jetty*. Andrew Lauder had employed Vic Maile to engineer and produce, a figure who would become a great ally to the Feelgoods even if they didn't always see eye-to-eye in the studio. The bottom line was that, as Lauder puts it, 'he was a beat-group kind of a guy. I wasn't going to have to sit down and explain it to him.'

There was an expectation from those outside the circle that the resulting release would just be 'a bunch of old standards. But we weren't into that at all,' said Wilko. This was an opportunity to shrug off the retro stamp they were in danger of being branded with and bring in a haul of tense, flinty Wilko originals such as 'All Through The City' (which contains the lyric that would be used for the album title), 'Keep It Out Of Sight', the nonchalant boogaloo 'I Don't Mind' and 'Roxette', which would outweigh a selection of covers including a live version of 'Bonie Moronie',[18] segueing into 'Tequila' and 'Cheque Book', written by Mickey Jupp. The aim was to capture the Feelgoods at their tough, wired finest – in other words, retain as much of a live sound as possible.

'The whole thing was really an introduction to the band,' Lee reflected. 'We wanted to show what we had been doing up until then, and to give some indication of where we were going. Another reason for not doing a lot of the standards was that I felt I couldn't do them justice on record – the originals are so great. We did try "I'm A Hog For You" but when we listened to it, it just wasn't good enough.'

In terms of preparation, they'd been playing so frequently that they were already 'fit for the studio', said Figure – the modus operandi was to stick microphones in front of them and record what they were like on any given night at any sweatbox in town. Just one original Feelgood track would see some major re-arrangement. The red-blooded 'Roxette' we know today was rather different to the 'Roxette' the band had been playing live up until that point. Hard as it may be to imagine, the song was originally Wilko's attempt to make like the Coasters and bring a little doo-wop into the Feelgood repertoire. The result was a melodic and somewhat benign number involving quite a bit of 'shadoodah-wop' backing vocal action from Wilko and Figure.

'We weren't happy with the way we'd been doing it,' admits Sparko. 'I think it was Lee's idea to use that riff, which is the main part of "Roxette". It makes the song.' The simple, three-note guitar riff in 'Roxette' was in turn, Lee confesses, 'nicked from a Lee Dorsey song'. Rock'n'roll is excellent at recycling – it's just what and how you recycle that matters. The new 'Roxette' now had an attitude that better suited its baleful lyrics, and it boasted a more interesting rhythmic pattern between the guitar and the vocals. 'Roxette' would be their first single, released in November 1974 with their bright, jagged cover of '(Get Your Kicks On) Route 66' on the B-side.

Recording took place over a period of about a fortnight, spaced between August and November – with the exception of their stay at the residential Rockfield Studios. The later sessions were necessarily sporadic as they had such a packed schedule. Wilko came into his own in the studio. Lee, on the other hand, was not exactly in his element.

'What was Lee like in the studio?' says Fred Barker. 'Go in, do one take, get out, go down the pub. But it wouldn't really be like that because you had engineers who'd go, "No, it's got to be done like this."

Lee would say to me, "Go out and get me some more harmonicas. You're bored, aren't you?"'

Suggestions to use Dolby sound reduction technology were dismissed by Lee altogether. On being asked what exactly the problem was, he quipped, 'Would *you* trust someone with a name like Dolby?' Evidently many did, but the concept did not blend well with the raw Feelgood ethic. The idea of 'noise reduction' was a superfluous one in Lee's eyes – it was like being at a live show and not being able to hear the electrifying susurrus of the crowd. (This is reminiscent of John Peel's famous distrust of CDs – on being told they cut down on 'surface noise', he protested that *'life* has surface noise'.)

Sparko: 'We were all involved every step of the way, including the mixing, but Lee didn't take much interest in the technical side. You'd have the big recording desk and usually there'd be a bit at the end, like a blank bit of counter, and there's a thing called a chinagraph where you mark positions on the desk, marking where the faders are. Well, Lee used to draw his own set of dials and knobs on the blank bit of counter to pretend he was using them. He didn't have much understanding of how it technically worked, but that was his fun, I suppose.'

Lee might have been turned off by mixing desks and the sterile, repetitive nature of performing their songs in a sound-proofed, brightly lit room, but the Feelgoods' time at Rockfield would be a happy one, and this was in no small part due to the discovery of the nearby Punch House hostelry in Monmouth. 'The landlord wears plus-fours, takes snuff, makes mutton with onion sauce, serves delicious pints of beer and they never close,' Lee declared to Charles Shaar Murray. How could any sane man resist?

'We had a great time,' says Sparko. 'We got on so well with the landlord we used to detour and go down for lunch there for years afterwards. He said, "When you lot first walked in, I thought you were bad news. Didn't like you much." But we ended up great friends.'

Much to their amusement, Lee, Sparko and Figure (Wilko being teetotal at the time) were invited to join the Punch House darts team. Sparko continues: 'We said, "But none of us can play darts." The landlord said, "But you can drink, can't you?" And that was our in, we used to go touring around the other pubs with the people from the Punch House and be part of their team.' Those of you alarmed by the idea of rock'n'roll's most dedicated drinkers being encouraged to fling sharp objects around in a confined space will be happy to know that 'there weren't many darts being thrown,' Sparko reassures. 'It was just drinking.'

The Feelgoods' notorious intake of alcohol was not yet at its peak – a later sojourn to the US would really tip them over into Olympic-level consumption – but it was already starting to cause a gradual separation. Wilko could be, by his own admission, moody and uncompromising, but his disdainful attitude towards downing a beer or twelve would increasingly alienate him from the others over the coming years.

Still, another element of life at Rockfield that would give Lee a welcome diversion would be the presence of Brinsley Schwarz, who were there working with respected guitarist Dave Edmunds while the Feelgoods were recording. 'We had a good time with them,' remembers Figure. 'Lee was at his comical best and we were just taking the mickey. We were being very Cockney with them and they were a little bit posh, but they were really enjoying it.' There was also ample opportunity for practical jokes. 'We'd put a hoover under someone's bed and trail the cable out of the window,' explains Sparko. 'Then we'd plug it in downstairs.' Then they would wait until the unsuspecting victim went to bed, bid them an innocent goodnight and, at a moment deemed opportune, switch on the hoover at the mains for heart attack-inducing results.

In addition to their time in Wales, there would be extra sessions in September at Jackson's in Rickmansworth, and the album would be mixed famously in mono for that cohesive 'live' sound, at Pye and Conway Studios in London.

As far as the decision to mix *Down By The Jetty* in mono was concerned, 'it wasn't planned that way,' Lee told BBC Suffolk's Stephen Foster. 'We recorded it in stereo, same as everybody else. What we did was refuse to do any overdubs. We were suspicious of the recording studio and the idea of playing two guitars … Vic Maile would keep saying, "Put another guitar on the track," and we'd say, "No, no, we can't do that, it'll destroy our natural sound."'

'We didn't actually put it into mono until we mixed it,' Lee explained to *Blues Bag*. 'Vic quite liked the mono idea, but I think he was frightened he might be overstepping his brief as far as UA were concerned. When we came to mix it originally into stereo, frankly, it sounded terrible. So we remixed it into mono and it sounded fifty per cent better. Then some UA bright spark said, "Perhaps we can make this a marketing ploy and play this mono angle up."'

'Of course, all the critics said, "Oh yes, they're going back to mono and it's a big …" you know, but it wasn't like that at all,' said Lee in later years. 'We just did it by accident.' Wilko wasn't happy about UA using the mono mix as an 'angle', concerned that it threw the band straight back into the nostalgic mode they were trying to avoid, but Lee regarded the issue with *sangfroid*. 'Looking back, [it] was quite smart really.'

Much to the band's chagrin at the time, however, the record company were keen to print the word 'mono' on the cover to make a feature of it. 'We didn't want it to be *called* mono, we just wanted it to sound good,' explains Sparko. But ultimately, what they arrived at was an album they were proud of – the album they wanted to make. 'It was our first recording,' Lee told Stephen Foster. 'We didn't have anything to judge it by – we all thought it was stupendous! We thought it was the best thing we'd ever heard. It was *us* on record.'

Once sessions were complete, the Feelgoods threw themselves straight into an ever more hectic gigging schedule. 'It had become very groovy to see Dr Feelgood,' confirms Chris Fenwick, and, as was becoming the norm, there was increasingly little time to devote to anything else. Therefore, the shoot for the album artwork had to be fitted in at the only opportunity they had. This happened to be at 3 a.m. after yet another evening's work, throwing R&B grenades at stupefied London audiences before screeching back down the A13 to Canvey.

The Feelgoods, still in their soaking stage clothes, headed to the historic Lobster Smack pub by the sea wall with a photographer, and, looking righteous if sleepy-eyed, proceeded to pose,[19] before wandering out to the jetty as dawn broke. They were shattered, unkempt and probably hadn't looked in a mirror for a while. It wasn't a typical band shoot. As the photographer took some black-and-white test shots by the jetty, Lee actually fell asleep standing up, leaning against the sea wall, arms folded against the brisk Estuary chill.

The initial plan was to use colour, but once the band had seen the striking monochrome shots, there was no contest. They fitted the band's saturnine image and chimed appropriately with their inescapably old-school feel. Even the picture with Lee mid-snooze was included on the back.

Chris Fenwick: 'For the moodiness we created, black and white was perfect. Everyone else was saying, "Are you sure, boys? Colour's the name of the game these days. People are buying colour televisions, you know!" But it was the right thing to do.' Perhaps it was also taken as a cosmic sign that when the glossy colour prints were presented to the band at Conway Studios, 'Figure immediately spilled a cup of coffee over them,' says Wilko. 'Straight away. It was awful. But it didn't matter, we'd already decided.'

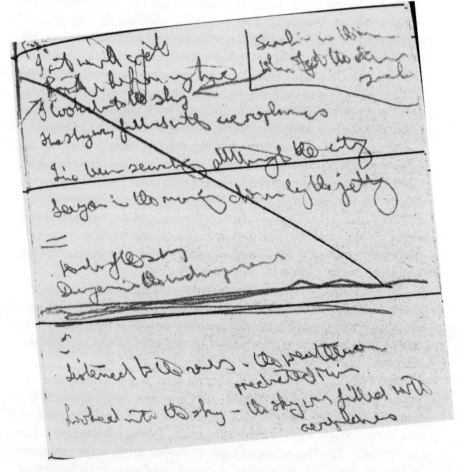

Scribbled lyrics to the defining song 'All Through The City' from Wilko Johnson's 1974 appointment diary.

Lee Brilleaux, resplendent in his now infamous
white jacket, on slide guitar.

During an era in which many recording artists were inclined to embrace rather more escapist themes than their perhaps unlovely local roots on the cover of their debut, the Feelgoods' decision to present themselves thus was significant, even if it wasn't completely strategic. 'All we were anti was people prancing around with make-up on,' says Fenwick. 'We did play that Canvey-Island-Delta thing consciously [though]. We come from the Thames Delta, there's oil refineries, it's bluesy ... And it had more of an edge to it than if the poor buggers had come from Swindon.'

The album was scheduled to hit the shelves in January 1975, appropriately marking the half-way point in the decade. After this, little, musically, would be the same – not that the Feelgoods could have known the far-reaching effect *Down By The Jetty* would have at that time. The band had, however, cottoned on to the fact that their 'Canvey mystique' was capturing imaginations up West, so really there could only be one way to launch *Down By The Jetty*, once the time came. "Bus 'em all down to Canvey, right?' says Chris Fenwick. Throwing parties was something the Feelgoods were very, very good at. They practically had one a day anyway – the general ethos being, 'Good day? Have a party! Bad day? Have a party!'

'Lee was always the first one up, last one to bed,' remembers Geoff Shaw. 'I'd be in the corner thinking, God, it's five a.m., I want to go to bed and never wake up, and Lee's turning the records up. His stamina was amazing. Sometimes we'd come back after a gig really late, but he just wanted to play music. It was a ritual: he'd make you smoke something and then he'd play you something you'd never heard, like Django Reinhardt. Back then, to even read about someone like Django, you'd have to go to a special shop or read a jazz magazine. He'd put it on really loud and just sit and snap his fingers, listening. He didn't want the night to end, he just didn't want it to end.'

Once Sparko had built the now notorious 'Cluedo Club' bar in Feelgood House, the partying really was 24/7, so when it came to hosting a bash for the great and the good in honour of *Down By The Jetty*, it was practically just another day at the Feelgoods'. They were single-minded when it came to what they felt would suit them best, and, again, UA had the guts to trust them. There'd certainly be no way they'd be poncing up to town for a civilised listening party; *Down By The Jetty* was a tangible statement of who they were, where they were from and what they were about. The Feelgoods might have had a handsome singer in his early twenties, but he was an unusual kind of 'star', being more excited by Thames barges and beer than limousines and cocktail olives. Forget the glitter of the contemporary glam movement, Lee Brilleaux was all sheepskin coats, scruffy hair, hard work and bad language. The launch would simply be an extension of the earthy, real Feelgood schtick. Which wasn't even really a schtick.

All UA had to do was provide endless crates of tequila; whether this was a cheeky reference to the inclusion of 'Tequila' on the album, or simply because it had become a preferred tipple of Lee Brilleaux's is uncertain, but either way they were soon 'gargling the stuff by the pint' according to Chris Fenwick. 'There's a Van Morrison song in which he sings, "The record company has paid out for the wine" ['Saint Dominic's Preview']. That became the catchphrase.' And so, under a grey January sky, Canvey Island played host to the Feelgoods' first record launch, taxing many a liver and destroying more than a few brain cells in the process.

Hopped up on R&B (and the rest) and dropping the odd aitch in an attempt to fit in with their formidable yet convivial hosts, the music biz illuminati observed the Feelgoods in their lair as if on safari before finally staggering back to the city to file their reviews. The only criticism would be that, in the opinion of those who had experienced the sheer force of their live shows, the blood-and-guts excitement of a Feelgood performance could not be conveyed on vinyl – or at least it hadn't been captured as yet. But, as *NME*'s Nick Kent put it, it still had the ability to 'grab you by the lapels [screaming] out, *"this is rock'n'roll."*'

'[And] people who want a live Feelgood album will get one when the time is right,' promised Brilleaux.

In an era of increasing aimlessness, the Feelgoods seemed to have the focus of a laser beam and a robust disregard for the zeitgeist. Even the Stones, who had originally hooked Lee into the blues, would be rejected by Lee (he wasn't a fan of their latter predilection for producing 'mawkish ballads' such as 'Angie'). Part of Brilleaux's appeal was that there was something old-fashioned about him. He seemed to personify a return to the kinds of things his dad might have done, the kinds of things that 1960s kids would have actively avoided doing. He was in his own world, from the books he read to the movies he watched (Richard Attenborough's *10 Rillington Place* was a Feelgood favourite). While everyone else was looking at the stars, Lee, and the Feelgoods, were earthed, gruff and unpolished, and looking straight ahead. They knew what they wanted, and no trend was going to change that.

Lee would view the vagaries of the music industry with a keen sense of irony, but close friends noticed the temporary conflict he was going through as the Feelgoods stood on the brink of real fame. Lee would brood upon his new position and where it put him in the scheme of things, at least in the scheme of things on Canvey Island. The Feelgoods had sweated in a bid to achieve the dream of 'giving up the day job'. Now, as with many working-class people made good, Lee was uneasy, not least because the better the Feelgoods did financially, the more they wanted to be generous, and, while the Feelgoods were undoubtedly Canvey's golden boys, the mood was just starting to turn. The more rounds the Feelgoods bought at the Jellicoe, the more they'd be accused of being 'flash bastards'. If they stopped, of course, they'd be 'tight bastards'. These were problems they'd never had to consider before.

'Early on, he was struggling with an identity problem,' remembers Pete Zear, who had become close friends with Lee by this stage. 'You know, "At night, I go out onstage and I'm Lee Brilleaux. In the day I'm feeling guilty thinking, I'm sitting here not going to work."

'I remember there was this one weekend Lee had been struggling with his demons and then he announced, "Right! From now on, I'm not going to snap back, I'm going to be like this *all* the time!" Good on you, mate, because that's what you are. There's the *NME*, you're on the front page – that is *who you are*. You're not a solicitor's clerk.'

Joan Collinson on Lee 'Angry Young Man' Brilleaux

He wasn't really an angry person. It was all an act. Seemed to go over all right, didn't it? I really don't understand any of it.

Jools Holland on the Physiognomy of Brilleaux

Lee had this great face, this amazing, very well-lived-in face. It was like a person from English history, but he could have been from all sorts of times; he could be an eighteenth-century highwayman, or a medieval baron, or he could have been a Dickensian villain.

Chalkie Davis

Lee Brilleaux looking very much the lord of
the manor at home on Canvey, watch-chain in
place, bow-tie and waistcoat … Long live the
Utterly Club.

'Milk And Alcohol' backstage pass, boasting
Wilko's infamous Dr Feelgood logo (which
now graces many a Feelgood fan's flesh in
tattoo form.)

THE ROCK 'N' ROLL GENTLEMAN'S GUIDE TO HUMAN INTERACTION

- Find the humour in everything (where appropriate).

- Embrace solitude. Even in places where other people are socialising, there is nothing wrong with taking time to observe the 'human carnival'.

- Be polite and generous: when people come in their droves to see you, it is natural to feel a little embarrassed. However, if you shy away from them, they'll feel rejected. Instead, slip into another character if you have to (this is a useful technique in all sorts of situations), buy them a drink and have a chat.

- If the above droves have indeed come to see you, but they are waving some sort of weaponry, have a homicidal glint in their eye or are just plain rude, it is perfectly acceptable to do one or both of the following:

    1) Out-mad them in a bid to distract your potential assailants; or
    2) use appropriate expletives to make your feelings known.

- A rock'n'roll gentleman may certainly lead an unusual life, but he does not boast or monopolise the conversation. He is more interested in asking the people around him about *their* lives.

- Retain a healthy sense of the absurd. Most people are pretty absurd so this will stand you in good stead.

- Question the rules and, in particular, authority. There's no need for people to be rude just because they're wearing a uniform, a stupid hat or are holding a gun.

- Parties are important. Have lots of them.

- Know when to keep your trap shut.

Dr Feelgood and Chilli Willi breakfast on the M1

Mick Gold

Tourmates Dr Feelgood and Chilli Willi and
the Red Hot Peppers stop off for yet another
roadside breakfast during the Naughty
Rhythms Tour of 1975.

7. THE MAN IN THE DIRTY WHITE SUIT

Well, I ain't never heard nothing like us before. Stop and think about it – neither have you.

Lee Brilleaux to Neil Spencer, *NME*

The year 1975 would be a hugely significant one for Dr Feelgood. They would release two albums, both of which would be held up as touchstones for the coming punk generation,[20] and an invasion of the continent beckoned ('most every country outside the totalitarian state jobs', as Lee reported). They would also make their first TV appearances, which would include waspish performances of 'Roxette', 'Keep It Out Of Sight' and 'She Does It Right' on *The Old Grey Whistle Test* and *The Geordie Scene*. What also helped to seal their fate was their inclusion on the evocatively titled Naughty Rhythms tour, which strode into the New Year, turned up the heat and promptly catapulted the Feelgoods out of the pubs and straight into the next league.

The tour featured mellow rock'n'rollers Chilli Willi and the Red Hot Peppers[21] and British soul band Kokomo. The three groups rotated the bill every night.

'That was about a year after we signed [with] UA,' Lee said in later years. 'The record company did a very good job in the way they promoted us, and the wonderful thing was that there was already a street buzz going, so all they had to do was to point us in the right direction to maximise our effect. It wasn't pure hype. In our case it was at least fifty per cent genuine, something I was quite proud of.'

This era was sadly not especially well documented in terms of live shows. The band's hometown show that November at Southend's Kursaal would be properly shot, and later released (*Going Back Home*), but further live footage is hard to find. All the same, anyone you speak to who was either involved directly or in the audience will tell you that this period, and the run-up to it, represented the group at their most electrifying.

'I don't think there are any really good films showing what it was like,' says Sparko. 'In those days, if you knew you were being filmed, the lighting would be a lot brighter, so you don't get the benefit of the light show. It'd be white lights on almost all the time. And everyone's thinking, God, they're filming, I'd better not make a mistake. You don't let yourself go so much.

'Most of the live footage I've got, it's all so fast. We couldn't believe it when we used to listen to the tapes, it just sounded like someone had taken the speed control and turned it up. There were nights when we'd be there to play for an hour and we'd come off stage and they'd say, "You've only done forty-five minutes." We'd be looking at the set list – we'd played them all, just too fast. Adrenaline. And substances.'

In the middle of the tour, the Feelgoods would break off to film their first TV appearances, and they would find that the resulting exposure instantly 'doubled, trebled our door at gigs – stupid,' remarked Lee to Neil Spencer, adding, 'I thought [*Whistle Test*] had a touch of class, meself.' And whether he was spoofing Bob Harris and the all-round middle-class air of the programme or not, well, one couldn't possibly confirm, but when Brilleaux announces 'She Does It Right' he does it in a noticeably plummy accent (look up 'Dr Feelgood Complete OGWT' on YouTube).

The experience of playing their music in a television studio was, of course, unnatural, especially as there was no response after their performances on the *Whistle Test* – there was no one there to respond apart from the camera crew, and they were a little busy themselves. But when the Feelgoods appeared on *The Geordie Scene*, Brilleaux was disconcerted that, while there at least was a studio audience this time, it was largely made up of 'nine-year-old girls!' he exclaimed. 'I thought, I can't do this act in front of these girls, it's evil, there ought to be a law against it … I mean, I'm not *that* much of a pervert.'

Former Feelgood roadie Neil Biscoe first came across the band while working on the Naughty Rhythms London show at the Rainbow, Finsbury Park, on 15 February 1975. Contrary to the Feelgoods' usual bare bones show, some special effects, including pyrotechnics, had been hired in. It quickly became apparent that potentially dangerous lighting effects and the Feelgoods did not mix well.

'They'd sub-contracted people from Britannia Row,' Biscoe remembers. 'Pink Floyd's warehouse was there, they'd started renting out equipment. My job was on the side of the stage setting off the pyrotechnics – it was just about connecting a battery.

'Nobody knew about Wilko's [erratic movements] … we'd set up flash-pots at the front of the stage and I kept getting cues on the headphones to get ready to set off the pyrotechnics, but then Wilko would start moving. We nearly blew him up – we never used them in the end. It was just too unpredictable and he moved so quickly. It was like, "Ready, set, NO!" He was completely oblivious to how close he was to having his testicles blown off.'

The tour was an opportunity to introduce the Feelgoods on a national level, and no matter who was headlining on any one night, the Feelgoods stole every show. By the end of that heady month-long run, Chilli Willi and the Red Hot Peppers were on the verge of splitting, Kokomo were heading out to the States and Dr Feelgood were, as Joe Strummer admiringly put it, 'the kings'.[22] From this point forth, the Feelgoods would headline their own tours.

Thanks to 'Naughty Rhythms' and the white-hot, pared-back might of *Down By The Jetty*, the Feelgood schedule was now rather lighter on pub gigs, with bookings at universities, civic halls, pavilions and Winter Gardens taking their place. Future Stiff Records boss and promoter Dave Robinson had wanted to book them for more shows at the Hope and Anchor in Islington, but it was clear that a move back to the pubs would be a move in the wrong direction. But apart from anything else, as Nick Kent observed, the pub rock groups who had been working themselves into the ground and 'paying their dues' throughout 1974 were now suffering health-wise (not that he was particularly a paragon of bonnie wellbeing himself). Chilli Willi guitarist Martin Stone was suffering from pleurisy, the drummer had malnutrition, and the Feelgoods were almost always down with the flu. For the Feelgoods' part, this new era would not only feed and shelter them a little better, but release them from the 'London stranglehold'.

Dr Feelgood would have about a month's grace until their own tour – appropriately titled Speeding Through Europe – which would take them through to the summer with hardly any time off, traversing the UK, charging into France, shaking Scandinavia by the scruff of its neck and providing the entertainment at Led Zeppelin's aftershow party at Earl's Court at the request of Robert Plant himself ('would have been bad manners to refuse,' said Lee).[23] They would also be spending a little more time in Amsterdam, just a few short years after their first visit, and they could fly straight from Southend and thus over Canvey. *Sounds* magazine accompanied them, recording the Feelgoods' excited banter as they tried to pick out their houses: 'Look, Wilko, there's some bloke climbing out of your back window!' 'There's Lee's Jag!' 'What's your old lady doing with all those geezers in the back garden?'

But before that, it was time to get back in the studio. They had some punchy new Wilko Johnson compositions honed by the road and ready to record (such as the moody shuffle 'Back In The Night' and 'Going Back Home', co-penned with Pirates guitarist Mick Green) as well as a mean selection of covers (including 'Rolling And Tumbling', which would feature Lee on characteristically forceful slide guitar, 'I Can Tell' and 'Riot In Cell Block Number 9'). It's symbolic of the Feelgoods' focused, rapid-fire trajectory that they would release two seminal albums within ten months of each other, both records clocking in at no more than forty minutes long.

Rather than return to Rockfield, the band would split the recording of their second album between sessions at London's historic Olympic Studios and Pye Studios, basically grabbing any time they could to lay down the tracks they'd selected. The record would be called *Malpractice*, and, in Lee's words, it would be a 'perfect continuation' from *Down By The Jetty*. 'I chose the title, a word used to describe an action contrary to the ethics of the medical profession.'

Malpractice suited Dr Feelgood's demeanour, and they were now playing more on the 'doctor' metaphor. In addition to the inclusion of the Wilko Johnson song 'You Shouldn't Call The Doctor (If You Can't Afford The Bills)', the imagery on *Malpractice* put the group over as a sleazy gang of blacklisted medical practitioners who'd inject you with something addictive as soon as look at you. Vic Maile was brought in to produce, with Doug Bennett engineering, although by now the group had some studio know-how, and were able to take more control.

As always, time in the studio would be kept to a minimum, Lee, in particular, becoming bored extremely quickly.[24] The lifelessness of the studio literally gave him nothing back when he sang; without the response of the crowd to complete the crackling electrical circuit of performing live, it just didn't make sense. So it was not for him the obsessive listening back of each song, the recording of take after take. 'The problem isn't composing, it's just that there is no audience in the studio,' Lee would explain. 'We don't want to create for the sake of creating, we want to produce energy and emotion.'

The Leiber and Stoller classic 'Riot In Cell Block Number 9' was a must for *Malpractice*. It had long been a key feature of the live Feelgood show, the intro of Figure's menacing, swinging drum pattern punctuated by the classic five-note blues lick as Lee, standing at the foot of the drum riser between Sparko and Wilko, looking every inch the hard-case convict, stares ahead, lights a cigarette and waits an audaciously long time before commencing to sing.

During one performance of this song, the poet Hugo Williams noted Brilleaux performing 'unchaste push-ups' on stage, and later hurling his Guinness bottle with all of his might into the crowd during the 'dynamite' line. 'In fact,' reports Williams, 'he let it slip out the back of his hand, but the effect was not lost upon his benumbed followers.' Pure confidence and rock'n'roll theatre.

According to Wilko, his own songs weren't quite doing it for the rest of the band at this point in time – 'Back In The Night', a song he rightly intuited would be a hit, initially failed to spark Lee's interest (although Lee would later claim this was a favourite of his to perform live, not least because it gave him a chance to play some slide guitar). Another nail in the coffin in terms of Wilko's relationship with not just Lee but the rest of the group would be hammered in when they discussed inviting Nick Lowe to write some material. Taking care of the songwriting single-handedly was a lot to expect for one already over-extended person, also a husband and a father, but, as Wilko remembers, all of these things were perceived, rightly or wrongly, as slights and would serve to drive them further apart.

'I was difficult to get on with then,' admits Wilko with a rueful laugh. 'It's embarrassing to think about it now but that's how it was. I'm a sensitive guy! The pressure of the songwriting, I don't think they realised what it was like. Also back then I did want to control everything. I had a total idea about what Dr Feelgood should be. Maybe that didn't go down too well. Sometimes I was a bit out of order – but so were they.'

The Speeding Through Europe tour would feature Lee's now infamous white suit. This outfit would become so legendary it was practically a band member in its own right, and it would never, ever be cleaned. There was no time, after all, but the sheer filth became a feature in itself, as would the contrast with Wilko's ubiquitous black whistle: two kings on opposing sides of the chessboard, stalking each other warily.

'They were so fucking hot. Nobody had seen anything like Lee and Wilko since Mick and Keith,' said Pink Fairies/Motörhead guitarist Larry Wallis, who would later write material with the Feelgoods

Top left: Lee Brilleaux in classic air-punching mode on stage. Bottom left: a refreshed Lee salutes the poet Hugo Williams behind the camera. Yes, the picture is blurry, but it's probably no clearer than Lee's vision at the time. Above: Lee behind the wheel of the bus. He was a good driver, but his duties were eventually passed on to someone with a calmer disposition, particularly after he once leapt out of the van to wave a baseball bat at the driver in front, who was a little slow for Lee's liking.

himself. As for Lee's attire? 'Arguably a suit possibly only slightly less historically famous than Presley's.' The defiance of wearing a pure white suit and then rolling around on a dirty stage in it was almost amusing. The smell, not so much.

'The main man and his poxy, stinking suits,' shudders Fred Barker. 'They were rank, and he knows they were rank. He'd throw them off, chuck them in a flight case and they were taken out the next night – we wouldn't touch them! Practically stood up in the corner of the room on their own.'

As the shows got bigger, the crew expanded, as did, inevitably, the number of people who wanted to wheedle their way into the inner sanctum. The band decided between themselves to stay separate from their audience rather than mingling with the crowd. This theatrical tactic of 'not breaking the spell' didn't just add to their enigma but ensured they weren't distracted during the crucial moments before walking on stage, psyched up and ready to attack, because 'even between the dressing room to the stage you get people wanting to have a conversation with you, right at that moment,' said Sparko. The rising tide of hero worship that was rushing towards the Feelgoods – Lee and Wilko in particular – was all very well, but not everybody respected their boundaries. That was where Chris, Fred and Geoff came in.

While Lee was kind to enthusiastic punters – frequently citing the old showbiz 'be nice to people on your way up …' mantra as well as keeping in mind that the fans 'put bread on my table' – ranks had to be tightened in order to maintain order. Even when it came to new crew members, 'it really was about whether they fitted with us or not,' says Fred Barker. 'Wouldn't take no fools. It was a tight team. The only fools we took in were the entertaining ones that could add something to it, otherwise you're out. It was very closed, it had to be. We had loads of guests, but they were our choice of guests that we tolerated. Wilko started getting these odd guests that no one really wanted around, but that was his choice and it was respected.'

Possibly another element that would add to the tension between Lee and Wilko would be the fact that it was Wilko who seemed to attract the most idolatrous attention from fans, groupies and lost souls, evidently hypnotised by his crazy-eyed gaze, ecstatic to have been impelled to 'stick 'em up' as Johnson pointed the business end of his machine-gun Telecaster at them.

'At the end of a show there'd be twenty crazy fans,' observed Barker. 'Nineteen of them wanted to see Wilko, one would want to see Lee.

Once you're all in the bus on your way home, you're all just blokes, so what? But it took its toll, naturally.'

Lee was, to be fair, more likely to give nutters short shrift rather than just tolerating or ignoring them if their presence was becoming vexatious to the collective spirit. Sparko: 'Lee said, "If ever you get confronted by a nutter," which you do quite often after a gig, "just pretend you're more mad than they are. It freaks them out." And it does. Lee would start flailing his arms about and shrieking. If someone weird was coming on to him or trying to talk to him you'd soon see them back off.'

Admittedly, most people took one look at Brilleaux onstage and assumed they were probably better off not meeting him at all. He looked like the kind of villain who'd look you up and down, bark out a humiliating list of your shortcomings, pour your own pint over your head and then punch you in the face. His dodgy-car-salesman-gone-berserk aura most likely shielded him from hassle, but the reality was that, if you were respectful, Lee would have time for you.

Family and friends were always welcome. Wilko's friend, the poet Hugo Williams, once turned up accompanied by the poet Thom Gunn, who loved every moment of it. Gunn was further thrilled when, backstage, he was politely greeted by Lee, who then told him, 'We used to do your poems at school,' before launching straight into a recitation of 'Elvis Presley'. The word-perfect performance was particularly notable because, as Lee later admitted to Hugo, he never actually liked the poem.

Lee's old school pal Phil 'Harry' Ashcroft would also attend shows, reconnecting briefly with Lee during the band's spring tour and meeting up with them at UMIST (University of Manchester Institute of Science and Technology). Lee put aside a backstage pass for Phil, gave him his first line of cocaine and invited him to watch from the wings.

'There was a lot of cocaine,' said Phil. 'Lee was smoking loads of dope, and they were drinking Carlsberg Special, so when they went on they had Carlsberg, cannabis, cocaine inside them, I don't know what else, but they were fucking tremendous. It was like being next to a nuclear reactor. I was just so proud. There they are, they've done something, it's something from my part of the world that's actually happened.'

Offstage, there was a moment of intimacy and a glimmer of the old days when Phil sat down with Lee for a conversation. 'That was just like being at school,' said Phil. 'It felt right.' Brilleaux had momentarily morphed back into Lee Collinson, before morphing straight back again. 'I have a letter from Lee from March 1975, we nearly started corresponding on a regular basis but the band suddenly got really big, and I found it a bit intimidating, this great Dr Feelgood machine. I went to some concerts when I didn't make contact with Lee afterwards. I was in my red loons and had long hair, beard. It was such a different vibe.'

The letter Lee had sent Phil, written during a rare period of downtime, started off cheerfully enough, making references to the tour, although he didn't mention the fact that said tour had concluded in Le Havre under something of a cloud. It was the first time Lee and Wilko 'almost came to blows', as Wilko remembers, and it happened onstage at the Salle Franklin in front of a crowd of rapt fans.

'We started to do "Riot In Cell Block Number 9". I can't remember if Sparko was late on the beginning, but I looked across and said, "Where are ya?" and both Sparko and Lee said exactly the right reply: "And where the fuck are you?" Lee threw his microphone down, the drums were still going, and we're squaring up, and the crowd were going apeshit. We got close to each other and suddenly it was like, "What are we doing? We're supposed to be working here." We both just turned away from each other and swung into the song. The atmosphere was fantastic. That was the closest we came to a fight. We were both obviously very angry with each other, but because I realised I was slightly in the wrong, it made me *more* angry.'

In the letter to Phil, Lee just conveys that he's now back home and hoping to do as little as possible other than 'duties' such as decorating the bedroom and 'visiting aged grandmother'. But by the next side of paper, the mood becomes reflective and then irate – albeit not towards anything directly connected to the Feelgoods. He is possibly just exhausted, and this has caused his defences momentarily to slip, but he opens up to Phil as he used to at school, letting rip about the people and situations that vexed and disgusted him. The letter seethes with raw memories, feelings of helplessness about the homeless, the battered wives, the wronged innocents, and fury directed at the exploitative 'sodomites' who had wormed their way into 'Sweyne Idiotsville'.

Wilko might have felt pressure as the band's songwriter, but being viewed as a leader, the life and soul of a seemingly endless party and, to some, even at twenty-three years old, an avuncular figure who always seemed to have the answers, Lee evidently felt pressures of his own that were not so openly expressed. Hence the courteous letter which soon transformed into a multi-page, existential and nihilistic rant, written as one fluent outburst with barely a correction. On the fifth and final side of paper, Lee wearily concludes that 'it is all hopeless and everything seems grotesque … I've given up caring about it … I am not afraid to admit "I am a human being; ergo I am too stupid and low an animal to comprehend anything other than my own life nor that I could be wrong about that." Sorry if this letter sounds like someone thinking out loud …' It's the sort of letter one might think twice about posting, one more like a furious diary entry than a correspondence with an old friend.

Lee was starting to 'veer into another world', according to Phil, a more showbiz world that would outwardly seem to numb some of his more introspective qualities. However, Lee obviously still contemplated things profoundly; what he chose to present to the world, especially after becoming well known, was far from the sum of who he was. He would still observe, brood, analyse, rage. Alcohol may have dulled the edges of his unusual sensitivity, as Phil observed, but this will have been a necessary protection within the walls of the 'cruel and shallow money trench' of the music business, 'where thieves and pimps run free and good men die like dogs,' as Hunter S Thompson famously put it, before concluding with the immortal line: 'There is also a negative side.' Wilko admits he saw Lee as more a 'man of action' than a 'thinker', an observation which does seem at odds with the evidence (although, as Wilko said, there was plenty that Lee wouldn't have shared with him), but it does, in turn, fit with the public image Lee put so much energy into projecting.

Lee learned not to take the industry and its associated mores too personally and he found a way to remain, largely, calm at the eye of the storm. That said, some people still managed to press his buttons. One person in particular. Wilko and Lee might have been close at first, but by the summer of 1975, mutual admiration had turned to irritation and worse, and the cracks were starting to show.

Christoffer Frances

Left: Lee playing slide guitar.
Right: A rare sketch of Lee and Wilko, the
ultimate rock'n'roll duo, drawn by Wilko
himself back in the day.

Do not approach these men. Dr Feelgood
in their spiritual home – at the bar – with
amphetamine kid Wilko prophetically if not
deliberately standing apart from the drinkers.

BRILLEAUX GLOSSARY

absolutely disgusting – tremendous, impressive (Larry Wallis remembers Lee reporting back about a shop on Carnaby Street which stocked an 'absolutely disgusting range of foot furniture')

as it happens – to commence or conclude a sentence or point (and to be said as often as possible. Same rule applies for jolly-up.)

beak lunch – daytime cocaine break

bit of a goddess – woman (for example, 'bit of a goddess, as it happens.')

'The book' aka 'The Bible' – originally either the *Good Beer Guide* or a guidebook compiled by the Feelgoods themselves – no doubt Lee and Chris – containing information about their favourite hostelries. This would then be kept in the van, updated according to their discretion and referred to while on the road: 'Pass the book, Whitey.' The aforementioned Feelgood-compiled guidebook would be left in a pub somewhere by the band's sometime tour manager Fred 'Borneo' Munt (the termination of his contract would not necessarily be entirely to do with this, all the same, *Melody Maker*'s Allan Jones observed Sparko looking 'distraught' at the memory.)

bunce – money

bunch of bollocks – nonsense

the business – good, excellent

the do it yourself – off licence

extra double buzz – particularly exciting, fun

foot furniture – shoes

jolly-up – party, or any visit en masse to a public house

primo – very fine

sharpener – an enlivening alcoholic beverage

swift arf – any drink at all, could be an actual half of lager, could be a brandy

uncle – mate, fella (informal noun, as in 'Fancy another drink, uncle?')

Mick Gold

A classic Feelgood tableau – Wilko is borne
aloft, apparently powered by some unearthly
energy, while Brilleaux, er, romances the
drums. The Marquee Club, Soho.

8. ANGRY YOUNG MEN

It's a better word than rock, don't you think? Rhythm, yes. Blues, definitely.

Lee Brilleaux in 'The Breeding of Dr Feelgood', Hugo Williams

In July 1975, the Feelgoods visited Finland shortly after the release of 'Back In The Night', the first single from the *Malpractice* album. During their trip, the band were interviewed by a journalist for a filmed segment now visible on YouTube, a rare opportunity to see not just Lee or Wilko being interviewed during this period, but all of the group members (although, as Big Figure put it, he favoured the 'morose', monosyllabic approach). This clip makes for interesting viewing not least because it is a visual display of the now unequivocal antipathy within the band.

We can only imagine what had happened earlier that day, but Lee appears to be in a foul mood, and the way the interview unfolds doesn't improve matters. The camera zooms in on the silver chain around his neck before zooming back out to reveal his dark expression as Wilko speaks. 'We were the only ones playing [R&B]. It's the best sort of music. People have been sitting around for the last five years listening to stupid synthesisers and things. Rock'n'roll's not about *The Hobbit* and things like that, that's for girls … This is for people who want to have a good time,' he sneers in conclusion, brimming with (proto)-punk attitude. Wilko is, admittedly, always good value when it comes to a quote, but he's already come up with a pithy soundbite before Lee has even had a chance to open his mouth.

The journalist tries to involve Lee, citing the fact that the *NME*'s rival, the *Melody Maker*, had recently caught up to the hype and pronounced Dr Feelgood 'ones to watch'. Lee gruffly responds, with a slight laugh, 'Well, they're right, I hope.' On being asked as to whether this gave them 'some kind of certainty of the future', Wilko steps in with a proclamation. 'The *Melody Maker*, as usual, is two years behind. Now it's nice and safe, they say we're a name to watch … Probably means we're not a name to watch now it's in the *Melody Maker*.' Wilko gives a smirk as Lee casts him a sharp look. You don't have to be especially perceptive to spot that all is not entirely dandy in the Feelgood camp.

While Wilko insists they 'never took [the tension] onstage with them', it was that very tension, whether staged or real or somewhere in between, that was proving ever more intoxicating as far as the audience was concerned. As the mercury rose during the summer of 1975, the Feelgoods only became more sultry and magnetic as they paraded from show to show, systematically grabbing rock'n'roll with both hands, cracking its neck and resetting it like some insane chiropractor night after night.

On 16 August, the band flew to Avignon, France, for the Orange Festival in a privately chartered Handley Page monoplane (during this flight, Wilko Johnson insisted on 'having a go' at being the pilot while the rest of the party prayed to gods previously ignored). *NME* editor Tony Tyler was present to document the experience. His piece would be titled 'Oil City Meets The Riviera – And Wins'. The fact that no one had said it was a war in the first place was neither here nor there.

The festival was set in a Roman amphitheatre, heaving with in excess of 12,000 fans by the time they arrived (it seated 9,000). There was something gladiatorial about the whole affair, and the general atmosphere in turn was not a little combative. They landed into chaos – 'the usual panic over hire cars,' said Lee – although the band didn't care: their ferocious tour manager Jake Riviera was a dab hand at speaking French, not to mention settling issues in whatever manner he felt would be the most effective. Lee Brilleaux viewed the maelstrom with detached *froideur*. 'Silly buggers, frogs,' he was heard to sigh as everyone around him flapped. (This may or may not have been the same occasion on which Lee suggested that France would be better off being turned into a giant golf course, with the French serving as caddies. It was, as we have previously established, the 1970s.)

The festival bill also featured Procol Harum, Tangerine Dream and John Martyn among others, but, as the ever adoring *NME* surmised, the 'best local group in the world' was about to sweep in.

Anticipation for the Feelgoods was building and, shortly before Lee, clad in trademark sullied white, prepared to walk up to the stage, a fracas broke out. The Hell's Angels had come down to the festival in force, having 'taken the festival over as "security",' remembers Geoff. 'Very scary. They had bats and stuff, as if it was going to be some kind of war. We were a bit worried, it felt like there could be violence.'

The horrific scenes at the Altamont Speedway Free Festival in 1969 were still fresh in people's minds, and at one point, it was not out of the question that something disastrous might occur at Orange. Twenty drunken, overheated Angels suddenly crashed the backstage area armed with cudgels. 'Brilleaux and Fenwick watch from their caravan door with narrowed eyes, Oil City natural reactions hovering on the brink. No need. The clowns are ejected. On goes the Doctor. The Doctor crunches the crowd,' writes Tyler.

Their natural cool was underlined by the fact that they apparently refused to come back for an encore after a set that had everyone on their feet, dancing. They'd had their wicked way with the crowd like a gang of rapacious highwaymen, torn and thrust their way through the Wilko compositions *du jour* and covers such as 'Riot', 'Route 66' and an obscene 'I'm A Hog For You Baby', with its brazenly long two-note, back-and-forth guitar solo (a kind of musical metaphor for the Feelgoods' staying power in the sack), Brilleaux molesting the drums, the floor, the mic, his beer and any other inanimate object that happened to be in his sightline. And then they disappeared into the fading light – and no amount of begging would bring them back. In actual fact, the Feelgoods were more than happy to perform an encore but, as Lee remembered, 'the organisers prevented us. They claimed there were sound problems. I think they were afraid of what we could do.'

Shortly after Orange, the Feelgoods would play the Reading Festival – another defining moment. The bill included everyone from Hawkwind, Southend pals the Kursaal Flyers and their Naughty Rhythms comrades Kokomo to Caravan, the Mahavishnu Orchestra and Yes, but, again, it would be the Feelgoods' set that would prove one of the most memorable moments for many; their so-called simple, good-time music reaching further than ever before thanks to the diverse nature of the festival audience. This was the sound of the past being grabbed by a swift fist and flung forcefully into the future. Cognitive dissonance at its most exhilarating. *Melody Maker* declared Dr Feelgood 'the success of the day'. *NME*'s Charles Shaar Murray, meanwhile, was now mentioning the band in the same breath as The Who and Led Zeppelin in terms of their live prowess.

One could be forgiven for thinking that, after these rapturous performances, the come-down might be a bit of a kicker, but for the Feelgoods, coming home from tour meant that another kind of party was about to start. The band, always organised, had 'quite heavy riders', Dean Kennedy remembers, and anything left over would be brought home and used to restock the Cluedo Club bar in the new Feelgood House (aka Feelgood House 2), a large 1930s building with a croquet lawn, plenty of rooms and a recording studio, built by Sparko, for the group to lay down demos.

Lee now lived in his own little Canvey 'shack' on Rainbow Road, a house originally owned by his grandparents, and therefore filled with the nostalgia of boyhood visits to Canvey. Lee's bachelor pad was a good place to be – there was always a warm welcome, some blues or the latest *Derek and Clive* album on the turntable, and 'always a line of something "afore ye go"', remembers Pete Zear fondly. 'All the things of the day, basically. You'd go round and if you had a problem you'd run it past him. He was always a bloke about whom you'd think, Yeah, I'm glad I know him.' 'He had a plastic 1960s bar there,' adds Lew Lewis. 'It was "Lee's Club".'

However, Lee still spent considerable time at the new band HQ, particularly after inviting Mickey Jupp, temporarily without digs, to move in with him for a while. According to Zear, Jupp's enthusiasm for fry-ups nearly drove Lee spare. 'Talk about the odd couple,' laughs Zear. 'Jupp had loads of frying pans and Lee was, "Bloody hell, he's got that frying pan on again."' There would be respite, of sorts, at Feelgood House, a place where drinks would be served in bounteous Feelgood measures, and, just like at Lee's Club, the music never stopped.

'Feelgood House was brilliant,' continues Dean. 'The bar was always full. If anyone came to town, like when Elvis Costello played locally, we'd invite him over. George Melly, Alison Moyet, Ed Hollis [Eddie and the Hot Rods] and his brother Mark [later of Talk Talk], Madness would come ... although I don't think they got in, because no one knew who they were. Higgsy from the Hot Rods. We'd get very drunk and play croquet at four in the morning with all the floodlights on. The neighbours thought we were mental.'

The band would have reason to celebrate – by November 1975 *Malpractice* would be in the Top 20, their first release to chart. The promotional tour would start in October, and this run of dates would feature an appearance at Southend's Kursaal which would be recorded, later turning up on the acclaimed live *Stupidity* LP in 1976 alongside tracks taped during appearances in Sheffield and at Aylesbury Friars earlier in 1975.

The atmosphere of a Feelgood show was hard to capture, but a live album would come close and also ease the pressure on Wilko when it came to churning out new songs in an ever more hardcore climate of touring and gleeful – or not so gleeful – sleep deprivation. The Feelgoods were packing out houses during the *Malpractice* tour, one of which was London's Hammersmith Odeon – 'House Full And Raising The Roof For Dr Feelgood' shouted the sign over the door as fans, friends and equally fervent members of the music press filed in.

However, tonight would be 'a weird one', Charles Shaar Murray would report. He'd attended the opening night of the tour in Hemel Hempstead a few weeks earlier where the Feelgoods, dogged by technical issues, 'struggled through on raging energy alone'. He'd also been present at the Guildford Civic Centre show – 'not so much a killer set as downright genocidal'. But when it came to what should have been the crowning moment at Hammersmith, there was a problem – a big one – which led those present to speculate as to whether Lee and Wilko had had a fight before the show.

It wouldn't have been the first time. Fred Barker remembers discreetly standing outside the dressing room many a time, waiting for the pair to stop screaming at each other, but in this case, Wilko, already in a 'bad state of health', had got wasted beforehand, descended into full-blown panic and became faint when he suddenly became convinced that his 'brain had vanished'.

The show began with a noticeably hesitant performance from Wilko, and it soon became clear that the rest of the band were getting distracted. Once they'd reached the middle of the set, Wilko took off his guitar and fled.

'Wilko just went absent for ten minutes. Just three of us left on stage,' says Figure, adding, with his customary understatement: 'What was it like? Well, it wasn't very good! Suddenly there was this big hole in the sound and we turned around and Wilko has gone. He was all right after a little while and came back onstage, but the *NME* the following week came up with the line: "Doctor – heal thyself."'

Wilko explains: 'I flipped. Everybody's going, "What's he ... where's he going?!" I was backstage thinking, what is this? This is a gig ... it's quite big. Who am I working with? I'd forgotten who I was. The sound was like it was echoing quite loudly and all the time, this confusion, I just didn't know who I was, and I was wondering how on earth I'm getting through all these numbers. There's a recording of it, and in fact, I'm not playing too bad at all!'

As soon as Lee noticed they were a man down, he growled into the mic, 'Our guitarist is taking a quick break. OK. "Train Blues",' and the remaining trio instantly went into a frantic, chugging 12-bar to cover the situation before Wilko reappeared, 'gripping Brilleaux by the arm as if to reassure him', writes Charles Shaar Murray, before continuing the show. The gig concluded with Wilko exiting stage right, the rest of the group stage left. The audience became hostile, prompting Lee to re-emerge and apologise to the crowd. 'It was entirely my fault for being out of it,' said Wilko.

This case may have been particularly dramatic, but, as Chris Salewicz remembers, 'Wilko was always walking off. He appears to storm off stage – in most cases he's just forgotten something – but people *loved* it, regardless of what the band felt. The crowd think he's throwing a wobbler. People get these reputations and it becomes part of the legend. It's like Keith Richards turning up late in the 1970s, gigs starting three hours late because no one could find Keith. People would stand and wait because they thought it was part of Keith's cool – it's absolutely egregious dysfunctionalism, actually! But people liked it.'

Fred Barker would be backstage to witness the fall-out. 'Well, Lee was angry like anyone would be. He punched a speaker cabinet once, gave himself a bad hand. "Fuck it!" Bang. Better than hitting a person.' Audience and music critics alike got off on the volatile nature of the Feelgoods, but the reality for the band could be exhausting.

There'd be little opportunity for a break from each other, however; 1975 might have been about to call it a night but the Feelgoods were more in demand than ever. Even Lee's white jacket could have done with a bit of time off, although this may have been wishful thinking on the part of the *NME*: 'This jacket will not be appearing at Liverpool Stadium and Hammersmith Odeon' announced the magazine, a huge picture of Lee's slush-white jacket,[25] the item recently and wittily proclaimed the *NME*'s 'Sleeve of the Year', emblazoned on the back page. There it hangs, defiant and crooked, thin of lapel, battle-worn and blackened, bearing the marks and scuffs of a hundred shows and never once having burdened a dry-cleaner. 'On the other hand,' continued the caption beneath the image, 'Dr Feelgood and the Roogalator will.' But no one had to read to the foot of the page to work out the connection. 'Everybody knew whose suit it was,' said Feelgood associate Larry Wallis. 'Now that's fame.'

All the same, it was probably time to spruce up the wardrobe a little. Being, as they were, at the peak of their powers, the band had signed an American deal with the major label CBS, and the Feelgoods would travel to San Diego at the end of January 1976 to perform at the record company's convention (trans. 'jolly-up'), bringing their English take on American blues right back to the States.

The Feelgoods would take their most trusted friends (including Nick Lowe, booked in under the name of 'Dale Liberator, Equipment Handler') with them on this potentially life-changing learning curve – and this would be the point at which they (with the exception of Wilko) *really* started drinking. America was lifting up its skirt to the Feelgoods and revealing, among other things, a free bar. It would have been rude to say no, and if there was one thing Brilleaux couldn't stand, it was rudeness.

Committed boozing would also galvanise these Brits abroad who would, by most, be treated as freaks, as Nick Lowe merrily recalled. In comparison to their slick US cousins, the Feelgoods and co. looked like 'a bunch of terribly dressed losers – they were horrified by us, which made us feel great'. Lee was regarded as quite terrifying by some of the delegates. He, on the other hand, was just bemused by the cultural gulf. 'I thought because Americans speak English they *are* English, except they live in another part of the world,' Lee said. '[This] I found to be a mistake. We might as well have landed on Mars.'

"Dépassez
la dose
prescrite ! "

LEE BRILLEAUX et le nouveau
traitement de choc
du Dr FEELGOOD...

Wilko Johnson's personal archive

From Keith Morris's Malpractice shoot, 1975. The band posed outside various Canvey establishments for the cover art, Canvey Island itself very much being part of the now irresistible Dr Feelgood appeal. Lee Brilleaux holds up a copy of Malpractice during a stop-off in Paris. The photograph is believed to have been taken by Jean-Yves Legras; this copy is kindly provided by Patrick Bataille.

THE ROCK'N'ROLL GENTLEMAN'S GUIDE TO OPTIMUM ADVENTURING

- Any opportunity for adventuring must be taken. Always have a bag packed for when the mood (or obligation) takes you. Pack the essentials – toothbrush, maps, a good book or two, a flask of brandy, a radio on which you can pick up BBC World Service, a harmonica.

- Learn about the place you're going to in advance so you have an idea of what you'd like to do and to avoid aimless wandering. (Although aimless wandering does have its place.)

- Take the train where possible; more time to stare out of the window, read and, lest we forget, there is generally a bar.

- No man or woman is a (Canvey) island. Talk to the locals. They'll take you off the beaten track and introduce you to the best eateries. Maybe they'll even cook for you themselves. Maybe they'll even teach you how to make the local cuisine. Watch and learn.

- You can't always go four-star when it comes to accommodation. Don't be afraid of roughing it where necessary and, should your digs be unsatisfactory, remain dignified and polite until an alternative is found if possible. If an alternative is not possible, locate flask of brandy and escape into book.

- Keep abreast of what's going on in the homeland while you're away. Lee Brilleaux would spend 'up to two or three pounds' (adjust this according to rate of inflation) on an English newspaper while abroad. This, and his trusty 'super radio', kept him informed.

9. SEALED WITH A KISS

I'm a bit disappointed [with the luxurious Rivermont Hotel]. It's too much like The Prisoner – *it's got sinister overtones. I wanted to spend my first nights in America in one of those places with a big neon Indian waggling a tomahawk over the roof of a teepee-styled motel. Now that would have impressed me.*

Lee Brilleaux to Cal Worthington, who documented the group's US debut for *ZigZag*

'We [had] a superb deal with CBS,' said Lee. 'We were on their A-list for promotion with an unlimited budget. They flew us to the West Coast for the convention. Roadies, mates, you name it, we could have it. Nothing was too much trouble.'

The hedonistic and, for some, almost fatal, CBS convention would see a diverse roll-call of eminent artists performing to a collection of drunken sales reps brought down to San Diego on the label's buck. Aware of the opportunity they'd been gifted, the Feelgoods at least tried to sit through the other artists' sets during the convention, although some were easier to endure than others: Boz Scaggs performed, the Charlie Daniels Band and, of particular interest to the Feelgoods, the mighty Muddy Waters. (Wilko recalls himself and Lee completely forgetting their studied nonchalance and heartily applauding Muddy's appearance.) Chick Corea, appearing with the jazz rock supergroup Return to Forever, on the other hand, were not their thing at all. Return to Forever played on the first night of the convention, and while the rest of the Feelgoods slunk off to do something more profitable with their time, Lee felt guilty and stuck it out as long as he could. Eventually making his excuses to the CBS executive nearby, he insisted it was nothing personal, and that he 'wouldn't be offended if Chick walked out' during their set.

Whether Chick witnessed them or not, Dr Feelgood would impress many and confuse most of those sufficiently *compos mentis* to take them in. Andrew Lauder remembers it was 'a dry crowd, basically hard-bitten sales guys going, "What the hell's this?" I think one bloke had a heart attack [not necessarily because of the Feelgoods], somebody fell off a balcony, somebody almost drowned in the hotel fountain. Usual things.'

There would also be a bevy of hookers and enough booze and drugs to keep any hardcore sybarite feeling suitably sybaritic. It's no wonder a majority of the guests found it hard to keep their attention on the music, even though that was, ostensibly, the reason everyone was there. Despite the distractions, Cal Worthington, who wrote about the Feelgoods' trip for *ZigZag*, described people dancing on their chairs during the group's appearance, and there was also speculation about Wilko's psychotic demeanour; Feelgood comrade Martyn Smith could be heard 'explaining' to gawping record executives that it was all down to 'centuries of inbreeding on Canvey Island'.

The twenty-five-minute set, featuring songs from *Malpractice*, was never going to be a typical Feelgood show, but after the group strode onstage, with thirty super-efficient Showco attendants at their beck and call, they had to then wait patiently for nearly a quarter of an hour as 'the cat from CBS was making a speech about major breakout areas/ demographic sales surveys/promo campaigns ...'

As they waited, Lee noticed that his microphone lead had been taped down at the back of the stage – he preferred it to be taped down in front to ensure it didn't become tangled during his frenzied performance. 'I dispatch a Showco guy to fetch some tape,' reported Worthington. 'And as he rushes off, he knocks Lee's slide guitar off its stand, breaking the neck clean off.' Everyone froze, but Lee took his set list out of his pocket and with a pencil coolly scored through a handful of songs, muttering, 'We'll knock those ones on the 'ead, then.'

John McEuen, guesting at the convention with the Michael Murphy band, saw the incident and offered to lend Lee his Stratocaster, but Lee politely declined for fear of destroying the guitar with his own frenetic playing. So there would be no 'Back In The Night' among others for the execs and reps present, but that didn't seem to matter. The Feelgoods 'tore the place apart', said Worthington, and the mood would only become more celebratory as the night wore on. 'To our great delight, we discovered a thing called Total Unlimited Credit,' said Lee. 'You could just go to the bar and order what you wanted.'

'Room service, whatever, you could just put it all on the bill,' adds Andrew Lauder. 'Sparko in particular had not blown this chance. I don't know how much good it did, it certainly didn't do any harm.'

It did do *some* harm, namely to the plumbing system. Thoroughly smashed, Sparko proceeded to attack the toilets, destroying every single fixture. (Ironically, he was probably one of the few people there capable of fixing the place back up again too.) Fortunately the label representatives thought it was hilarious rock star behaviour and there would be none of the expected chastisements.

Another classic Sparko moment during this double-vision extravaganza came when he spotted a tall man in a smart red jacket approaching in the hotel corridor. Assuming him to be a porter, Sparko promptly asked him to take his bags to his room for him. The porter looked confused. This was because he wasn't a porter. The man Sparko was preparing to tip (or not, seeing as he didn't exactly snap to it) was Led Zeppelin drummer John Bonham.

Once the hangovers had started to lift, there was time to drive, explore and do some shopping before heading north to set up camp in 'Feelgood House LA' – a 1940s timber cabin previously owned by Byrds/Flying Burrito Brothers star 'Skip' Battin. The house was way up in Laurel Canyon, the perfect Californian base, situated snugly in the secluded valley of the stars (famous neighbours included Joni Mitchell, various Mamas and Papas and all manner of frightful long-hairs).

Lee was in his element in LA, stocking up on albums from obscure blues labels, records he wouldn't otherwise have been able to find. As happy as he was with how their American stay was unfolding so far, he was still a little crushed about what had happened to his guitar. It was an inexpensive Guild, but it had significant sentimental value – as a teenager he'd learned how to play slide along with Elmore James records, and he'd finally bought the Guild when the band were given their first record advance. Showco refused to have it fixed, presuming it to be a waste of time – they'd pronounced the instrument deceased.

Chris Fenwick knew what it meant to Lee and took it down to Arturo Valdez, a guitarmaker on Sunset Boulevard who had crafted guitars for Eric Clapton, John Lennon, José Feliciano and the Doors (and he is still working at the time of writing). Not only did Valdez fix the neck, he inlayed the name 'Lee' on the fretboard in luminescent mother of pearl. 'Looks great,' observed Worthington. 'It ought to. Cost more than the guitar.'

It would be during this stay that the Feelgoods would see their blues hero John Lee Hooker play live at the legendary Starwood venue. Anticipation was, naturally, high, but the old warhorse was disgruntled and below par, leaving the boys feeling less than euphoric. The Feelgoods, legend has it, drowned their disappointment with a succession of White Russians – vodka, Kahlua and milk (I imagine you know where this is going) inspired by the 'milk, cream and alcohol' of

Hooker's 'It Serves You Right To Suffer' – before jumping in the hired car to head back to their digs. But Chris, behind the wheel, accidentally missed a red light. The police picked them up, hauled them out of the car and lined up these loaded limey reprobates at gunpoint on the sidewalk (just a tad over the top). 'Up against the wall stuff,' sniffed Lee to *Smash Hits*' David Hepworth. 'We didn't realise you had to be a bit cool on the streets.' The whole cocktail-fuelled evening would plant the seed for 'Milk And Alcohol', the song that would be their biggest hit. But this was all to come.

The Feelgoods still had some time before the start of their first US tour, and Nick insisted they use some of this hiatus to track down a Bay-area band called Clover, a country rock group based in Mill Valley, California. Clover were, in his opinion, every bit as great as The Band, although they didn't have much in the way of status. The group were fronted by a young Huey Cregg – aka Huey Louis, later Huey Lewis, who would have considerably more success with his 1980s pop group Huey Lewis and the News.

It would be drummer Pete Thomas, formerly of Chilli Willi and the Red Hot Peppers, who would bring them together. Thomas had moved out to Malibu after joining the John Stewart Band, and there was no question he was going to hook up with his old Naughty Rhythms tour mates while they were in LA. Clover hailed from further north, but Thomas had previously lived near them in Mill Valley, and they'd had a few jams together. Pete suggested they head to the Palomino in North Hollywood where he knew Clover were playing.

This evening would mark something of a meeting of minds, and Clover quickly took the Feelgoods under their wing, insisting they drive in convoy to San Francisco, showing them around before their next show at River City in Fairfax. The Feelgoods, hurtling up the highway in a rented Lincoln, checked in to a smart Japanese hotel before checking straight back out again ('It was obvious the staff didn't like us one bit,' noted Cal, this just one of many proprietor-versus-Feelgood incidents). They settled in to a Howard Johnson's motel instead before joining Clover for the gig.

One of the people attending the show was a hip, vivacious young woman called Shirley Alford, known to all as 'Suds'.[26] Shirley had been studying drama in Marin County but eventually dropped the course ('I had an aversion to getting up in the morning'), she loved rock'n'roll and, being a regular gig-goer, she'd become friends with Clover manager George Daly.

Clover were 'always a big draw', says Shirley, and everyone knew they were in for a good night. What they didn't know was that they would be blown off the stage by not just one of their new pals, but the 'quietest' one. To be fair, they hadn't yet seen the Feelgoods play, and they weren't convinced whether someone as understated as Lee could cut it on stage. The suit just compounded matters – to them it screamed (or mumbled) 'conservative'.

Lee wasn't expecting to be invited onstage. When Huey called him up during the show, Lee was quite happy occupying himself at the bar and actually needed some prodding to respond, only adding weight to Clover's impression of him being, perhaps, a little too self-effacing to rock. Eventually he was persuaded, and, with his trusty gob-iron in his jacket pocket, weaved his way through the crowd to the stage. After some brief conferring, it was decided they would play the standard 'Checkin' Up On My Baby', a mutual favourite with both Feelgood and Clover. Cal Worthington was among those watching and, unlike most people in the club that night, he knew to expect something explosive, but the crowd's reaction was almost as entertaining as Lee's performance.

'Fuck me, I just wish I'd had a camera to catch their faces,' he wrote. 'As soon as the music started, Mr Modesty became a wild animal, sinews and veins are sticking out over his sweating, contorted, snarling face ... the band cannot believe it. They can NOT believe it! People are clustering around the stage to take full stock of this madman. They've never seen anything like it in Palo Alto.'

Shirley was one of the many people dazzled by Lee that night. 'The whole place was like, "Woah, who is *that*?" Short hair, suit jacket. I just thought, wow! That is radical! And everything that I saw in his face ... it was just like this personal energy that he had going on, and he always had it, right up to the end, he had it.'

At one point, Brilleaux swung round to the drummer and barked, 'Come on, you fucker! Give it a bit of fucking stick!' 'The drummer,' reported Cal, 'totally unprepared for such an outburst, just snaps into gear ... The partygoers went berserk and Clover fell in love with Lee after that – they were all over him. The song ended and Lee reverted to Mr Modesty. "Er, thanks a lot, fellers."'

The following night, Clover were booked to play a private cowboy-themed birthday party in San Jose, and the Feelgoods, now very much the heroes of the hour, were urged to join them as guests. As was 'Suds'. George had introduced her to Nick Lowe, and the subject of the party had come up in conversation. They arranged to meet her at the hotel the following evening and drive up to the party from there.

Shirley recalls: 'The next day I went to the bar at Howard Johnson's to meet Nick, and Lee was there. He stood at the bar next to where we were sitting. Nick looked over my shoulder as we were talking and said, "Oh, there's Lee! Hey, Lee." I turned around, he looked down and my first impression of him was just of the most intense person I had ever seen. I was like, "Woah, hey, er ... nice to meet you." He bought a drink, slammed it back and then walked out of the room.'

Shirley had driven up to the hotel in her MG, so she and Nick rode to the party together. 'It was a crazy private party with about forty to fifty people attending, lots of food and booze and everything, everybody was having a good time.'

Evidently by the end of the evening – a cornucopia of cocktails and cowboy boots – Lee had become quite attached to 'Suds', because by the time she and Nick Lowe headed out to the parking lot to leave, they found Lee, in his cups, installed in the back of her tiny car, 'wedged behind the front seat'. Shirley laughs. 'I mean, it's a two-seater, maybe there's space where you can fit a small suitcase, or a body, but he was contorted behind the seats. "I'm going to ride back with you guys, OK?" Nick said, "Lee, get out of the car. Go and ride with the band." It was amusing.'

One person was notably absent from many of these jolly-ups: Wilko. 'There was a rift within the band that I suspect had been there prior to them going to the US,' says Shirley. 'Wilko really wasn't around in San Francisco on that first trip.' The separation – at least partly due to a disparity in social habits – was becoming more pronounced, and inevitably the more separate Lee and Wilko were from each other, the deeper the resentment became.

'It was a shame because we had a brilliant friendship,' muses Wilko. 'Certainly at first. But deep animosity was going on. We couldn't stand each other. I was getting isolated from the whole of the band. When we went to America it really started to go wrong – things were getting big. It was worrying for me because I'm the songwriter and I've got to come up with another album, and I'm freaking out and taking loads of amphetamine. I'm up in my room writing songs and they're down in the bar drinking and talking about ... well, me, probably.

'There were times when Lee would be on stage and he would be drunk, and it really diminishes your performance. You're kind of flat-footed. He would sing the same verse three times over. "Bloody hell, I wrote that!" If I felt that that was happening, I would complain. I said, "I don't care what anybody does as long as they can do their thing." Sometimes Lee was past that point and that used to make me angry, and I would sulk, and that used to make *them* angry.'

Lee, on the other hand, was heard to mutter, 'He's speeding again,' on seeing Wilko one morning, just because the guitarist had given him a rare smile. But Lee could probably be forgiven for assuming Wilko's beam was chemically induced, being as he was more used to Wilko brooding wordlessly and, as a result, creating something of an atmosphere.

'We were on the road and they were having a go at me for something or other and Lee said, "It's just these fucking *silences!*" Maybe there's some justification in that, but he didn't like these silences, and I thought, yeah, *you* never sit there in silence, thinking about things … I remember when I was in these silences that Lee found so … [infuriating] sitting there thinking, you don't understand. There's some lack of communication here, I could see myself being spiteful and sneering but I didn't want to do that. I was doing it in reaction. I thought they were misunderstanding me, although I probably didn't realise at the time that I was misunderstanding them as well.'

Geoff Shaw admits the roadies didn't take too much interest in the friction between Wilko and Lee, although after America 'there were lots of bad vibes; that never really happened before, it was just normal bitching that you get between four human beings. They were all difficult at some time, with the exception of Sparko. Wilko would go completely quiet, and Lee probably didn't understand. If Lee was in a bad mood, he would be more likely to say something sharp. You'd know about it instantly, there wasn't any blockage in that department, he'd just let you have it. But at some point a wall went up.'

Lee did see that Wilko's 'misery' was at least in part due to the fact that he was often homesick and lonely while he, on the other hand, was a single man, smitten with life on the road to a far greater extent than anybody else. There would be elements of the experience that wound him up, of course; the Feelgoods were still learning how the majors worked, hyping up the band sometimes to the point of total falsity. There weren't many places to escape to.

'Sometimes when you're out on the road, record companies say things about you which are not true, and sometimes you say similar things which you really believe at the time,' said Lee. 'Come the night of the gig, you're fucked up, it's your fourteenth day on the road, I haven't had a break. I'm away from home, I've got all these record company people around me, I couldn't give a fucking Empress of India, I'm going back to my hotel room …'

While some might initially have thought the Feelgoods were bringing the proverbial coals to Newcastle in steaming over and blasting audiences with 1960s R&B, spat out in an American accent (with the exception of Lee's very Estuarine between-songs shout, 'Thangyewverymuchladeez'n'gennuhmen!' Or sometimes just an abrupt 'TA!') what they were really doing was 'very English', says Andrew Lauder. 'There was no tradition most people there could relate to because they'd never heard of Johnny Kidd and the Pirates. We always knew it would be difficult but that a few people would get it and some critics would champion it, and that the live show would do the rest as long as you could get it in front of an audience.'

One way of doing that, of course, would be with a plum support slot. A well-timed opportunity to tour ten major cities in the central and Southern states had arisen that spring, Lee recalled, 'supporting KISS, of all people'. Incongruous as this was, they had the chance to play stadiums in some cases and they weren't going to pass that up. They flew in to Mobile, Alabama, for the first gig of the tour to find there were just two dressing rooms, 'occupied, needless to say, by the members of KISS,' recalled Lee. 'They needed them for their make-up and costumes, all that shit.' KISS's road crew barred the Feelgoods' way before they could get any further. 'They said that no one was allowed backstage,' Lee continued. 'Kiss couldn't be seen without make-up.' This was laughable, but the situation soon stopped being funny when the Feelgoods, laden down with their guitars and cases, were then informed they could 'go and change in the toilets front of house'.

'We dropped everything and looked at each other,' said Lee. 'We told them no. The management told us to fuck off. So we said, "OK, we won't play." We'd previously asked them to provide a caravan. They said it was too late. We didn't want to change in the bogs with people pissing next to us.

'Wilko threw a complete wobbler, refused to go on and stormed back to the hotel. We were sacked from the tour and returned to base in Laurel Canyon. Wilko sulked there for a week while Chris went to New York and got a massive carpeting from the president of CBS. We never even met KISS. The record company started to get the hump because they'd spent a lot of money on promoting us and then found the band didn't seem to be co-operating. So really,' Lee concluded, 'we had a good chance to give it a go in the States but it was a chance we let slip. The Feelgoods missed their opportunity in America.'

Lee would largely blame the crumbling of their American dream on how the situation with KISS was handled. They were treated disrespectfully, but the ultimate reaction from Wilko – who, to the KISS camp, was simply a mouthy member of a support group they didn't know or care about – obviously upset the wrong people at a crucial point. There would still be shows to play in the States, but it would, in the main, be on too small a scale for them to catch fire in a significant way. Worse still, the resulting resentment would make for an uncertain future for the Feelgoods as a group. Lee's mother Joan remembers her fuming son ('Wonderful boy, he'd ring me from wherever he was in the world') telling her he'd been 'racking his brains as to whether they had capital punishment in the state they were performing in, because he thought he'd come off stage and kill him'.

'Wilko was very unhappy [in America],' said Lee. 'We had arguments all the time instead of having fun … In the end it just got so bad. Looking back on it, poor old Wilko must have been very miserable and depressed. That episode sort of marred what should have been a wonderful period of our career,' he told *Blues Bag*. 'We never really got a fair crack of the whip because Wilko didn't enjoy being in the States. Being far from his family … it's difficult to live in those conditions. Personally, it suits me perfectly.'

Lee Brilleaux Talks Touring Pressure

(using a gloriously Southend metaphor): We've all got our faults. If some bloke puts an excessive amount of salt on his chips, and he does that every day for three weeks, you start thinking to yourself, 'That cunt puts too much salt on his chips.' But you have to learn to live with it. It's up to him. It's his chips. If he wants to ruin them with salt … They're the sort of things that get to you.' (as told to Roy Carr, *NME*)

*Lee Brilleaux (in his beloved sheepskin coat)
takes on New York.*

10. FROM LEW LEWIS TO LOUISIANA, WITH LOVE

Rock'n'roll isn't about satin trousers and limousines and massive banks of amplifiers and thousands of roadies everywhere. It's about people. They're important.

Lee Brilleaux

Dr Feelgood would return from America in the spring of 1976 for a short break before going straight back in May. The pressure was on to record a new album for their already scheduled autumn tour. The best solution, however, was the simplest one, and it was a solution that was already in existence. Brilleaux had promised that fans would get a live album when the time was right. That time was now.

Recordings of the previous year's shows in Sheffield and Southend had at last bottled the spirit and energy of the Feelgoods at their peak. Other than listen back to the recordings and select the best tracks, 'there wasn't much to do other than mix it,' said Wilko, who set to work with Vic Maile on readying the release. What transpired was 'the ultimate Dr Feelgood album', in Lee's words.

'Some of it is out of tune, some of it's too fast because we were so out of our brains on amphetamine, some of it doesn't even bear listening to. I think it's more interesting as a historic document rather than a piece of music,' but there was, as Lee put it, a 'magic' about it.

One of his favourite tracks on what would become *Stupidity* was their version of 'Johnny Be Goode', Lee snapping the words rhythmically over a long, dynamics-driven blues workout. UA were dubious about its inclusion. 'We were told, "Don't put it on the record – it's been done to death by everyone."' said Lee. As usual, they did what they wanted, and it was the right decision.

By April 1976, Wilko took a much needed holiday with his family before the next American sojourn, which would take them back to San Francisco and also to New York, among other places, to play to the burgeoning punk crowd at the Bottom Line club. Closer to home, the rest of the Feelgoods and an assortment of pals were about to lay down some tracks with the eccentric and talented harmonica player Lew Lewis. Lewis was a character of whom Lee was very fond. They'd grown up on the same street – Lew had played in the Southside Jug Band as well as The Fix – and Lee still looked out for him.

'I'd gone to Borstal training, sort meself out a bit,' explained Lew, 'and when I came out, Lee said, "Why don't you join Eddie and the Hot Rods?" They were looking for a harmonica player. I knew them anyway, but he got that together, absolutely.'

The band had started playing in town, but one night, 'Lew freaked out,' Pete Zear remembers. 'It wasn't the first time; it had come to a head. [Hot Rods manager] Ed Hollis told Dave Higgs, "We've got to drop this guy."' Lew: 'After I left the Hot Rods I was like a fish out of water – one minute I was in a band and the next minute I wasn't. I was slung out of the band with just two rusty harmonicas. It was terrible, well out of order.' Lee took offence at the development and, as Pete Zear recalls, 'decided to help him out. I got a phone call. "We're doing some recording, are you interested?" I went round and they were trying to get this song together. It was "Caravan Man". Lee had the riff. Sparko, Figure, the drummer Bob Clouter was there, Geoff Shaw ...'

Lew continues: 'I'd called in and Lee said, "Lew, let's do a song! Let's do a song about Ed, about what a bastard he is! He lives in a caravan ... let's call it 'Caravan Man'." But I'm not going to waste precious lyrics saying "Ed Hollis is a bastard" and all that. So I said OK. Lee really wanted it to be about Ed, but the idea at the back of my mind was of a Native American in a caravan. Nobody knows that, really. It's not about Ed, it's about territorialism, people stealing other people's land. That's what I was thinking about.'

'It was a combination of compassion and respect for Lew's talent,' adds Geoff. 'Lee was doing it from the music stance as well. Lew could be a massive pain in the arse, but we loved him, he was a soulful guy. He was always a bit troubled. He's bright and funny, kind, but there was the other side which was self-destructive. There was a gig he did at Dingwalls once. We had to tie him to a post to get him through the gig, he was so out of it.'

'Anyway, Lew's all nervous, trying to please,' continues Zear. 'We got through the recording and then I remember it being said, "Well, now we gotta do a B-side!" Didn't think it would be a single, seriously. Sparko said, "Start on guitar." So I said, "All right," and we did 'Boogie On The Street'. Made it up in one take.'

Lee played the recording to Jake Riviera, the Feelgoods' some-time tour manager, who was now working with the promoter Dave

Robinson, having just founded the now legendary independent label Stiff Records.

When Jake was still planning the enterprise, Lee asked him how much they would need to set Stiff up. Jake responded that 'four hundred pounds would get it going,' Richard Balls writes in *Be Stiff: The Stiff Records Story*. Lee immediately wrote him a cheque for £400 and handed it over, and he subsequently became a shareholder of Stiff Records alongside Chris Fenwick, Nick Lowe and the photographer Keith Morris. Elvis Costello told a Southend audience in June 2015, beneath a projection of Lee Brilleaux, that without him, his first album might not have come out, although Dave Robinson has since said he doesn't think the cheque was actually cashed. (Apparently a cheque from Wilko Johnson was framed and hung on the wall.)

The Feelgoods would use pseudonyms on the release as they were UA artists, so it is 'Lee Green', rather than Lee Brilleaux, who is vamping away on rhythm guitar throughout 'Caravan Man' (very Canvey title). Sparko became 'Johnny Ocean', while 'percussion' was provided by 'The Sheikh of Araby'. Contractual reasons aside, this would also mean they didn't steal any thunder from Lew.

'It didn't sell a lot,' says Zear. 'But it had a vibe about it, and people like Frank Zappa said he liked it. I was lucky enough to catch his radio show one time and he put "Caravan Man" on. All through this, Lee was like the rock keeping it all going. UA heard about it and said, "We want you to do one for us as well." We recorded a single, "Out For A Lark", and "Watch Yourself". Lee was playing guitar and we were both doing the riff.'

Another reason behind the Feelgoods' decision to start working with Lew Lewis was because there had been a row within Dr Feelgood, and Wilko had, ostensibly, 'left'. 'It was *one* of the times he'd left,' clarifies Sparko. 'We were going to carry on doing the Lew thing, but then Wilko came back and we carried on.'

Stupidity was soon to be released and tour dates were booked, but another trip to America was not about to cheer up the increasingly over-wrought Wilko. 'Someone reported back to me that Sparko had said, "Wilko ought to have a drink, because then he'd be less uptight and we could be mates."' said Wilko. 'There was probably a lot of wisdom in that; Sparko is a wise person in lots of ways. But I was a teetotaller and it emphasised the differences between us, particularly between me and Lee. You know when someone just really gets on your tits? Everything they do. If one of us was in the room the other would walk out.'

The fundamental problems within the band were self-perpetuating, and the individuals involved were now sadly bringing out the worst in each other like never before. By the end of the year, they would hardly be speaking.

The tenth of May 1976 – Lee's twenty-fourth birthday – was one of two nights the Feelgoods would headline at New York's Bottom Line, with the Ramones in support. The Ramones, with their driving blend of bubblegum pop and trashy punk, would later be garlanded as the East Side's punk pioneers, but Lee wasn't sold on them. 'They seemed too nervous, embarrassed,' he said. 'I had the impression [we were] dealing with four intellectuals who were playing at being little punks.' The Feelgoods, on the other hand, were completely in command and Lee was wilder than ever. It's hardly surprising the Ramones were nervous in their presence.

Patti Smith would also be written off as 'too intellectual, too poetic. Sorry, Patti. I don't want to be mean.' Lee just didn't like the combination of art and rock'n'roll, which was the direction in which many New York punk groups were heading. He might have been uninterested in them, but they, on the other hand, took much from the Feelgoods – Patti included (see the cover of *Horses* – black-and-white image, skinny tie, man's shirt). All very well, but for Lee's part, give him The J Geils Band any day.

Of all the American acts the Feelgoods met, interestingly the all-girl band The Runaways stood out to Lee, and not for the reasons one might assume. They might have been put together by svengali Kim Fowley and encouraged to 'rock out' in skimpy clothes, but the reality was they took what they were doing seriously. 'We found ourselves in the same hotel as them,' said Lee. 'They didn't consider themselves a gimmick. The whole conversation was technical detail, comparing monitors and sound systems … in short, no different to any male rock musicians.'

Meanwhile, back on the West Coast, Shirley Alford had heard on the radio that Bad Company were playing at the Winterland, supported by Dr Feelgood, on 15 May. 'I was like, "What? That's crazy, I've got to go."' Shirley had stayed in touch with Nick Lowe since meeting him with the Feelgoods back in January, and assumed he'd be with them on this trip.

'I go down there and I was fairly late. I was coming along the sidewalk alongside this huge old venue in San Francisco and was making my way up to the front to try and get in, get a ticket, whatever. As I approached – you couldn't make this up – the stage door was right there and it opened, and out came Jake Riviera and Lee, Wilko, Sparko and Figure.'

Shirley realised the only member of the band she'd actually met was Lee, and she called his name. 'He came up and went, "Oh! OK, get in the car." I'm bundled into the car, sitting in the middle, Jake was driving, and Sparko and Figure were there. I said, "Where's Nick?" And they're like, "You know Nick?" It dawned on me they had no clue who I was. Lee didn't remember me.

'I eventually got over the fact that my vanity was a little wounded, you know – he really didn't have any idea who I was. I was just someone who knew his name and that obviously qualified me to get in the car.'

All the same, fate had brought them together again, and this time they would connect properly. 'I remember hanging out with Lee and going partying with Lee and Chris – we had a fantastic time together. That was the beginning. Once they left we ran up enormous phone bills. I was like, "I've got to get to England." I was crazy about him.'

'Lee was careful about who he got together with,' said Pete Zear. 'He wouldn't be sure whether someone was interested in him as a person or because he was in the band. I knew him well enough to know this – he wasn't always looking around to play away. And there was no doubt that when Lee got married, it would be to someone wild and American.'

Other than meeting the woman who, it quickly transpired, would be the love of his life, the American tours would be written off by Lee as 'a sorry tale. We spent a lot of time striving to make it, and neglected our UK and European fans. And [we were] too British. Bit Tony Hancock. The Southend feel, they didn't understand it. I remember a LA record executive saying to me, "You've got to talk more to the audience!" He was probably right, but it's not me. I'd come across phoney, corny.'

In addition to this, while the Feelgoods had been chancing their arm once more in the US, the British kids who had idolised them in the preceding years were now punks, and anything that had occurred pre-1976 risked being dismissed as dated and irrelevant. 'All those bands were coming to see us,' remembers Wilko. 'But we didn't see this coming at all, it was happening in town. It really kicked off when we were doing these tours of America.' The Kursaals, on the other hand, were on the ground watching it unfold.

'The punk thing was happening and I loved all that,' said Will Birch. 'In fact when the Kursaals headlined at the Roundhouse, bottom of the bill was The Clash – they watched us soundcheck. They looked the business. It was Joe Strummer, Mick Jones, Paul Simonon, Terry Chimes and Keith Levene. The minute they walked in, I just knew it was all over.'[27] But the Feelgoods' finest hour was yet to come.

Stupidity, the Feelgoods' hotly anticipated live LP, was released in September 1976. Within days, it had topped the album chart, making it the first live album to go to number one in the UK within a week of coming out. The Feelgoods knew *Stupidity* would do well – 'we were undisputedly the best and most famous live band in England at that time,' said Lee – but no one expected a number 1 hit.

'By the time of its release there was a real buzz going round,' Lee told *Blues Bag*. 'We were quite famous people, but bearing in mind that nowadays so-called "stars" get into the pages of the tabloid press and become household names, the exposure we got back then wasn't the same. However, we couldn't walk down the street without being recognised.

'We were, I suppose, a little bit big-headed, so when *Stupidity* did chart we weren't all that surprised – but when it hit number one that was another thing, a magnificent moment for us.' The band were touring the album around the UK when they heard the news – 'either on the radio or in the paper', says Figure. Sparko recalls they were 'in a car park in Manchester'; Lee, on the other hand, believed they were in Portsmouth, and that it was also his birthday, 'which was extra double buzz'. (Lee's birthday is in May. It probably just *felt* like his birthday.) Wherever they were, as Figure remembers it, 'we celebrated ... and celebrated ... and celebrated ...'

The band, drunk as one might expect, migrated from pub to restaurant and traumatised the *maitre d'* by demanding to have all the tropical fish out of the tank, tried to eat them,' recalled Lee, before adding the disclaimer. 'We didn't in the end; animal lovers will be pleased to learn we gave them back.'

Wilko was particularly vindicated by the news. He had locked horns with Andrew Lauder during the mixing stage; Wilko was adamant there should be more ambience – it had to be 'a really live album' with minimal fixes, 'bum notes and all', and he wanted much of the recording to be taken from the audience microphones.

Lauder still doesn't agree that this was the best way forward, even if the album did top the charts. As for the rest of the group, they were less inclined to get involved, and also keen to avoid a combustible situation. As Wilko at one point told Lauder to 'leave the studio', Lee and the Feelgoods can't have felt comfortable. They may have been at the top of their game, but the fact that they – a purportedly 'unfashionable' band playing R&B – were now a phenomenon was almost an anomaly, hardly a given.

'Wilko is a very single-minded chap,' said Lee in later years (to Stephen Foster). 'He knows exactly what he wants and he had very fixed ideas about how the records should be made. Whereas we were always willing to listen, Wilko would be the one who would argue with the producer. That's fine in itself but it kind of led to a destructiveness.'

Andrew Lauder: 'I remember Wilko saying, "This is what it sounds like when you're at a gig at the back of the hall," and I said, "I don't want to be at the back of the hall at a gig, I want to be down the front."' An exasperated Lauder eventually told the producer Vic Maile to 'let Wilko have his way, the album will die and then he'll have to do as he's told'.

'It was getting to the stage that they had to schedule the record,' Lauder continues. 'They had a tour to do. We couldn't just sit here in limbo. Wilko had made his mind up. I remember him saying, "It's gone to number one, I was right." Well, you're not right because if you'd done it my way it would have stayed there longer! We'll argue to the grave about that one.'

In September 1976, the week *Stupidity* was released, Shirley would arrive in London for the first time, five days after her twenty-first birthday. The plan was to stay with friends, see Lee and have a couple of months' holiday before going back. At that point, Shirley had no real clue as to how famous Lee now was. The Feelgoods were away on tour when she arrived, but Shirley went to visit Nick Lowe, who was staying at Jake Riviera's flat in Queensgate, West London, at the time. Nick told her the band would be playing London's Hammersmith Odeon on 1 October.

'He said, "It's all happening, you've got to go – we'll put you on the guest list." And that was it. That was the first time I saw Lee in England, and the first time I saw them perform as the Feelgoods, the four of them. *Stupidity* had hit number one and they were *huge*. HUGE. Biggest thing in the UK – and it was overwhelming because I had no idea. They were not big in the US.

'For years I've had people make jokes, like "Oh, you were a groupie." Well, guilty, I guess … but I'd never heard of them, so does that make me a groupie? Was I supposed to be impressed by the fact [that] he had no fame in the US? It doesn't make sense. But he certainly had fame in England. I was astounded when I got to London, there were posters of them everywhere. It was fantastic.'

This was the major London show, and as Shirley walked through the doors of the Hammersmith Odeon that evening amid droves of fans, all wearing the merchandise and talking about the Feelgoods in excitable tones, the magnitude of what was happening began to sink in. This show would also be the first time Lee's parents had ever seen him perform with the band. Lee knew it was going to be a potentially rough night (and he was right. 'Everybody was just going crazy,' said Shirley. 'I really was nervous that I was going to get inadvertently punched in the face.') Lee wanted to look after them, but Arthur was determined to experience it just like a punter. Sparko: 'Lee wanted to arrange transport for them but his dad said, "No, no, I want to travel with all the fans!"'

It was hard to know what they would make of it all – not just the often suggestive spectacle on stage, but the madness of the fans: people were tearing up the seats, fighting, slam-dancing and basically trashing the joint. 'It looked like a bomb had gone off,' said Shirley. As for Mr and Mrs Collinson's reaction, they couldn't have been prouder.

'We had a wonderful time,' said Joan. 'Incidentally, we'd done a lot of our courting in the back row [at the Odeon], so it was quite something to see Lee there. My husband was crazy about it. I was terrified he was going to go over the edge of the circle, I was hanging on to his coat-tails, he was as bad as all the youngsters.

'We'd had strict instructions from Lee that we were to go home before the last number because of the rush – he reckoned we'd get trampled to death getting to Hammersmith station. And my husband said, "We're staying. I'm seeing them right to the end." Outside the theatre there were four cardboard cut-outs of the Feelgoods, [some fans] stole them and they were in our carriage – Collie, the old big mouth, said, "That's my son!"'

'We were so exhilarated, there's no way of describing how we felt. We couldn't stop talking about it.' And it wasn't just parental pride – they really had just seen the Feelgoods at their best.

As the various acolytes and journalists staggered off to the Tube, the latter already constructing ecstatic reviews in their over-stimulated cerebra, Shirley made her way backstage thanks to a little help from Fred Barker. The promoter of the show had dismissed her as a chancer ('an immediate blow to my ego'), but Fred recognised her and ushered her straight to the dressing room where it seemed like 'a million' people had managed to squash themselves in. 'There was a party back at the hotel around the corner,' says Shirley. 'They had this huge suite, amazing food and booze, and everyone I got to know later on from Canvey seemed to be there. It was a big deal. *They* were a big deal.'

After the party, Lee whisked Shirley away in his Jaguar, and before she knew it they were flying down the A13, with industrial East London, the foggy, spectral Essex marshes and ultimately the flaming tower at Coryton Oil Refinery whizzing by as Shirley kept 'pressing an imaginary brake. I was so tense because I was on what I considered to be the driver's side … He's driving, overtaking on the other side of the street, it was crazy. But we finally get to Canvey Island, still alive.'

Shirley was charmed by her first moments on the Island, although it's worth bearing in mind that it was very dark when she arrived. Once the sun rose on Oil City and a bleary-eyed Suds eventually got up and peered out of the window, her impression of Lee's stomping ground would be a little less romantic.

'He takes me to this tiny bungalow on Rainbow Road which had belonged to his grandfather. It was adorable. I was like, "Oh my God, I'm in *England*, this is amazing!" The next day I get up and look out the window, and there's a roundabout and a playing field, all these little ticky-tacky houses, the refineries in the distance … I'm thinking, where am I? What is this place? It was flat and bleak and marshy. Actually it looked like Southern Louisiana – there's a place upriver from New Orleans, a refinery town called Norco. I thought it looked a lot like Norco.'[28]

All the same, Shirley would be absorbed into the Feelgood way of life almost instantly, and a significant part of that would be hanging out at the Admiral Jellicoe. The Feelgoods might have been the stars of the hour, but their everyday habits were more like those of a group of boozy old geezers than a bunch of cool young dudes with a hit album. Shirley soon realised that the daily routine, if the band wasn't gigging, was: get up, have breakfast, make a cup of tea and then go to the

John Denton

Top left: Shirley 'Suds' Altord, soon to become Mrs Brilleaux, brings some Southern glamour to Oil City. Bottom left: Suds and Lee, Canvey's golden couple. Top right: an early 1980s shot of Shirley, pianist John Denton and Lee in the Grand, Leigh on Sea, Lee Brilleaux's 'home-from-home'. Bottom right: Buzz Barwell (who would join the Feelgood line-up in 1982 on drums), John Denton and Lee.

John Denton

John Denton

'Jellie', shoot some pool and hang out with the various characters who happened to be in that day.

The presence of the glamorous Shirley with her Southern belle accent would be novel in any 1970s old man pub, but she was the honoured guest of Canvey royalty and would be treated with respect (with the exception of a few times when the occasional patron would enquire as to why she was in the pub with Lee, rather than at home cooking dinner). Shirley paints an evocative portrait of an average day at the Jellicoe, bearing in mind it was not your average pub ('people would ride their bicycles straight into there,' remembers Pete Zear. 'Mad things. Lew would be playing harmonica into a beer glass, somebody would come in with a chicken and throw it up in the air …')

'My first visit to the Jellicoe, I was like, "OK …"' said Shirley. 'I liked to drink, and I'm from New Orleans, so you know … but I wasn't prepared for the magnitude of the band's habits. I remember people asking me, "How do you like it here? Have you been down the seafront?" Sparko was killing himself. He was like, "Oh yeah, because Canvey seafront really makes the California coastline look like shit. Once you've experienced Canvey Island you'll never go back to California."

'There'd be working boys, labourers, people on the dole, a lot of old men with their little peaked caps hunched over their pints, and Albert, this old pot-man, who would shuffle around with a biscuit tin emptying ash trays and complaining about the weather. Bernie behind the bar, he was hilarious, muttering things about people under his breath … and then there were people who started showing up when they worked out it was the Feelgoods' local. Lee was such a gentleman. He'd sit down and talk to them, buy them a beer. He'd never turn anyone away if they came looking for him – not without reason anyway.[29] There were people he told where to go, but they would be people who turned up to give him a hard time – there were plenty of those too.

'For far too long, I tried to keep up with the drinking. Thank God Lee wasn't there all the time, because I'd probably be dead by now. They were so famous, they were facilitated at every turn by the record company, the media. Everyone was talking about these "hard-drinking lads". It was part of the legend, and I bought into it as much as the next person. We were all really drunk a lot of the time.'

Winter was looming, and Shirley's return ticket to San Francisco was starting to burn a hole in her pocket, but it was clear that her original plans to stay in England for 'a couple of months' vacation' had long since been abandoned. 'Basically I went home with him in October and never left.'

Shirley Brilleaux

Shirley Brilleaux

Top: Larry Wallis, Lee, Tommy Montegut
(a friend of Shirley's from Louisiana) and
Shirley celebrate Christmas in The Proceeds,
the Leigh on Sea home they would move
into after leaving Canvey Island in the early
1980s. Bottom: hanging out on tour and
looking cool (even when he was taking the
piss). To Lee's right is Kursaal Flyer and long-
time pal Will Birch.

Photographer Chalkie Davies took this picture of a crazy-eyed Lee chomping into Shirley's elegant hand in an ironic tribute to the cover of the Rolling Stones album Love You Live (released September 1977), which featured an image of Jagger biting a woman's hand.

11. OIL CITY BLUES

'Most reprehensible'

Lee Brilleaux on drinking outside pub opening hours (to Shrink
Wrap, *Melody Maker*)

Domestic bliss might not have been the ideal term for what Lee Brilleaux
was now enjoying – Lee and 'Suds' were both strong characters – and
quarrels, smashed household items and even the odd period of full-on
estrangement would not be uncommon, but he had the perfect partner
in crime, a fellow adventurer who was, like him, fiery, intelligent and
not a little mischievous.

Lee was keen to take Shirley away from damp, chilly Canvey for
a breather, but there were still a number of dates on the Feelgood
calendar in this, the band's biggest year so far. The most significant of
these would be 19 December at the Hammersmith Palais, a historic gig
for various reasons, not least because it would be the Feelgood's last
live show with Wilko Johnson – not that they knew that then.

The white jacket was back, lapels tinged with requisite filth, and there
was a noticeable but thrilling increase in the nervous energy onstage.
Lee was especially fierce that night, although that may partly have been
because he was channelling his temper into the show after a row with
Shirley at the Portobello Hotel, where they'd been staying.

'We were just heading out to the cars to go to the venue,' recalls
Wilko, 'and there was a ruck between Lee and Suds. Somebody threw
a telephone. I remember thinking, fucking hell, fancy smashing about
like that just before a gig. I didn't realise I would have my turn at all of
that, of course.'

While the Feelgoods were always mean onstage, tonight there was
also a little humour in the show. As an acknowledgement to the growing
wave of punk that was about to push the Feelgoods, the Kilburns and
almost every other associated act aside (after a bit of looting in the style
and attitude departments), Lee had had a huge safety pin made and
wore it 'like it was going right through him,' said Wilko. 'That was us
satirising punk.' Admittedly, a bunch of snotty kids who weren't very

good at playing their guitars didn't seem like that much of a threat. Lee was more interested in going on holiday than worrying about punk. The band had a new album to record, more tours in the book, and 1977 was already shaping up to be a non-stop year.

During the Christmas break, Lee took Shirley to southern Spain with Chris Fenwick and his then girlfriend Linda for some time away and, hopefully, some winter sun. One might assume an airport was the last place Brilleaux would want to see, but some distance was required. While Canvey and the Feelgoods were inextricably linked – 'he was intensely passionate about the Island,' said Shirley – that link was starting to show signs of wear. Being recognised had long been par for the course, but the Morrissey song 'We Hate It When Our Friends Become Successful' gives a hint of the feeling, at times, on home turf (Wilko would soon move off the Island altogether, opting for a home in Westcliff over the water, unfortunately creating an even bigger, and now physical, gulf between himself and the rest of the group). Lee needed a chance to relax, preferably somewhere with few Feelgood associations.

The two couples stayed in Chris's parents' villa in Almeria, close to where Sergio Leone shot his spaghetti westerns, and David Lean filmed scenes for *Lawrence of Arabia*. From there they would take a flying visit to Tangiers, load up on pastis and spend New Year's Eve 'playing Canasta drunk in the hotel, it was just the most bizarre experience,' said Shirley.

Almeria was, in Lee's opinion, 'a pretty funky sort of joint', and the Brilleauxs would holiday there with the Fenwicks for many years, taking their children there in the 1980s and 1990s. But back in the 1970s, it would be on one of these trips that Lee and Chris decided to purchase a pig farm as an investment, and also (Lee will surely have been jesting when he said this) as a place to rehearse for tours. The idea came to them when Lee nearly won a pig farm in a game of cards. Just another day on Planet Feelgood.

It was also during one of these visits that Lee announced that he desired a fez, but an authentic fez, as in from the *town* of Fez. Thanks to the efforts of Spanish Feelgood comrade and sometime road manager Jerome Martinez, a boat trip was organised and Lee's wish would be granted.

By the time Lee and Shirley returned to Rainbow Road, 1977 was still looking deceptively innocuous, but plans in Camp Feelgood were already afoot. It had been decided that two weeks at Rockfield Studios were in order, as a fourth album was urgently required. On the other side of the Atlantic, executives at CBS had had their enthusiasm for the Feelgoods revived by the phenomenal success of *Stupidity*.

They insisted it was time the band tried their hand in the States again with a new album – a second bite of an exceptionally rare, sweet and occasionally poisonous cherry.

CBS wanted the next Feelgood album to be a slicker affair with an American producer at the helm, so Lee and Wilko were invited back to the States for another convention, this time in Atlanta, to meet the man they had in mind. Lee was keen to make sure they hadn't earmarked 'some arsehole sort of geezer'. Fortunately, the producer in mind was not an arsehole at all, but the soul producer Bert de Coteaux, who had worked with everyone from Stevie Wonder to Martha Reeves and BB King. But it was his work with Stax legend Albert King that would convince Lee that de Coteaux and the Feelgoods could be a good fit.

'Yeah, Albert King's last album [*Albert*] was the one,' Lee rhapsodised (in his way) to Nick Kent. 'There's a parallel [with the Feelgoods] 'cause he's always had a rough sound, very straightforward. [On *Albert*] he sounded modern, but still had all the bollocks of yer old Albert King. And I thought [Bert de Coteaux] could do it for us in the same way.'

Lee and Wilko flew out to Atlanta, and while, at this stage, the idea of these two individuals having to spend time together in the very place that had tipped the Feelgoods over into all-out toxicity may have seemed like a bad one, the pair appeared to be rekindling their affection for each other. 'In reality things were really good down there,' Lee admitted. 'I mean, comparatively …'

'We were getting on, we had a couple of laughs there,' said Wilko. 'I remember Lee bursting up to Boston – we'd never heard of them but they were huge – he stalked up to them in the corridor asking if they had any cocaine, and they were fucking frightened. They were like, "Ooh! Er, we'll have to ask our roadie for that." I'm standing there watching Lee, and they're wondering who these Englishmen are, coming over and frightening everyone. Good times.

'After [we came back], Lee would come over to my house with a bottle of tequila. I knew that he was trying to be friends again. I appreciated it. We both knew what we were doing. We seemed to be getting back to a friendship but … well, "Of all sad words of tongue or pen, the saddest are these: it might have been."'[30]

From Lee's point of view, not least the rest of the group, he never quite knew where he was with Wilko. The trip to America had gone well, all told, but the situation could easily turn, and sadly one of the pivotal moments that would seal the end of their relationship – certainly the moment Lee would often hark back to – was just around the corner.

It had been agreed with CBS that, after the fourth album was released, Dr Feelgood would return to America for a tour later that year. Everyone, with one exception, was looking forward to the chance to take on the States again, but there was trepidation about how the tour would play out with Wilko – whether it would even play out at all.

Sure enough, back in the UK, shortly after Lee and Wilko's return from the US, the Feelgoods were driving home from a meeting in London and decided to stop at a café on the A127 to load up on caffeine and bacon sandwiches. It was here that a decidedly agitated Wilko blurted out that he had no intention of going back to America at all. After a moment of shocked silence, Lee 'just went ballistic', remembers a friend. 'For years after, if ever we were driving down the A127, he would point out the café [now no longer there]. "There it is," he'd say. "That's where it happened. That's where it really ended." Even years later, it upset him.'

In Wilko's opinion, he didn't want to leave the band, he just wouldn't play ball when it came to America, a country he 'loathed'. But this announcement marked a major shift, representing possibly the most significant sign yet that Wilko's modus operandi was starkly different from the rest of the band's.

'Things were building up,' remembers Figure, who was often the referee in some of the epic Lee–Wilko battles. 'Wilko's ego, and Lee's ego, had become quite contentious. I was the placater because I'd known Wilko the longest. It was just part of keeping the band together.' But the rift was doing no one any good, and patching up the rips and attempting to move forward was becoming harder.

Part of the problem had been that, as always, Wilko was expected to come up with quality new material, but there'd been little time to actually focus on writing, and the resultant stress didn't make it any easier to get focused and start composing. Given the 'bad feeling' between them, for all of Wilko's previous attempts to encourage Lee to write lyrics, the opportunity for any Johnson–Brilleaux co-writes had now well and truly passed. 'You've got to feel quite close to somebody to sit and write a song,' Wilko explains. 'You've certainly got to feel friendly.'

Other songwriters would send tapes of songs written with the Feelgoods in mind, but the band hardly had any time to listen, and when they did, as Sparko recalls, 'only about two per cent would be suitable'.

'There'd been a lot of pressure on Wilko,' admitted Lee. 'He found it very difficult to come up with the goods. Wilko was a great songwriter who demanded a lot from himself. The [situation] caused huge frustration which almost made him ill.' Just half of the songs chosen for what would become *Sneakin' Suspicion* would be Wilko's compositions,[31] the rest would be covers – a marked difference to the Feelgoods' previous output. It didn't help that the stakes had never been higher.

Wilko had been anxious to inject a new flavour into the usual Feelgood style, given that the past three albums, while successful, had been very much of a kind. But Lee was more of an if-it-ain't-broke-why-fix-it? kind of a chap, and he couldn't see the point in changing what, up until this point, had been a winning formula. Wilko had written with Lee's voice and persona in mind, and it had always worked. But some of the songs he was now putting forward were not songs Lee felt comfortable singing (including, famously, the deeply personal 'Paradise' which we will come to a little later).

'When he started to experiment outside the Feelgood [remit], that's when things started to disintegrate between us,' said Lee several years later. 'I think Wilko felt under great pressure to come up with something new all the time, whereas me being a very conservative person by nature, I was saying, "Well, why? This is what we wanna do, this is what we've been doing, that's what people want. If it goes out of fashion, too bad."'

'It was all going very, very, very well – and then the trouble starts,' continued Lee. '[We were saying] "Come on, if you don't provide the songs, we're going to come up with them," and this caused some resentment and bad feeling, as it always does. I look back now ... if we were all a bit older and saw things a bit more sensibly, we probably could have sat down and discussed it.'

But a 'terrible falling out' was looming, a row that would leave considerable psychic scars on both sides, a row that would be impossible to come back from. Although it wouldn't be the worst falling out in the Feelgood camp, it would be, in Lee's opinion, 'the straw that broke the camel's back'.

'Lew Lewis had a song called "Lucky Seven",' said Shirley. 'Lew was Lee's protégé, and Lew ... well, Lew is Lew. Very talented guy, but to try and have a conversation with him ... You ask a closed-ended question and he'd flick his hand and crack his knuckles and go, "Oh! Oh! Snap dragon in half!" And it was like, "*What*?" It was like he was speaking another language. And he was! He was speaking fluent Lew Lewis. But he wrote brilliantly.'

Lee perused the lyrics to 'Lucky Seven' and knew instantly this was a very Feelgood-appropriate song – all trains, alleyways, boogying in hot basements, sex with 'high-headed honeys' ... It had just the right balance of energy and sleaze, Lee could imagine himself singing it, and he also thought the use of 'Lucky Seven' would 'temporarily relieve Wilko'. To say it would have the opposite effect would be an understatement.

Rockfield awaited, cosy and bucolic, the perfect juxtaposition to the heavy black clouds that would soon be descending once the full complement of Feelgoods were in situ – Wilko turning up several days later than the rest of the band. United Artists, well aware of how fragile the situation had become, had wisely decided to introduce an outsider into the group, session pianist Tim Hinkley. Lee had long been open to the idea of adding keyboards, even as a permanent fixture, not just to add an extra dimension musically but also to take off the heat and allow the rest of the band to 'lay back a bit' live. But the introduction of an extra, if temporary, member would also supposedly ensure good behaviour. This theory was unfortunately not Feelgood-proof.

Hinkley had never met the Feelgoods before, but his initial impression that they were 'beer-drinking pub yobbos' was quickly dissipated. After a hearty meal and some alcoholic refreshment at the Punch House, Tim realised at the end of the evening that he would be billeted with Lee in Rockfield's farmhouse. As he unpacked his bags and wound down for the night, he was intrigued to observe Lee reading a book by the Irish writer Brendan Behan. 'I thought, hang on a minute, this is a bit different,' said Tim. 'Every now and then he'd say, "Let me read you this passage." We'd laugh about it and talk about literature and music. He was a smart guy. He was different.'

The atmosphere at Rockfield for those first few days was friendly and relaxed. Bert de Coteaux was charming, they were jamming in the studio, listening to music ... 'Then Wilko arrives on the third day, and the vibe turns,' said Tim. 'He had a cottage, and I don't think I met him before he had locked himself in and wouldn't come out.'

After another night at the Punch House, the collective, *sans* Wilko, were in the mood to expend a bit of energy in the studio. Bert de Coteaux had secretly told the engineer to press record whenever there was any playing in the studio, even if it was just a jam. Tim picked up the guitar, Bert sat down at the piano and the band played around with 'Lucky Seven' before lurching off to bed. The next morning they assembled in the kitchen for breakfast, but there was still no sign of

Wilko. Sparko, as Shirley recalls, 'would just laugh at the whole thing', but Lee in particular was starting to get agitated. Fortunately Bert had the secret recording of the previous night's jam – a dynamic, driving blues – to distract them.

When Wilko eventually emerged, they played him the recording, but he dismissed the track, telling the group flatly that it just didn't sound like Dr Feelgood. 'I didn't want to discourage them from writing [but] the way they'd done it, I didn't like it,' said Wilko. 'It wasn't R&B. When I write songs, I used to think, can I imagine Bo Diddley singing this? This song failed that test altogether.'

As Wilko returned to his cottage, the rest of the group took solace in the pub. That night, back at the house, Lee 'just exploded,' said Tim. 'I mean, it was a really vehement tirade.' By this stage, as Shirley recalled, Lee had become so aggravated by the situation with Wilko 'it became almost impossible for him to concentrate on anything else'.

The Feelgoods would get through a few more days of recording despite the ill feeling, although Hinkley observed they were keener to get back to the pub than to bother recording extra takes. There was also some discomfort around the fact that Wilko had, at one stage, both his wife Irene and son Matthew and also his girlfriend present at the sessions, and he'd proposed the inclusion of the song 'Paradise', which made reference to both women. (The lyrics have since been changed so that the only woman in the song is Irene.) Wilko had also written a ballad, unusual territory for the Feelgoods. Both songs left Lee cold, but Wilko believes the band were also searching for a scapegoat to get rid of him. Creating a stink over Wilko's song choices seemed like a surefire flashpoint, although it wouldn't quite work out that way. That night, Lee banged on the door of Wilko's cottage and told him he didn't want to sing the ballad. Contrary to the reaction he'd expected, Wilko shrugged and told him to forget about it.

'They were expecting an argument over this, but there wasn't one,' he said. 'I thought, they're trying to provoke something. The next night, I hear them screeching back from the pub, they're slamming the doors, and I knew something was going to happen.' Sure enough, moments later there was a knock on the door. Lee, Chris and Sparko came in and 'the row started'.

'We're in this row and I'm saying, "While we're at it, I don't like that fucking song!" ['Lucky Seven']. I said, "There's always been this unwritten rule, if one guy don't like something, we blow it out." Lee [said] he didn't like the ballad. I said, "Don't do it. But you're now arguing with me that you want to do this fucking thing and I don't like it.' It started hinging on this but it wasn't really about the song. This went on into the night. At one point, Lee banged on the table and said, "Why is it that whenever you argue about anything you sound like you're fucking right?!"'

By the following morning, Wilko was no longer in the band. He says he was pushed; they say he jumped. It's not difficult to believe that a situation was engineered to precipitate a drastic change, as Wilko suspected. As Shirley remembers, 'they were not on good terms in any respect, and I think they used that ['Lucky Seven']. Had it not been that, it would have been something else.'

'There was other things going on there,' adds Lew Lewis. 'They weren't getting on, but unfortunately they used "Lucky Seven" as the reason for Wilko leaving. It was a scapegoat. Well out of order – it was nothing to do with me! It upset me terribly. Wilko years later said that too; that it wasn't fair to use [the song] like that. Wilko still hates that song … brings back bad memories, I guess.'

On being asked, repeatedly, about those final moments, Lee would later recount the story to journalists with characteristic diplomacy. Wilko had a huge following, after all. This needed careful handling, something Lee was skilled at. 'We split up,' he said. 'It wasn't a question of kicking people out. That's how I see it. Wilko might see it differently. [But] Wilko is a very big personality, he needs to be on his own.'

Wilko insists the 'Lucky Seven' argument was an aside, albeit a significant one, but Lee would counter that this was actually at the heart of the fight, prompting Wilko to give the band an ultimatum, although Lee later conceded that 'there were many other reasons as well. That was just the last thing. He more or less said, "If you want to do it this way, then I'm going to leave." And we said, "Well, OK, old son. Go." Obviously he was probably the most important single member of the group, [but] he'd made us all so unhappy, and himself unhappy. It was a relief to say goodbye to him.'

The negativity which had mushroomed within the group had turned into a poisonous boil, which, as Lee explained to Wilko's brother Malcolm in later years, 'had to be lanced for everybody's sake and sanity'. Even so, as the shell-shocked guitarist walked away from his old bandmates for the last time, Lee must have felt a flicker of conflict; this might have been a much needed change on a personal level, but he knew even then that they had lost 'not just a guitarist – probably the most gifted of his generation – but somehow the soul of Dr Feelgood'.

David Corio

'What it boiled down to was that Wilko didn't
fit in with the rest of us,' Brilleaux said in an
interview with Blues Bag in 1990. 'Looking
back on it, poor old Wilko must have been
very miserable and depressed.'

*Dr Feelgood storm ahead with new guitarist
Gypie Mayo. He came in with a roar, no two
ways about that.*

12. AND THEN THERE WERE THREE. BRIEFLY

Occasionally onstage, I get this flutter inside ... I turn around suddenly and think, God, where's Wilko? I miss him a lot.

Lee Brilleaux to Nick Kent, *NME*

The loss of Wilko was viewed as potentially disastrous by record company and fan alike, and speculation was swirling. Did Wilko really leave of his own accord? Would Mick Green be replacing Wilko, his *protégé*, in the line-up? Or would Lee Brilleaux leave the band and join the Pirates? There was even a petition, signed by well-meaning Wilko fans unaware of the angsty fullness of the situation, to 'bring back Wilko', but it wasn't to be.[32] Lee and the rest of the band's priority now was to plan the immediate future, find a suitable replacement, and get out on the road as quickly as possible to show the outside world that everything was as it should be.

'We were all in a state of panic because many people were quite rightly saying that Wilko was a very important part of the band,' Lee said. 'Some people were even going so far as saying that Dr Feelgood would collapse without him, and a lot of people lost interest after he left. You accept that as an inevitability.'

Guitarist Chris Spedding would cover a couple of shows for the Feelgoods, as would Henry McCullough (although as Lee recalled they couldn't afford him long term). Their dream guitarist was Mo Witham, who played with Mickey Jupp. Witham was a musician long admired by Wilko, and Lee was ready to offer him the job 'unconditionally', but he'd been working with a songwriter and had just signed a deal. The idea of potentially splitting up a partnership didn't sit right with Brilleaux and the idea was dropped.

The inevitable ad was placed in the *Melody Maker*, inviting hopefuls to send in cassettes of their playing before holding auditions at Feelgood House on Canvey, but the right person was just a recommendation away. American musician George Hatcher, one of the Feelgoods' UA cousins, had happened upon a gifted Harlow-based guitarist called John Cawthra – soon to be more widely known as Gypie Mayo (yet another

Lee Brilleaux christening, inspired by the fact that Cawthra always had a cold, a bad back, always had 'the gyp' – and also to cut down on the number of Johns in the Feelgood operation). Hatcher urged the band to try him out. Trying to find him was the first challenge. 'He was sofa surfing at the time,' Sparko remembers.

'They left a trail of messages all over the place,' said Gypie. 'Finally I spoke to Lee and he explained the situation, which I'd read about anyway. He said, "Forget all you've seen in the papers and just be yourself. Don't try doing Wilko, don't try to play like him. Nobody can do that. Just do what you do." It was tense for all concerned. They didn't know if it was all over for them.'

The Big Figure drove to Harlow to pick up Gypie for a try-out, brought him back to Canvey and 'he fitted the bill perfectly'. He was accomplished and musical, and his inclusion would take the Feelgoods from raw 'beat' territory into a thicker blues sound. It didn't hurt that Gypie also looked cool – tall, lean and with a resplendent rock star haircut – and he also liked a drink and was enthusiastic and funny. The Feelgoods were anxious to get this right, but needn't have worried; they would enjoy considerable chart success with Gypie, Lee later referring to him as their 'winning lottery ticket'. For Gypie, joining the Feelgoods was like being absorbed into a warm, supportive, if slightly loopy, family.

'Lee was such an unusual character,' observed Gypie. 'Very hyperactive and quick-tempered. He was about three or four different personality types in one. He could seem very angry and uptight, and then five minutes later everybody would be rolling around laughing because he's saying all these funny things. I've never met anybody like him. In fact, I've never met anybody like the Feelgoods.'

With Gypie aboard, the new guitarist would, as Lee put it, 'be applying for citizenship of the dominion' (relocating to Canvey) and moving in with Sparko after something of a domestic reshuffle. As we know, the Feelgoods liked to keep things in house, and that went for property too, where possible. Lee's grandfather's old bungalow had been fine for one travelling man and his record collection, but now there was a second person to accommodate, and it was time to upsize.

The bungalow would be bought by Sparko, while Lee and Shirley moved into a larger property previously belonging to Chris Fenwick's parents on Kellington Road on the quieter end of Canvey, moments from the house Lee had grown up in during the 1960s. It was an upside-down house – bedrooms downstairs, kitchen and living room upstairs – and it had a balcony with a romantic view north over the Estuary towards the lush green hills of Hadleigh and its ruined castle.

'That castle's the only bit of culture Canvey's got, and that's on the mainland,' Lee observed wryly to *Melody Maker*'s in-house Feelgood comrade Allan Jones.[33] 'All those people in posh houses up there, what do they get to look at? Us and these crummy little houses. We get the view of them. Funny really.' The new house was called 'Borde Del Mar' ('Beside The Sea') – nothing to do with Lee, I probably don't need to add.

Aside from its natural charms, it would take a while for Lee and Shirley to make Borde Del Mar their own, and not only because Lee was away for much of the time. Lee's previous home was full of old furniture that had belonged to his grandfather, and the future Mr and Mrs Brilleaux were more than happy to get rid of it. As a result, when they moved to Kellington Road, they had little more than a bed, a pool table and a custom-made cabinet for Lee's vinyl.

'We did eventually have some rudimentary lounge furniture so you could actually sit down,' said Shirley. 'But Lee was gone a lot of the time, I was working at the pub[34] not earning very much. It didn't seem to be a huge priority to me to feather the nest. We were young.' Sparko, in the meantime, set to work fixing up Lee's old bungalow which was 'a nice enough place,' he told Jones, 'except for the holes in the walls.' 'Holes in the walls?' snapped Lee. 'They were serving hatches. Did them myself. With a hammer.'

Part of the media's ongoing fascination with the Feelgoods was their resolute determination, at this point at least, to remain on Canvey. Most artists felt compelled to move to London, but just like Canvey itself, the Feelgoods had their own thing going on and it worked. London could – and would – come to them. The excitement of the capital was one thing, but Canvey had its 'own brand of madness,' said Lee. 'Much more fun …'

The band rehearsed the live set with Gypie, preparing to unveil him officially at the album launch at Advision studio before an intimate set at Bardot's and the ensuing promotional tour for *Sneakin' Suspicion*. In the meantime, Lee found he was not only taking on more of a father-figure status, he was now the sole mouthpiece for the band, and it was his responsibility to prime the press for the coming changes. He'd have little to worry about – the presence of Gypie would be roundly embraced.

Sneakin' Suspicion would be released in May 1977, and while it still obviously rang with Wilko's songs and guitar playing, the album artwork would be necessarily different to the preceding Feelgood albums.

The cover is more theatrical than previous affairs, and obviously couldn't feature a band shot, of either line-up. Instead, we have a dimly lit tableau with a furtive Brilleaux in the foreground, clad in his sheepskin and lighting his ever-present cigarette while a brassy-looking couple canoodle behind him in the doorway of 'The Alibi Club' (actually the Canvey Club). The only evidence of Wilko is the neon pink Dr Feelgood logo, designed by the guitarist, behind Lee's shoulder.

Regarding the record itself, it would peak at number 10 in the UK album chart, possibly assisted by the much reported upon circumstances, and the lead single 'Sneakin' Suspicion' would be the band's first to enter the singles chart. On being asked as to why Mayo hadn't been overdubbed onto the album, Brilleaux was aghast – 'that'd be a desecration' – while the suggestion that Mayo might dress in black onstage, à la Johnson, was 'hideous'. Brilleaux still respected Wilko, and he was rightly reluctant to criticise the guitarist publicly, least of all at such a sensitive time. Several songs would also be dropped from the set, not least 'I'm A Hog For You'. 'We can't ask [Gypie] to play that solo. It'd be an insult, and if we changed it, it'd lose all the magic.'

Mayo had plenty of magic of his own, and his public debut with the band at Bardot's was as much an introduction as it was a positive statement of intent. The Feelgoods knew they had to work hard to prove themselves. 'We were eager to get over that lump in our career, if you like,' explained Figure. 'We all felt the pressure, but Lee, being at the front, all the more.'

Still, amid the eddying rumours, get over it they would, and the talented Mayo, with his mischievous eyes, striped matelot T-shirts and legs-akimbo rock god stance, would win over the audience and allow the Feelgoods to soar straight into a promotional tour with confidence and no small amount of relief. Lee would often physically push Mayo forward for a solo, aware of the delicate psychology of making this new situation work for everyone involved, fans included. If Mayo himself was to charge forward too soon, the crowd, all of whom naturally still loved Wilko too, might resent him. But if Brilleaux urged him to take centre stage, then that would be respected.

'Gypie could take it all in his stride,' said Figure. 'He just needed that tug on the sleeve and he was away. He was fantastic.' Lee was 'very much in favour' of introducing keyboards to the line-up to give Gypie a bit more of a chance to 'stretch out' and concentrate on playing lead rather than rhythm, 'but he said no'. As a result, this would create noticeable spaces in the music when Gypie flew into one of his virtuoso guitar solos, but this was 'a new chapter,' as Lee put it, 'and I thought, if he's happy, I'm happy too.'

Only occasionally would there be a bit of heckling from individuals in the crowd, something Lee would give short shrift. During the show on 21 May at the University of Salford, for example, a female fan repeatedly shouted out Wilko's name during the gaps between songs. Gypie had expected a bit of this, but Lee wasn't standing for it. When it was time to play 'Hey Mama, Keep Your Big Mouth Shut', Lee located the offending heckler, fixed her with a stare and delivered a chorus customised just for her: 'Hey bitch, keep your big mouth shut.' And one would imagine that she did.

Lee, while it may not have been outwardly apparent, was nervous – and that was no reflection on Gypie's abilities. He had grown accustomed to being one half of a famous double act, and now most of the attention was on him. As a result, the sets got faster, the delivery more breakneck – if there was no time to think, there was no time to worry.

'The more gaps Lee had on stage the more angsty he was,' confirms Figure. 'He was happier pushing things along at a fast tempo. It was always, "Let's go, let's zip it on." It got a bit out of control. I'd often have to say to Lee, "Come on, mate, we've got a bit too much roll here and not enough rock. It's not having the impact. It's so fast we don't have time to breathe, there's no space in the music."'

Figure concedes that Lee's urgency to bolt through the set, again, reflects his innate shyness, despite the finger jabbing, the strutting, the mock-ejaculating ... We're talking about a serious rock'n'roll Jekyll and Hyde, and the clothes, the props and the physical elevation – not to mention the various substances – all came together to manifest the transformation, even if they couldn't quite transcend the nerves. That said, the transformation would also take effect in the event of any petty unfairness that happened to take place within his orbit, especially when it came to matters alcoholic.

Pete Zear remembers supporting the Feelgoods on the *Sneakin'
Suspicion* tour, and after loading in to the venue in Manchester at about twenty to six in the evening, he noticed the bar was filling up with punters. There was just one problem: the metal shutter was still down on the bar and it would not be rising until 6 p.m. It was a warm evening, people had come straight from work, the minutes were ticking by, and the room was getting busier. Cue the revolution.

'Lee's looking over,' recalls Zear. 'Finally he starts. "Look, there's a bar here! There's a lot of people thirsty – we've got to do something about this." He had a hat on, short-sleeved shirt; he looked like Hawkeye out of *MASH*. Immediately everyone noticed, you know, this is a man you can follow. "This is an injustice!" He got the whole room up. We were all like, "Yes, this is ridiculous!" And he got the bar open, basically. They were aiming to open at six, but no, we got them open at quarter to, and Lee started it. He would have been a great politician.'

While it was essential to introduce Gypie live as quickly as possible and show the world – or at least parts of it – that the Feelgood machine was still very much in motion, they wanted to get in the studio with their new guitarist as soon as possible. A new album would be symbolic on several levels: another strong statement of intent and forward motion, and their first without Wilko taking control.

'For so long we'd been dominated by Wilko,' said Lee, '[and] it was nice to have an opportunity to just be as we are. Teacher had left the classroom and now the pupils can be naughty ...' The band wanted to make a no-frills, straightforward R&B album with the chaotic, warm, tipsy feel of a live show, but some outside help would be required to bring out the best in them and, at last, successfully encourage them to write material themselves.

Feelgoods cohort Nick Lowe was brought in to produce the release which would be *Be Seeing You*, a reference to the TV series *The Prisoner* with which the band was currently obsessed, although certainly appears to be a bit of a comment on Wilko's departure as well. As Sparko remembers it, however, it was the record company who suggested using the *Prisoner* connection; they would pick up on what Lee in particular was into at the time and use those references however they saw fit, and in ways they felt would capture the public imagination – and, increasingly, Lee would be more than happy to let them do exactly that. Now the visionary Wilko was no longer there to steer the good ship Feelgood, it was often left to whoever was putting up the money to make the aesthetic decisions while the band did what they did best – had as much fun as they possibly could, and poured every ounce of energy into entertaining people live.

Larry Wallis, underground star of The Deviants, the Pink Fairies and Motörhead, now a solo artist, was hanging out at the Stiff Records office when the phone started ringing. Canvey calling. It was Chris Fenwick checking in prior to Nick's visit to Feelgood House to work with the band on what they wanted to record. Teacher might have left the classroom, but he'd taken his songbook with him, and Lowe was 'freaking out' because he couldn't think of enough material for them.

'In a moment of madness, I piped up. "I'll write 'em a song!"' says Wallis, 'to which Nick replied, "You've gotta have it here for eleven a.m. tomorrow." Off I toddled, with my stupid suggestion terrifying the crap out of me as I'd never written a song for anybody else in my life. I put myself in Lee's place, thinking, what does this guy sing about? Whisky, women, maybe gambling, all suitably redolent of smoke-filled rooms in the bad part of town.'

After meditating on these themes, within twenty minutes Wallis had conjured up the darkly mesmeric 'As Long As The Price Is Right' (featuring the classic line, 'I said, "oui, babe", 'cause that's French for 'yes".' There's something pleasingly Del Boy Trotter about that lyric.) The next morning, as agreed, Wallis leapt in a cab with the demo in his hand and delivered it to Nick, who listened, approved, tore over to Canvey with the tape and played it to the Feelgoods. 'As Long As The Price Is Right' was in. Lowe, meanwhile, would provide the catchy 'That's It, I Quit'. (Fellow Stiffster Elvis Costello offered up 'You Belong To Me' – a song almost impertinently reminiscent of The Rolling Stones' 'The Last Time' – to Lee Brilleaux, who leafed through the lyrics before protesting, 'This is like bleedin' *War and Peace*, Elvis.')

In addition, there would be the usual handful of strong covers, including a saucy, swaggering version of 'Ninety-Nine And A Half (Won't Do)', 'My Buddy Buddy Friends' and 'Baby Jane', but for the first time, Lee's own name would be on the songwriting credits of some of the tracks – lead single 'She's A Wind-Up', a high-energy canter bemoaning the perils of the prick tease, was a band co-write while 'I Thought I Had It Made' and 'I Don't Want To Know' were composed by Mayo and Brilleaux. Lee 'had a way of putting his own vocals over better than anybody else,' said Figure. 'Lee became a very able composer, especially on the last two or three albums we did.'

They might have been eager to record but Nick Lowe would generally have considerable trouble getting them away from the bar and into Pathway Studios. *Melody Maker*'s Allan Jones was writing a piece on 'a day in the life' of the Stiff Records HQ when he encountered the band in a pub nearby with Ian Dury's maverick publicist Kosmo Vinyl, discussing the allure of Canvey Island, a place Vinyl, like many Londoners, used to visit as a child. When Jones walked in, Lee was busy filling Vinyl in on the sexual habits of jellyfish. 'Jellyfish don't fuck,' he was heard to confirm. 'They split up like worms. I hate jellyfish, as it happens. No time for 'em.'

Jones sidled up to enquire as to how the new album was shaping up with 'Basher'[35] as Lee threw yet another brandy (referred to every time as a 'swift arf') down his throat. 'He's a bastard,' Lee replied grimly. Why? 'He doesn't understand the complications of British licensing laws. Pubs close at three, he wants us in the studio at two.' 'I can't get them out of the pub,' Lowe was heard lamenting back at the Stiff office. 'They just won't move.'

Eventually they did leave the pub (when it closed) and came up with a strong record which would earth the band's new direction and present Gypie's chunkier, rockier guitar sound on vinyl. The most important thing, to Lee, was that people could hear the band were having a good time on the record, and it would take the right producer to foster that combination of hard work and application and sheer drunken fun.

'To get Nick on board at that time was really good,' agrees Figure. 'He got the best out of us. He was able to listen to what we were doing and go, "If you did this and this it'll sound more like this …" He was actually working with us rather than just producing the songs.'

Perhaps it was Lee's habitual modesty that made him initially come across as fairly casual on the subject of this, the first album he'd actually written some material on; he would joke that 'the sound wasn't of the highest quality but it was an opportunity to drink dozens of pints of lager with Nick Lowe'. (Jake Riviera, Lowe's long-time manager, noted that working with Dr Feelgood had done nothing for Lowe's physique. Riviera complained that he'd 'just had him slimmed down, looking like a proper rock star, and the Feelgoods send him back looking like a tub of butter.')

'It's not particularly well recorded,' Lee continued, 'because we only recorded it on an eight-track machine, but there's feeling and power there. I like it because it was different and back to the roots, unpretentious.' *Be Seeing You* was, he later declared, his favourite Feelgood record – and one can't help but sense that Lee was perhaps making a point, being as it was their first without Wilko. That said, as Shirley points out, because the dynamic in the band had changed so fundamentally, and the strength of purpose in terms of production values was largely no longer stemming from within the band itself, 'every record the Feelgoods did [from that point] seemed to be influenced by whoever happened to be producing the album. The original Feelgoods sound was kind of history by that point.' It was perhaps unfortunate for them that Mick Farren, a close friend of Wilko's, would be the one to review the record in *NME* – and he would register concern that the

Feelgoods were allowing 'conservatism (with a small "c") to creep in'. [36] (He reserved praise for fellow Deviant Larry Wallis's track, however.)

Be Seeing You, in addition to its *Prisoner*-inspired artwork (featuring Dr Feelgood in blazers, Patrick McGoohan-style, on the beach in front of the Labworth on Canvey) boasted a cover image of the band drinking with new boy Gypie in the Jellicoe – a scene you would never have witnessed with Wilko. The release peaked at number 55 in the UK album chart, with the single 'She's A Wind-Up' entering the Top 40. 'It wasn't unsuccessful,' Lee reflected in later years. 'It wasn't a huge hit … it paid the milk bill.'

Brilleaux Musings

'No matter what you do, even if it's selling dodgy ballpoints down the market, you've gotta be a grafter and if you're prepared to put in the hours then the chances are you'll succeed.'

'People have said, "Why don't you do something about your image? Become like pop stars or something?" But that isn't us, you know? We couldn't afford the razor blades.'

'I always think, if you don't know what to do next, go back to your roots and have a think about it.'

'The important thing is always to keep one step ahead of your hangover.'

Christoffer Frances

Dr Feelgood onstage in Sweden (new guitarist Gypie Mayo on the left). It's important to stay hydrated.

Hangover Cures

One method Lee would prescribe was a 'coffee and a digestif' (the digestif being a brandy). Another remedy would be to scarf down a pot of cockles from Leigh Beach – 'pure protein,' Lee would enthuse. 'Great for hangovers.'

But 'generally,' says Shirley Brilleaux, 'Lee's way of curing a hangover and avoiding turning into a "three-day drunk", as he called it, was this: you should have two or three drinks the following day and then stop yourself there, if you're able. The ability to stop after putting yourself out of your immediate misery … sometimes he had better luck with that method than others.'

Above: Dr Feelgood onstage: The Big Figure, Lee (in his incredible palm tree jacket) and Sparko.Right: Be Seeing You promotional tour information. The cover (and album title) paid tribute to the band's obsession with the TV series The Prisoner, but the words 'be seeing you' must surely have been a reference to Wilko Johnson's recent departure too. The other side featured the band in their favourite Canvey pub, the Admiral Jellicoe, drinking with Gypie.

Be Seeing You

ALBUM UAS 30123
CASSETTE TCK 30123

On tour

OCTOBER
4 TUE   HANLEY, VICTORIA HALL
6 THU   MANCHESTER, FREE TRADE HALL
7 FRI   LIVERPOOL, EMPIRE
8 SAT   BIRMINGHAM, ODEON
9 SUN   BRISTOL, COLSTON HALL
10 MON SWANSEA, TOP RANK
11 TUE CARDIFF, TOP RANK
13 THU CANTERBURY, UNIVERSITY

14 FRI   BRIGHTON, TOP RANK
15 SAT   HAMMERSMITH ODEON
16 SUN   HAMMERSMITH ODEON
18 TUE   PORTSMOUTH, GUILD HALL
19 WED   BOURNEMOUTH, WINTER GARDENS
20 THU   OXFORD, NEW THEATRE
21 FRI   CAMBRIDGE, CORN EXCHANGE
22 SAT   SOUTHEND, KURSAAL

David Corio

Rock'n'roll's favourite Jekyll and Hyde gets into character backstage at the Winter Gardens, Malvern, 1977.

13. EXTRAORDINARY VOYAGES: RETURN TO THE US

It's a high in a way, but not a pleasurable high. You're definitely hurting yourself. You're pushing yourself further than you should.

Lee Brilleaux on performing live

The Feelgoods toured *Be Seeing You* that autumn before embarking on their pivotal trip to the States. CBS wanted to give the band another high-profile support slot, but the money would be rather more scant than it had been when they'd first tried their hand in America.

The band had a great affection for oddballs, so it was hardly surprising that they would bring the intimidating 'Borneo' (on account of his wildness) Fred Munt into the firm as tour manager to take over from Jake Riviera. Munt was formerly of psych-surrealists the Bonzo Dog Doo Dah Band, which should give you something of an idea of the man. (Fans of the Bonzos will recall Munt getting a name check as 'the Wild Man of Borneo' in the classic 'Intro And Outro' track.)

When you spent as much time on the road as the Feelgoods did, you had to surround yourself with relentlessly entertaining people to allay the inevitable monotony of travelling, or to distract you from the more stressful psychological aspects of being away from home. Life was certainly never dull with Munt around, although his presence wasn't exactly a stress reliever for the road crew, being as he was more interested in partying than working, and the psychological aspects … well, let's not go there.

'He was absolutely off-the-scale bonkers – and they loved bonkers, but this guy was mental,' remembers Geoff Shaw. 'I don't know if I liked him or not, but he was interesting. He had a walrus moustache, one tooth, bit dishevelled, red gypsy bandana like David Essex on heroin, waistcoat, bit of a travelling thing. Loudest voice you've ever heard. He was like a sophisticated Bernard Manning.

'He'd come down in the morning in flippers and a mask, goggles and a tennis racket. Walking into the breakfast room, everyone's in there not talking, pissed off, trying to charge their batteries, and he'd walk in like that, or in something even madder. He was hard to work with, but he was fun and they loved him. Bring him out, put him at the bar and he'd entertain everyone all night. You could just sit and look at him.' Munt would be the one chopping out thick rails of coke at the aftershow, as Allan Jones observed, with Brilleaux sauntering over shortly afterwards. 'Don't mind if I do,' Lee was heard to say. 'Just to be sociable.'

Now that the hedonistic Gypie was on board, the parties would get wilder and Brilleaux's frequent announcements that he was suffering a 'terrible thirst' while en route were no longer inhibited by anyone's disapproval, not that, one might argue, any consternation from Wilko ever really stopped him before. ('Jolly-up, *must* have a jolly-up,' Brilleaux would sing as they sped along in the van. 'It's been half an hour since the last jolly-up! No sense to this!')

It would be during this very UK tour, after the band's show at Leicester's De Montfort Hall, that the Feelgoods would repair to the Holiday Inn and, according to Allan Jones, proceed to '[drink] the entire profits of their UK tour in one night'. The more time spent enjoying themselves, the better – that was surely the whole point of the operation – and so with every minute being treated with respect and economy, such fripperies as sound checks were jettisoned, Brilleaux in particular feeling that the time would be better spent 'reading a book or having a shit'. The Feelgoods were supported on several dates of this tour by the San Francisco group Mink DeVille, who evidently did require a sound check at each venue, giving rise to Brilleaux's almost poetic retort (quickly becoming a Feelgood maxim) '"Sound checks are for poofs and Mink DeVille,"' as former roadie Neil Biscoe recalls. 'They sound checked at the beginning of the tour and that was it, anything more would be wasting time. So yes, sound checks were for poofs and Mink DeVille.'

Allan Jones, who travelled with the Feelgoods for much of this tour (and apparently ended up 'recovering from its excesses in hospital', which one can readily believe) reported on the group as they traversed the country, swearing, boozing and, indeed, fighting as they went, at least in Lee's case; all hopped up on booze, substances and attitude, he would bellow abuse out of the window as they drove through Edinburgh, remonstrating with bemused passing 'Jocks', making a few choice remarks about kilts and the like, and, at one point, jumping out of the van and starting a fight. This behaviour was related to drink, as Sparko observed at the time, that is, Lee needed one. Lee would remember nothing of this *contretemps* at all, incidentally, when he received his alarm call the next morning (Fred Munt hammering on the door, howling obscenities in a bid to help them start the day).

On the same trip, coked up after several 'beak lunches', the boys went down to the Edinburgh nightspot Tiffany's, where Lee became incensed by the sight of a fellow drinker's kipper tie,[37] yanking it as he snarled, 'A tie shouldn't be thicker than your finger. *That* is a bleedin' bedspread.' Shortly afterwards, during an in-store appearance to sign *Be Seeing You* in a record shop in Aberdeen, Jones remembers in his much loved *Stop Me …* column in *Uncut* that, before long, 'Lee gets into an argument with someone who tells him music should be free. "No fuckin' go, mate. Rock'n'roll is a business. We need money to live." As he wandered off Lee was heard to mutter, 'Overgrown fucking gerbil. If I had a hammer handy I'd have caved his head in. Anyone fancy a drink?' The angry young man hadn't quite disappeared, and the startling transformation from a shy and retiring gent to a crazed individual with a purportedly casual attitude towards violence didn't exclusively happen onstage, depending on the chemicals and circumstances involved at the time.

They were forcing themselves to go further on this tour, aware they had more to prove, and the shows were duly 'psychotic', Allan Jones noticing with alarm how haggard the singer looked post-performance: 'Brilleaux told me that some nights he feels uncomfortably close to death, so ferocious is the intensity [of the show],' he wrote. 'Tonight looks like one of those nights.'

It would take some control to cope with the next run of dates without committing multiple homicide. What was about to kick off would surely make Brilleaux long for the kipper ties of Edinburgh and the 'fucking gerbil' of Aberdeen. It was time to board the plane and make for the States, where they would be supporting the prog rock band Gentle Giant on their Missing Piece tour – a mystifyingly bad idea, it has to be said. Punk and prog were pitted against each other in the music press – you either liked one or the other – and Dr Feelgood were almost doomed to fail no matter how well they performed. It wasn't out of the question that whoever booked the tour knew the band's contract with CBS was soon to be terminated, and just no longer cared enough to put the band with someone appropriate. The Feelgoods' touring experience this time around would also be somewhat different. There was less of a budget, and less confidence all round. Lee, as the band's leader, worked hard to remain pragmatic and keep up the band morale, but he had to admit that after having 'made it' in the UK, starting all over again and eschewing 'luxuries' like having one's own hotel room with a shower could be hard.

'Out there they're conditioned to having everything hyped up, and believe me, we were hyped up something wicked,' said Lee. 'No wonder a lotta kids were confused. We made a half-hearted attempt to go along with it – whatever *it* was, but we quickly realised it was destructive. Images can be useful to a point, but they can be dangerous if you're stupid enough to start believing in them.'

Gentle Giant were 'gentlemen' to the Feelgoods – Lee was always keen to point this out – but their audience were, in the main, decidedly unpleasant, and made their disapproval of the choice of support very clear. 'We had a rough time of it. I was getting worried,' said Lee. 'People were throwing things and they'd hit you in the eye, it was frightening.' Without fail, the crowd would yell for the headliners to come on within minutes of the Feelgoods starting their set. On one occasion, Lee cracked and was heard to yell, 'OK, you'll get your bloody Gentle Giant!' before storming off stage mid-song. Various members of Gentle Giant would take Lee aside on more than one occasion to ask why Dr Feelgood continued to put themselves through it.

'You come off stage very angry,' said Lee. 'You feel like killing all of them. You hate them, and then you calm down and see the funny side. It was ridiculous – drive five hundred miles to have people slag us off.' It was an isolating situation, no doubt felt all the more keenly because, back home, Stiff Records' Live Stiffs Tour had commenced, featuring the Feelgoods' mates and contemporaries (Nick Lowe, Larry Wallis, Ian Dury and the Blockheads, Elvis Costello and Wreckless Eric) basically having a party onstage every night.

Lee, rightly determined to extract something positive from the situation, was also convinced that the hellish slog of being abused by thousands every night had pulled them up. The UK tours had been going so well, Lee confessed they might have become a touch complacent. 'It's all very easy if you become successful in one country. You start walking around with your head in the clouds. You've got to go somewhere you don't mean nothing. It can be a jolt to the ego. If you can get over that, it's a good way of making a band work hard, do what it had to do in the first place – winning over audiences.'

They also had the opportunity to return to New York and play the punk club CBGB; here they would be treated as heroes rather than howled at by outraged prog lovers, and photographer Ebet Roberts' images from the end of the show display an unusually boyish-looking Lee gazing calmly down the lens with a hint of a smile.

All the same, by the end of 1977, a supremely stressful year for the Feelgoods all told, the band would return to England emotionally bruised, exhausted and minus a US record deal. Drowning his sorrows in the company of Larry Wallis, Lee let slip the positive, dignified front he reserved for press interviews, concluding flatly: 'The septic tanks?[38] They don't like us and we don't like them.'

The chaps might have needed a little time licking their wounds – not long, mind – but 1978 would see a reversal of fortunes for the new line-up. Before long, Lee would even have no small reason to gloat in the face of the doubters and cynics convinced it was a matter of time until they folded without Wilko.

The mission for this new year was to head back to the continent as quickly as possible, where they were loved and missed. A series of events awaited, including Belgium's Rock & Blues Festival in Werchter alongside Nick Lowe, Dave Edmunds and Rockpile. This show would largely be memorable for Lee because the Feelgoods and Rockpile had been travelling together in the same van, and 'gentleman as ever,' Lee remembered, 'I closed the [van] door and slammed Dave Edmunds' fingers in it. I thought, oh my God, one of the finest guitar players in the western hemisphere, and I've just chopped his fingers off.' Lee looked over at Nick who simply stared, horror-struck, which probably didn't help. Fortunately this would not mark the end of a prestigious career and Edmunds would, somehow, play on.

As usual, the live shows would give the Feelgoods a chance not just to promote their most recent output, but to polish up new material. They wanted to make a killer new album that would chainsaw its way through any negativity and put them, if not back on top (they were realistic – they knew they'd gone from being 'extremely hip, the bee's knees', as Lee put it, to being leapfrogged by the punks and new wavers) then at least in a stronger position than before. They were determined to build on their post-Wilko catalogue and prove they could still make the operation work on their own terms.

Plans for Dr Feelgood's next album were underway, and if *Be Seeing You* was reflective of the band's insularity, warm-blooded pubbiness and sandpapery charm, its follow-up would be a harder, shinier affair. The fact that it would be called *Private Practice* gave it a loftier aspect (or saucier, depending on which way you looked at it), and lined up for the job of producer was Martin Rushent, who had a longstanding relationship with United Artists and had previously worked with Jerry Lee Lewis, The Stranglers – great admirers of the Feelgoods – and Buzzcocks among others. It made sense to pair the 'godfathers of punk' with such a producer, but sadly it wasn't to be. Shortly after sessions began at Eden Studios in Chiswick, West London, Rushent was taken ill with hepatitis, only working with the group on the Brilleaux–Mayo co-write 'Every Kind Of Vice'.

Andrew Lauder suggested the producer Richard Gottehrer, who had previously worked with Richard Hell and Blondie, as a replacement for Rushent. After 'checking the guy out', Lee was satisfied. Gottehrer was in and work could continue.

The Feelgoods, as we know, were always prepared. When on the road, for example, when fuel strikes threatened to strand many a touring outfit, Dr Feelgood kept jerry cans of petrol in the van. And when it came to that other kind of fuel, namely beer, there was no way they were going to rely on whatever happened to be on hand. Rather, kegs of locally brewed and extremely potent Canvey ale were transported with them to West London for the *Private Practice* sessions. McVitie's chocolate biscuits provided the solids until the band could break from the studio to get a curry late at night. 'Their stomachs [were upset] most of the time,' remembered Richard Gottehrer, as well he might.

In addition to his status as producer to the great, the good and the ineffably cool of New York's new wave *cognoscenti*, Gottehrer was also a member of 1960s band The Strangeloves, a garage rock trio – but not just any garage rock trio. The Strangeloves were a band of New York songwriters and producers who pretended to be three sheep-farming brothers from Australia, who went by the names of Niles, Miles and Giles Strange – just the sort of thing that would appeal to Lee's sense of humour. When ideas for covers were being knocked about, Gottehrer suggested The Strangeloves' 'Night Time' and showed them 'his way' on the piano. 'We tried but it wasn't working,' said Lee. 'So he said, "OK, you do it your way."' The Feelgoods kicked off by jamming the groove, Lee singing along all the while, and then, as Lee put it, 'I just jumped out of the way and said, "Keep going."'

Other songs on the record would include 'Take A Tip' (which pays tribute to various Feelgood chums including then Clash tour manager Johnny Green), written by Gypie and Lee, and 'Sugar Shaker', a wry song that tells the tale of 'losing your faith in human nature' while propping up a bar. (Doesn't sound like much of a jolly-up to me.) The band suggested including their current encore number, the Eddie Floyd song 'Things Get Better' – a rare low-key moment of warm-hearted,

Jezebel-free romance in the Feelgoods' repertoire (make the most of it) – and the whole album would open on a hard-boiled shuffle straight from the pen of Mickey Jupp, 'Down At The Doctors'. It was crammed full of sex, drugs (about a 'Dr Feelgood' character dishing out 'shots of R&B' at all hours as if they were flu jabs), fat guitar hooks and underlined by a heavy groove. It was, as many Feelgood fans well know, also to feature eight bars of piano. Lee explains: 'Richard, God bless him, he's not the world's greatest piano player, right? He said, "I'm going to put some piano on it, man!" OK … so I shouted out, "Eight bars of piano" to give some atmosphere and he was going to dub on some piano afterwards. He did dub it on. We mixed it out!'

What is especially amusing is that Lee's call for 'eight bars of piano' would be deliberately left on the track, and indeed Lee would say the words live onstage and during television performances, always preceding eight bars during which the band, totally straight-faced, would vamp purposefully and accompany the imaginary keyboard solo. 'Lewis Carroll would approve,' noted Charles Shaar Murray, adding that 'eight bars of piano' became something of a catchphrase after the single's release in September 1978, with his *NME* co-worker Danny Baker becoming 'positively besotted with it. "A definite case of eight bars of piano," he would say, when anything which had been promised failed to materialise.'

During sessions, the Feelgoods had developed a strong rhythm track based on a riff Gypie Mayo had come up with – the kind of hard-hitting riff one could happily do 'The Ace' to and not feel remotely ashamed – but, as Lee recalled, 'we were having our usual trouble writing lyrics, so we called in the man who can write words for every occasion, off the peg or made to measure'. The Feelgoods played Nick Lowe the backing track, gave him a whisky and sent him away. Twenty minutes later, Lowe returned with the finished song.

'People say, "that Nick Lowe writes songs on the back of a fag packet",' said Lowe. 'But I think on this occasion I actually did. They cut the song that night and off it went.' The song would be 'Milk And Alcohol', inspired by that illusion-shattering night in LA that Lowe had spent with the Feelgoods, watching an ageing John Lee Hooker trudge through a lacklustre show ('main attraction nearly dead on his feet') – a hero long past his prime. The song, sparse and penetrating, basically tells the story of that evening right down to the Feelgoods' arrest after going through a red light. It was perfect.

Richard Gottehrer observed how Lee simply read through the words a couple of times, stood up and prepared to record his low-key growl of a vocal take. 'I said, "How about a couple of run-throughs first?" but Lee said, "No, no, I've got it." There he was standing with a pint of beer and his biscuits in his other hand and holding the lyric out in front of him and he just sang it. That was it; he just sang it. I asked him, "How did you do it?" He just told me, "I know the story."'

The track would take the Feelgoods veering into lower-gear, head-banging mainstream rock territory, but, Lee insisted, 'I've got no regrets. I've never regarded Dr Feelgood as a purist rhythm and blues band, we are a rock'n'roll band that plays blues.' 'Some of [the record's] a bit more laid back than what we've done in the past,' Lee would explain to Allan Jones. But it's not like JJ Cale on mandies[39] or anything.'

During these West London sessions, the band would cut two tracks under the name of the Oil City Sheiks with Lew Lewis and Jools Holland, who, with Squeeze, had supported the Feelgoods in previous years and was always touched by how kind the band were to them. When he received the call to join the band and lay down some keyboards, he needed no persuasion.

'They were all really nice to us – they didn't need to be,' remembers Jools. 'They were all what you would call proper gentlemen. I remember once being on the side of the stage, about to go on. Lee was going to watch us, and he said, "Good luck." He had a Mac on, he looked like a private detective from some 1960s crime novel. I said, "You're nice and wrapped up there." He said, "Well, don't think I'm an old mum, but you can't have enough layers on, can ya, mate?" As I went on stage to this pogoing crowd, I thought, I doubt they'd realise that's the conversation myself and Lee have just been having. Lee always made me laugh. He had huge volumes of charm. It was that understatement, and mixing the mundane with the extraordinary.'

The A-side of the single they would record together would be 'Don't Take But A Few Minutes', written by the assembled 'Sheiks'. 'It was all verging on the edge of chaotic,' remembers Jools, 'but they just pulled it together. The Big Figure had this Dodge Challenger car. I'd never been in anything so amazing, and he gave me a lift home in it. I remember being propelled through the narrow roads of Bermondsey in this car at a speed you just couldn't believe. And to be honest, we all got right off our nut in the studio, which I never really did before, and then I got a lift home. It was just great.'

Back to the main task in hand, the front of *Private Practice* would feature a close-up of a deranged-looking 'doctor' looming over some poor victim – us – with a medical gas mask ('We found him in an actors' catalogue,' said Lee. 'He looked crazy enough.') The artwork on the rear shows our shifty heroes, suited up and looking grubby and murderous, heading towards their 'surgery' on Harley Street, a pretty nurse waiting anxiously on the steps (a similar scene is displayed on the front of the 'Down At The Doctors' single). On the street is one of 'Steve's Cabs', Lee's preferred taxi company, all the way from Canvey Island (one would hope they waived the fare), and a much used service indeed, as Lee would often require assistance transporting himself home from the Jellicoe after taking a few too many sips of the healing waters.[40]Come October 1978, and the album would be launched in time-honoured Feelgood fashion, a liver-blasting bacchanal at the Admiral Jellicoe. But this would be a party with a difference. This would be a party with strippers, and their presence would engender a mixture of, from a safe distance, laddish cheer, and from a less safe distance, embarrassed consternation. Jones recalls everyone suddenly moving back when the women bounded in, as if fearing a demand for audience participation. The mood relaxed when Lee and Lew politely invited them to play a game of pool.

Chris Fenwick proudly announced that the following week 'we got album of the week in three papers, which just goes to show', although it would be unfair to assume this hallowed position was merely clinched, so to speak, by the presence of breasts jiggling about in cupless bras as the record played. The 'solid rock', even metal-inclined sound of *Private Practice*, seemed to rejuvenate the Feelgoods and, as *NME*'s Phil McNeill, unimpressed by *Be Seeing You*, wrote, 'Brilleaux's performance is simply superb … evidently they've been practising in private. And they're still the best-looking band in the land.'

The Big Figure

While on tour in Yugoslavia – 'Milk And Alcohol' was in the Top 10 there – we were dining in a government-sponsored restaurant. The staff were all trainees. We were playing just down the road, a ten-minute walk.

The orders got completely confused – probably our wine starter wasn't helping – anyway it took hours, but food comes first. By the time we'd finished, our government-installed guide said we were late … so, full of whatever it was, we arrived at the gig in a bit of a sweat, only to be confronted by a gun-waving doorman refusing entry to us. After a second's thought, Lee confronted him, waved his gun away, told him not to be so ridiculous and gained entry, with us as the battering ram.

You see, it's not all chocolate and roses.

Above: Lee Brilleaux sporting a grinning Dr Feelgood tie-pin. When it came to his various outfits and accessories there was often, as Lee's old schoolfriend Phil Ashcroft observed, 'a sense of irony'. Top right: Lee looking understandably exhausted just after coming off stage during the Be Seeing You tour in Scotland. Melody Maker writer Allan Jones, who accompanied the band on the tour (much to the chagrin of his liver), recalls Lee telling him that some nights after a show he felt 'uncomfortably close to death. This looked like one of those nights.'

Six days on the road

Christoffer Frances

*Lee in full ejaculating-beer-bottle mode –
à la his hero Howlin' Wolf – at CBGB's,
New York, 1977. Note the righteous
heels … He was already over six feet tall
in socks. (Support act The Ramones were
understandably 'nervous' in his presence.)*

14. THE CALL OF THE WILD (PARTY)

The idea of machinery making music is interesting and obviously it has a place in the society we live in. But I also think we need raw basic rock'n'roll in our lives, with human feeling. If you hear BB King just play guitar and sing, there is energy and emotion there. You could get a machine to make the same notes but it wouldn't sound anywhere near ... not to me anyway. That music stirs my soul.

Lee Brilleaux, Radio Stockholm

The Feelgoods promoted *Private Practice* with a typically relentless European tour, fitting in a session for John Peel and a *BBC in Concert* recording along the way. Lee in his denim and Aviators, shoulders back, head forward, still mean, still drunk, still sexually intimidating the drum riser, charged forth with his band of (really rather nice) villains – pushing, pushing, pushing the record, pushing the sound, pushing the band further and further, his frenzied fist shaking practically generating power and speed in its own right. 'Let's have another fast one, eh?' But Lee's manic desire to propel them forward, faster and faster, could cause the music to suffer, as Figure had warned, and the band were becoming exhausted.

A few casual appearances in an intimate club in Spain before Christmas finally convinced Brilleaux to cool it. The London shows at Hammersmith Odeon, which had taken place on 28 and 29 October, 'weren't very good. Well, it's the old adrenaline. It's what Figure keeps going on about, and he's perfectly right. The temptation is to play loud and fast all the time. We played in a club in Ibiza, jammed and laid back a lot. We learned a lesson from that. We've not slowed down but we're letting things swing a little more.' Still no risk of coming over all 'JJ Cale on mandies' then.

Any concern onlookers may have had that the Feelgoods were taking a chance to kick back would soon be smashed into the water, however. In the New Year of 1979, the tough but radio-friendly 'Milk And Alcohol' went straight into the charts, peaking at number 9. Cue appearances on *Top of the Pops*, myriad interviews and that aforementioned gloating. 'For those critics who said, "Oh, they'll never be the same without Wilko," it was nice to be able to say, "Well, at least we got a top ten single with Gypie."'

Lee insisted he 'wished Wilko the best' when pressed by journalists hoping to stir up gossip, but at this stage at least the scar tissue was still tender and a streak of competition still burned. 'They were doing really well but there was always this sore point,' Shirley admits. 'Whenever they saw Wilko succeeding or releasing something.' Wilko's debut album with his band the Solid Senders had come out around the same time as the chart-bothering (number 48) 'Down At The Doctors' a few months earlier – a coincidence, but the timing was certainly noticed by the music papers.

'Down At The Doctors', incidentally, would have its own music video; in it we see the band playing in a dimly lit studio, and it's probably one of the few music videos of this era to show a group, all five o'clock shadow and sleep-deprived squints, sweating, chain-smoking and, in Gypie's case, wiping his nose on his hand as Lee, truculently lashing his mic lead about like a bored psychopath, oversees the scene while managing to look simultaneously fervid and as if the whole thing is a bit of an inconvenience. It's magnificent. Go and have a look at it on YouTube right away if possible, then come back and we'll continue.

Lee Brilleaux
The Feelgoods were an accident – like getting a parking ticket, throwing it away, having the computer foul up and never getting fined. If you've got that kind of luck going for you, it's best to stick with it.

Dr Feelgood were something of an aberration; they were not 'pop' but key members of the pop press were still hooked, still watching their every move, still intensely interested in what they were about to do next – and the band had a Top 10 hit in the 'pop' chart without compromising their style during a time of seismic change. They'd never been in fashion, as Lee always said, so they'd never be out of fashion. That said, Lee Brilleaux would express revulsion at the fact that rock'n'roll was now being taken over by electronica. At least the punks were using guitars. As popular music became more processed,

Lee Brilleaux wrinkled his nose, slammed the door and poured himself another drink.

Synthesisers were not for Lee. Organs, pianos – he could work with those, but these apparently cold, soulless machines were anathema to him, representing something rather different from the R&B-loving, snuff-taking, detective-novel-reading world that Lee had worked so hard to create. In conversation with *NME*'s Charles Shaar Murray, Lee summed up the sound of German synth pioneers Kraftwerk: 'I thought it was a load of ice cream vans gone wrong.' Murray was exasperated. 'Oh, come *on*, Lee.'

New wave – which would encompass synth pop, pop punk and, within a few years, new romanticism (don't get Lee started on Duran Duran) – was everything the Feelgoods weren't. Its advent represented the nudging aside of the sweaty sexuality of the 1970s and the welcoming in of something cleaner, still fun, but clinical and stiff with hairspray. What was coming would be wilfully artificial, brightly coloured, often androgynous, sometimes childlike. Dr Feelgood, on the other hand, exuded testosterone and experience, made good-time music and came from a good-time place – Canvey Island, Southend, places where 'women were women and men were men', places where people would go to let off steam, to gamble, dance, eat bad food, drink too much, get in a fight, have a dirty weekend.

The record sleeve for 'Milk And Alcohol' was inspired by the classic Kahlua bottle design, the single was pressed up in both milk-white vinyl and coffee-liqueur brown – 'surely there can't be anybody stupid enough to buy both, can there?' Lee scoffed to *Smash Hits* (UA's marketing executives no doubt with their heads in their hands) – and sponsorship for the launch would come from 'not Nike, not Marshall amps, but from Kahlua,' said Jools Holland. 'You could have as much Kahlua as you liked. Lee said, "Bring anyone you want." He was very well-mannered and inclusive; that's a proper gentleman. He had almost royal manners.'

Generosity and *noblesse oblige* aside, there might not have been much in the way of royal manners immediately in evidence at the launch party at Nick's Havajah restaurant in Soho, especially with good old 'Borneo' Fred Munt still on the scene. Ribaldry was assured – it was a Feelgood party after all – and as the 'dirty boilers' (milk and Kahlua cocktails, lovingly named by Stiff's Dave Robinson) were poured down every throat present, Munt would bellow out a volley of eye-watering anecdotes before joining Lee (sporting sunglasses and a badge emblazoned with the words 'I'm Best') at the piano. There, Jools Holland, his head bowing lower and lower with inebriation, was working his boogie-woogie voodoo with Gypie by his side. A vigorous if not melodious singalong rounded off the evening.

The bash might have been 'just an excuse for a piss-up', in Lee's words, but it would be this very evening on which they would not only toast the success of their single, but also unveil Lew Lewis's new release on Stiff, his own version of 'Lucky Seven', as well as the Oil City Sheiks single, the cover a blithely amateur-looking affair of the Feelgoods and Jools Holland 'in disguise' – all strategically arranged head-gear and shades – beaming and mugging for the camera, an array of empty wine glasses in front of them. They were just having a good time and doing what they damn well liked, which is what they had always done. You probably wouldn't find a label like UA putting a single like that out today. (In fact you wouldn't find a label like UA today either.)

'That was a great thing about Lee, that couldn't-care-less-ness about him,' said Jools. 'Couldn't care less whether you liked it or not, this is what we're doing, which is a very important factor for music. Unlike the [TV] talent shows today, not to knock them, but [it's] all people who are desperate to be liked. Lee was above all that, that wasn't his point.'

Lee and Chris had an almost obsessive drive to keep the Feelgood machine producing, producing, producing – they had both the record label's and their fans' expectations to keep up with – and so far the band had released at least one album, sometimes two, a year. Then there were the live shows, the television appearances, the BBC sessions … Naturally, there had been little time to work on anything new, even though they still technically had a 'new' album out in *Private Practice*.

They wanted to release something before the summer, and decided to 'play the live card', as Lee put it. It was about time their fans had another live album after all, and it would be their first to feature Gypie. The record would be titled *As It Happens*, a *double entendre* but also, of course, a favourite phrase of Lee's. It would feature, on one side, a live recording taken from a show the band played at Hemel Hempstead's Pavilion the previous October, and on the other, a set recorded at Rayleigh's legendary Crocs (a key South Essex venue, later known as the Pink Toothbrush, which did originally house a pair of crocodiles in a tank). In a blazing red sleeve covered with black-and-white images of the individual band members in full flight, Gypie takes the main spot on the front top left, Lee beneath him, one hand over his face, wiping the sweat from his brow.

Numbers on the fast-paced romp that is *As It Happens* include 'Take A Tip', 'She's A Wind-Up', 'Milk And Alcohol' and 'Ninety Nine And A Half (Won't Do), and at one point we hear Brilleaux chastising the increasingly rowdy audience. 'Please don't push,' comes the voice from the front of the stage. 'We want to make a live album, we want it to be a good groove ... so don't fucking PUSH.' *As It Happens* would tide fans over until, well, September when the band would release yet another album.

Whether there was some neurosis about not letting people's attention drop, whether they were concerned not to appear to be slowing down, it's hard to say, but while three fifths of the Feelgood operation were starting to hanker for a bit of time off, Lee and Chris were doggedly steaming ahead. To be fair, they didn't yet have families to miss – Sparko remembers Joan Collinson giving him a baby's comforter she'd initially made for Lee for when he had children. 'It was a beautiful little [blanket] that goes on a cot,' said Sparko. 'Really intricate, it must have taken her months. She said, "I might as well give it to you for your baby, Lee's never going to have one."'

'It was kind of crazy but Lee just loved working,' adds Figure. 'Well, we all loved being on the road, but I love my family as well; they're growing up, all the usual stuff, and when you're on the other side of the world you miss that intensely. To try and get a break in the band with Lee's work ethic, which was just to go on and on and on, was desperately hard.'

Another person feeling the effects of the Feelgoods' extreme workload was, naturally, Shirley. It was very clear that, when the road called, which was most of the time, Lee would be off – and so it was around this time that Shirley decided to take off herself in turn and go back to America for a while. The lyrics to Lee's favourite song 'Roadrunner' were all too appropriate, and being with Lee was never going to be easy: when he was home, the situation could be volatile, when he was away ... well, he was away. 'We broke up a couple of times,' said Shirley. No doubt Lee's way of dealing with this was to work even harder.

Meanwhile, rumour had it that the Feelgoods' intention to release *As It Happens* was down to the fact that they had one last record to put out with United Artists before their contract was up, 'and we had some live tapes so we just decided to smash 'em out,' said Lee. 'Well, we knew all along they was wrong but we weren't in a position to say so, because matters were still being negotiated. We put it out because we wanted a live album, it's as simple as that. There was no politics behind it.'

Above: promotional information for the Nick Lowe-produced A Case Of The Shakes, a record powered by copious amounts of white wine (Lee had been told to lay off the gin for a while by his GP). Shades of Utterly Club style can be seen here in Barney Bubbles' design (note the monocles). Top right: Sparko and Lee onstage. Bottom right: Lee and harp. Courtesy of Christoffer Frances.

The Feelgoods would negotiate a new contract with UA, who would then be absorbed into EMI. By 1980, the UA name would have been dropped altogether, with Liberty Records being used for all artists taken on during the UA years. The Feelgoods' first release on the new contract would be *Let It Roll*,[41] which they immediately started work on before the live dates started in earnest that September. Sessions would take place at DJM Studios in Holborn, central London.

With Brilleaux's favourite producer Nick Lowe unavailable to work with the band on this occasion, Dr Feelgood agent Nigel Kerr suggested the esteemed Mike Vernon (Fleetwood Mac, John Mayall, Chicken Shack). 'Great name in blues production,' said Lee. 'He inspired our respect. We had a lot of fun working with him.'

As the group jammed in the studio, there 'was an element of the ninety-ninth hour', Lee joked, but the Feelgoods would pull together six strong originals, including 'Put Him Out Of Your Mind' – a Mayo–Vernon co-write, group compositions 'Shotgun Blues' and 'Hong Kong Money' and Mayo's laid-back 'Keeka Smeeka', an instrumental, much to Lee's delight (more time at the pub), while the choice of covers was unusual and inspired (such as opening track 'Java Blue' aka 'Java Blues' by The Band's Rick Danko).

Where Richard Gottehrer had drawn more out of the group in terms of performance, Vernon was 'more interested in sound and tone,' Brilleaux told journalist Ian Ravendale. 'He was interested in feeling. He'd go, "Gypie's solos are better after ten o'clock at night, so we'll adjourn for an hour." He'd break things up. I like the way he works."

Let It Roll is something of a departure. It's a step into glossier territory, boasting more of a soul pop sound, but it's also a chance to hear other dimensions in Brilleaux's voice. Here we have everything from snippets of *Sprechgesang* to all-out soulful elasticity, no doubt encouraged by this new influence in the studio. It's also a treat to hear some gruff Feelgood humour in the spoken word moments within the irreverent Brilleaux–Mayo song 'Bend Your Ear'.[42] Lee evidently had a good time making the record, and he would look back on it as a favourite Feelgood release. One thing was for sure: they 'didn't want to keep making the same album,' Lee told journalist Ian Ravendale. 'That would be a waste of time and a waste of tape.'

The artwork for *Let It Roll* would feature the now famous Dr Feelgood Toby jugs, each portraying a member of the band. 'Lee was the one who used to collect Toby jugs, he loved antiques,' said Sparko. 'But it wasn't his idea to use them for the album. We left it to the label a lot of the time, although a lot of those things would have come from Lee's ideas.' The reverse of the record would show the group lurking in the Cluedo Club in Feelgood House.

Three and a half months' worth of touring lay ahead, and, as roadie Neil Biscoe observed, the band became jaded as the weeks wore on. 'That tour was hard, a massive stint. You could tell it was draining. When you do the clear-out after a gig, early in the tour there's nothing left from the rider. Couple of weeks into it, there's *loads* of booze left. They just wanted to get out of there. It was exhausting and you completely lose touch.'

It didn't help when the few opportunities they had to sleep while on the road were decimated thanks to having to do promotion, much of this being on Lee's shoulders. There would be an abortive 'punk summit' interview arranged by *Melody Maker*, which was intended to feature Brilleaux, The Stranglers' Hugh Cornwell and Buzzcocks' Pete Shelley all questioning each other. On the first occasion, Brilleaux had been partying too hard the night before and didn't turn up, much to Cornwell's chagrin. On the second occasion, Lee was the only one to appear. During the one time the magazine successfully got them together, the trio were photographed looking awkward alongside a 'tame' bear. ('Sure he's tame, as long as he's got a pound of prawns to eat,' grumbled Brilleaux.) It was an exercise the magazine conceded they would not be trying again.

When the band were expected to turn up to an in-store signing to push the new record in Berlin, in an incident redolent of a scene in *Spinal Tap*, they would find that little promotion had been done, and hardly anyone had turned up. On entering the record shop – a place referred to by accompanying *NME* writer Paul Du Noyer as reminiscent of the '*Clockwork Orange* Korova Milk Bar' filled with 'slumped, zomboid youths' – the band are good-humoured. 'Let's all hold hands and see if we can contact the living,' Lee is heard to say. A few of the faithful have turned up, however, and, albums in hand, nervously approach the group. 'Sometimes I think they're frightened of us,' Lee tells Du Noyer. 'They think we're like we look onstage. We'd never try to be like that … there's enough fucking aggravation in the world without us adding to it.' Sharpeners are imbibed before the weary but always witty collective conduct a group interview with Du Noyer, during which Gypie Mayo apparently collapses, out cold, onto a bed while mid-sentence.

The players were in need of some R&R, but this isn't to say that the shows were suffering – far from it. It was on this tour that the Feelgoods played a major festival package in Berlin alongside more mellow rock'n'roll fare such as Barclay James Harvest, Dire Straits and Lee's pals Whitesnake. (Yes, you read correctly. Two years earlier Brilleaux had been brought in to play some harmonica on Whitesnake track 'Keep On Giving Me Love' during the making of *Northwinds*, thanks to Tim Hinkley who was playing on the album). The Berlin audience had had 'six hours of melodious rock', and were drifting happily into the arms of Morpheus as the soporific chords floated over the site. The Feelgoods, meanwhile, were backstage: 'idle, for six hours, with lots of alcohol,' said Biscoe. 'They were steaming by the time they got on stage. They came on and just kicked ass, *so* hard. Mark Knopfler had half his band begging to get onstage with them, because anyone could jam with the Feelgoods. It wasn't technical stuff, everybody just wanted to go on with them, because they were so, so good. Everyone thought it was going to be a disaster, but they rocked the place and woke everybody up. It was the number one show I have ever worked.'

Dr Feelgood could not survive the rigours of the road on drink alone though; there had to be other forms of recreation in order to stave off insanity, and Lee's love of a good practical joke was as healthy as ever. When the band returned to Spain, they reconvened with Spanish tour manager and all-round character Jerome Martinez, who was also fond of a bit of japery. Once he and Lee got together, all manner of silliness would occur, one stand-out incident being at the expense of Dean Kennedy who was, he admits himself, 'young and naive. Very gullible. Lee sent me on false errands quite a lot. For example, I told him I liked artichokes and he told me they came out of a sheep's arse. I believed him and stopped eating them.'

'After the concert in Seville,' said Jerome, 'I accompanied the group to the Parador Hotel of Carmona, an old restored castle. We got together in my room to have a few drinks, but in the silence of the night we heard a strange noise, like someone breathing loudly. Lee said, "What's that?" I winked at Lee and said the castles in Spain were inhabited by lost spirits and ghosts. Lee said, "Ah yes," and we looked at Dean. He got nervous and, believing this, he didn't want to go to his room. Lee [wanted to continue] the joke and said, "What shall we do?" I put a white sheet on and knocked on Dean's door. What a shock he had. He was livid. Lee was in the corridor laughing his head off. In the morning we asked what the noise had been – it was just the watering system in the gardens.'

There's no doubt that Lee will have approved of staying overnight in a strange old castle rather than a characterless hotel. Lee, as he was as a teenager, was still fascinated by ancient buildings and architecture, sites of interest and natural beauty. This was one of the reasons he loved being on the road. 'When we went to Spain,' said Sparko, 'Lee wouldn't be satisfied with just hanging out. Lee would be like, "Right, Monday I think we should visit the caves." There'd always be something. "Let's drive to Granada tomorrow." He wasn't a person who could relax. I don't have that problem. His main thing was being on the road … you're always going somewhere, which he liked.'

Another way of allaying any touring tedium was, of course, dressing up – something Lee had always been partial to. It was only a matter of time before Lee tried to revive the spirit of the Utterly Club within the Feelgoods, including the introduction of snuffboxes from specialist shops in Charing Cross Road, watch chains and waistcoats, even a short-lived attempt to introduce silver-topped canes. It was, as Gypie remembered, like a 'mobile Regency gentlemen's club'. But even if Lee's dandified leanings weren't adopted by the collective long term, one thing was certain: service station food would never darken the Feelgoods' gullets again if Brilleaux had anything to do with it. Yes, this would, by all accounts, be the tour during which Lee took his first real steps towards becoming a bona fide gourmand.

As we know, the *Good Beer Guide* was never far from his grasp on tour, and, when he was home, Lee and Shirley would try out Delia Smith recipes,[43] but the Michelin and Egon Ronay guides had since been added to this library of gourmet guidance, as would the much loved *Just off the Motorway*, written by fellow *bon viveur* John Slater. The Feelgoods worked hard, and as a band they were largely frugal when it came to everyday expenses – 'no more four-star hotels for us,' Lee had announced (unless the promoter was paying). 'Like all industries in this country, we're economising.' But similarly, Lee quite rightly thought that when it came to fuelling up, they deserved something special to look forward to during those monotonous van journeys.

Country pubs and restaurants would feature strongly in Feelgood tours, and Lee would do his homework. If he noted that a promising eatery was vaguely on the way to where they were going, then he'd work a visit into their schedule, even if it meant everyone had to get up two hours earlier. It was almost always worth it. Curries, Guinness stews and fry-ups would remain Brilleaux favourites, but this was the beginning of his famous love affair with fine food and drink: we're talking about real ale, expensive wines, brandies and many, many gin and tonics.

Lee's enthusiasm was not always reciprocated by the proprietors of some of these establishments. As they had with the landlord of the Punch House near Rockfield Studios in Monmouth, the band would sometimes come up against prejudices based on their collective appearance, a problem the Feelgoods had endured since the early days. (If ever one needed a silver-topped cane …)

Lee had, on one occasion, booked somewhere especially smart on the way to a gig, reserving a table for the band. 'The woman who ran the restaurant saw us and thought, they're not the sort of people I want in my restaurant,' said Sparko. 'You know, Gypie with his leather jacket; someone else might have looked a bit scruffy. And she said, "No, we're fully booked." Lee said, "Well, we did phone and book, we've got a reservation." She wouldn't let us in.'

Lee wouldn't stand for this. Having bought a pint at the bar, he looked the restaurant owner in the eye and slowly poured his drink onto the carpet in front of her. 'Lee said, "If you want animals, we'll give you animals,"' remembers Sparko. 'Those were the sorts of injustices he railed against.

'Lunchtime was important. You can't eat just before a gig, especially if you're going to eat a lot, which we all probably did. We'd all drink a couple of bottles of wine each, brandies … We used to joke that it was more important than the gig.' The quality of the food and drink was vital, but what Lee also loved was the atmosphere, the sense of occasion, ritual and reward, the idea of being kind to yourself, the inviting glow of various hidden treasures that were off the beaten track. 'Lee would read from the Egon Ronay guide as if he was giving a reading,' adds Sparko. '"This sixteenth-century coaching inn, with a wealth of beams and …" It was like a recital of Shakespeare.'

It wasn't just the band who would enjoy a good meal. Lee was insistent on taking care of whoever was there on his watch – sandwiches and beer might be distributed to support bands by Lee and Chris in person, for example, and the crew would also be treated to proper grub, even at the risk of being late loading into the venue.

'In Sheffield, we stayed at this specific hotel,' remembers roadie Neil Biscoe. 'Lee had chosen it because they did the best Sunday lunch, and the gig was on a Sunday. The crew were not allowed to leave the hotel until we'd had lunch. I don't think we pulled up at the gig until about four p.m. But that was Lee. "You're not going to the show until you've had your Sunday roast, that's the reason we're here!" It was coming to the end of the 1970s, very much the Feelgoods' decade, and they were damn well going out well fed.

THE ROCK'N'ROLL GENTLEMAN'S GUIDE TO OPTIMUM ADVENTURING

- Don't be afraid to try the local cuisine when you're travelling. Be curious.

- The best cooking is the simplest. You can never go wrong with good home-cooked fare.

- Don't eat too close to the show. Having time to digest one's comestibles before physical activity will help you to avoid all manner of unpleasantness.

- If you are travelling, you'll need to be organised lest you end up subsisting on turgid service station coffee and Ginsters pasties. (Other pasties are available, but you probably shouldn't eat them either.) This is where your Michelin Guide comes in.

- The social aspect of eating out is important, but if you have a yen to try out a particularly swanky restaurant, it is more polite to slope off alone rather than to expect everyone in the touring party to shell out for a meal they might deem unnecessarily expensive.

- When at home, learn to cook some hearty meals. Brilleaux's favourite cookbooks included Elizabeth Luard's *European Peasant Cookery*, Delia Smith's *Complete Cookery Course* and *Feast Days* by Jennifer Patterson. (His copy contained a letter from Patterson – later known as the dark-haired chef of *Two Fat Ladies* renown. It was a reply to Lee's correspondence correcting her spelling of 'Maldon', in reference to the sea salt.) To the bookshop with you.

- Don't be too reverent with these kitchen tomes – they're going to get stained anyway (or they should, if you're using them often enough) so make like Brilleaux and write notes and thoughts in the margins, customise recipes to your own liking, draw pictures of the pie of your dreams … This inscription of Lee's, for example, was found in the back of *Delia Smith's Complete Cookery Course*: 'This book has served me very well. Mrs Smith has taken the mystery out of ordinary procedures and practice. When I have been sober and fastidious, her recipes have served me well indeed, my children fed conveniently, economically and myself smug, off to the pub, and considering my domestic duties well acquitted. Please God forgive me my pride.'

Chalkie Davies

Lee and his dog Bo survey the mainland (and the creeks where Lee and Chris used to play pirates) from Canvey's sea wall close to his home on Kellington Road.

15. LEAVING CANVEY ISLAND – AND THE LADY VANISHES

We have thought about adding piano to the line-up, but any musician joining us now would find it difficult to fit in with us.
What type of people are you?
We're crazy as hell.

Lee Brilleaux in conversation with Ian Ravendale

1980. Lee Brilleaux was still only twenty-eight but after a check-up at the doctor's, he'd been advised to cut down on his drinking, which probably didn't come as much of a shock. A brief and not always adhered-to ban on gin and tonics, beers and brandies was underway – white wine, however, was permitted. And so, as Will Birch recalls, 'they all embraced it and took it literally. There was white wine everywhere, they were all glugging away.'

As Nick Lowe had a window in his schedule in the early summer of 1980, the Feelgoods booked Eden Studios in Chiswick and engaged his services once more for their next album, the aptly named *A Case Of The Shakes*. On learning of Brilleaux's white wine diet, Lowe ordered in twelve cases of the stuff, which arrived just as the Feelgoods rolled up. There was, I'm told, the usual availability of amphetamines, cocaine and marijuana too – 'It's not true that alcohol was the only drug,' said Larry Wallis, 'but it was the most important.' The 'party method', that of inviting a crowd of songwriting pals and choice drinking companions to the studio, was employed once more.

'I went down one night,' remembers Will, 'and there was a narrow corridor through to the control room – it was filled with what seemed like dozens of cases of white wine. You had to squeeze past them. I went into the control room and they were all there knocking it back. Even Figure was there with a glass of white wine, pinky raised: "A superb vintage!" You remember that cheap wine Hirondelle? They referred to that one as "Horrendo-del". Someone would take a sip and go, "Hmmm! The year … one o'clock." But they cut a few songs on that.'

A Case Of The Shakes would feature live favourite 'No Mo Do Yakamo' featuring Lee singing in an unusually low register, requiring a restraint Brilleaux had little patience for onstage – the live vocals for this song would generally be roared out an octave higher instead. Then there was the Brilleaux–Mayo composition 'Drives Me Wild' and the punk-inflected 'Best In The World', a Nick Lowe song from the Rockpile slushpile. Larry Wallis, who would wait for the call from Brilleaux to let him know when it was 'Feelgood season', was also brought back into the fold. Larry would write 'Going Someplace Else', his favourite self-penned Feelgood song. Wallis would also work with the band on the fast-paced hard-luck story 'Punch Drunk', which would be chosen as the album's opening track.

One of the covers chosen for the record would prove a departure in terms of what was expected of the group, the swing-inflected R&B song 'Violent Love', written by Willie Dixon. It was a song Lee had always wanted to record, having owned and loved the Otis Rush recording for years.[44] The subsequent Feelgood version would be hailed as an offbeat classic with a light touch, and it would be one of the few tracks which would afford us a chance to hear Brilleaux's real voice, without the Howlin' Wolf affectations. It was also a rare opportunity to hear the Feelgoods 'unplugged'.

While in the studio, Lee was telling Nick how much he'd hoped the band could record a version of it. Lowe, unfamiliar with the song, asked Lee and Gypie to show him how it went. Gypie picked out the chords on his acoustic guitar while Lee commenced crooning. 'Bash went, "That's great, why don't you do it [like that]?" said Gypie. 'We had our doubts, but anyway, Sparko learned the changes in the control room and plugged his bass straight into the board. Figure used brushes instead of sticks, the engineer set up a mic for the acoustic, and we did it. First take.'

As soon as Liberty Records heard 'Violent Love', they were convinced the Feelgoods should release it as a single. The band weren't so sure – it was so different to what their fans were used to, and their priority was to please their audience rather than indulge their own whims. All the same, they relented, even making a tongue-in-cheek video[45] to accompany it – the band, every inch the sleazy lounge lizards, playing acoustically to a group of flirty elderly ladies with whom a shark-like Lee eventually disappears, not before flashing the camera an oily grin.

By September 1980, *A Case Of The Shakes* was out, boasting distinctive Barney Bubbles-designed artwork[46] in pink and blue, featuring the Feelgoods trapped 'inside' bottles of booze (the fortifying 'Horrendo-del', perhaps?). While the album wouldn't chart, it would become a popular post-Wilko release over time, and it still sounds fresh, every track flying straight out of the gate like a slightly mad racehorse.

The album would be promoted via the band's biggest tour yet (by now 'Dr Feelgood touring schedule' was an industry joke – a phrase that would simply double up for the word 'everywhere'), including a jaunt to Australia and Japan and culminating in a return to the US. But while they were praised as 'still effective' by the *Los Angeles Times*' Don Snowden, who attended their Christmas show at the Whisky a Go Go, it was also observed that they were like 'a slightly over-the-hill boxer' who had 'lost its knock-out punch'. The manic thrill of yore had been replaced, in Snowden's opinion, by 'workmanlike reliability'. Everyone – members of the band included – was starting to yearn for the Ghost of Feelgood Past, or maybe just the Ghost of Feelgood Pause, which, up to this point, didn't seem to exist.

'Travelling is very tiresome,' Lee would admit. 'You sit on an aeroplane for twenty-four hours and go to Australia, and then get off the plane on the other end and walk on a stage, you're jet-lagged out of your brains, you don't know where you are … There you are in Sydney, you left winter and there it's the height of summer. Then [someone comes up and says, 'Which one's the Doctor?'] and wonders why you turn around and snap his head off.

'Having said all of that, I'm very grateful that I've been successful enough to have the chance to travel like this. I've seen more things in ten years than many people would see in their lifetime.'

Lee was always careful to counter any complaint with a positive conclusion – he knew how lucky he was – but there was growing unrest in the camp. Family life was a pull in some cases, but also the standard of living was lower than before and the perks that make that almost unceasingly nomadic lifestyle bearable were not always present. There was, Lee had to admit, a 'drop in interest' in the Feelgoods thanks to 'a generation of kids who were more interested in electronic music and all that nonsense', he sniffed to *Blues Bag*.

'Our fortunes had also taken a dive partly through our own fault. We'd gone on *Top of the Pops*, told somebody to fuck off, that sort of thing – they don't like it on that programme, you don't get asked back! We'd been uncompromising about quite a few people, but that's fine, providing you're prepared to take the consequences.'

Support, as a result, was becoming thinner on the ground, the journeys were longer and harder, they weren't at their peak, and frankly, they were feeling it. 'To keep up with the drinking was [hard], let alone anything else,' said Figure.

Alcohol consumption had come to define the Feelgoods. It was 'like a joke', as Sparko puts it. This wasn't the angst-ridden alcoholism of a neurotic artist, rather the Feelgoods had the kind of attitude towards drink that seaside postcard artists have towards sex. Lee would sometimes dash into a bar and shout, 'Brandy! Quick! I'm a doctor!' and then down the shot himself once it appeared. One of the books Brilleaux had taken with him for the tour was the pulp novel *Beat the Devil* which featured a character who always replied, 'Busy drinking' when anyone disturbed him. This, naturally, delighted Lee and it quickly became a catchphrase. But the Feelgoods had been 'busy drinking' for years, and it was time to dry out for a bit. Expressing that, however, was not easy. 'No one could refuse a drink,' said Sparko. 'It was like, "Excuse me? You don't want a drink? Can you write that down?" No one was allowed to refuse.'

The band took a much needed six-week break after Christmas 1980 to recover from the tour, punishing even by Feelgood standards. The next year would be one of change on every level, a year of coming together and splitting apart. Lee, especially, would need all the strength he could muster – he'd find himself at the eye of a storm that would leave behind a fair amount of human wreckage. Barman, an extremely large G&T, if you please.

Lee Brilleaux
We undertook two world tours with Gypie, worked very hard and burned ourselves out.

Let's just take things onto a personal level for a moment: Lee had insisted that he never wanted private life to 'get in the way' of the work that was so important to him, but similarly the man was not made of stone. He was in love with Shirley, and after their last bust-up, he didn't want to risk losing her again. It was time to make a commitment. 'We got married on the twenty-fifth of July 1981,' said Shirley. 'Four days before Charles and Diana.' The pair were spliced not on Canvey but in the Alfords' family church in Hammond, Louisiana, 'to please my mother,' explains Shirley. 'It meant a lot to her.'

Chris Fenwick would be the best man, and he would also be the only guest to make it over from the UK. Lee was a little put out that Sparko ended up getting married on the same day, so they were both unable to attend each other's weddings, but post-ceremony, the party at the local Country Club rocked, the champagne flowed and 'for years afterwards I was hearing stories about what had happened to various people who'd attended our reception,' said Shirley. 'One friend of mine woke up in one of the golf carts and had to hitch a ride back to New Orleans, a number of people nearly got divorced after that day ... We really had a blast.'

The bubble burst when, two days later, Lee grabbed his bag, kissed his bride and rushed off to the airport with Chris. He had a show booked – and the Feelgoods never cancelled a show (so, if you happened to see Dr Feelgood in the late July of 1981, I hope you appreciated it – Brilleaux had to eschew any chance of a honeymoon for your entertainment). 'I was like, *really*? I was so annoyed,' said Shirley, who then elected to stay in Louisiana for nearly two months. 'What was the point of going back to England if he wasn't even there?'

The Feelgoods were touring Scandinavia during the summer of 1981, and one show in particular stands out in Big Figure's memory. It was a council-sponsored afternoon event in Sweden ('I can't remember which town'). Lee no doubt was missing Shirley, and his mood was not enhanced by the fact that 'in the council's wisdom, they had decided to enforce an alcohol and drug-free policy. Of course, we were struck with horror,' continues Figure, 'as not only were we deprived of a pre-gig drink, Lee was deprived of his gin and tonic. Any bottles on stage were forbidden.' Fortunately, and as one would expect, the Feelgood mobile contained a well-stocked rider and this, and Figure's ingenuity, saved the day. Figure had noticed some crockery in the kitchen next to the dressing room: 'teacups, teapot ... you can probably guess the rest.' Grabbing the gin and several bottles of tonic, he commenced mixing a teapotful of G&T, filled the sugar bowl with ice and on went the show.

'Lee spent the gig quite disgruntled that he had to have his favourite tipple poured from a teapot and supped from a teacup all presented nicely on a tray on stage,' said Figure. 'There was a complete lack of understanding on the promoter's face – the tea being poured was transparent and came with ice cubes, and by the end of the gig it had had an effect on Lee that was quite different from tea. I remember Lee holding the cup up and wishing good health to the audience, a blank look on their Scandinavian faces. We got away with it.'

This would be the first year the Feelgoods didn't release a new studio album. Like many classic blues artists, they had been turning out records at a prodigious rate, but 1981 would be different. The live *On The Job*, released in August, would be their last album to feature their 'winning lottery ticket' Gypie Mayo, while their second release that year, *Casebook*, would be a compilation and career retrospective, harking back to the Wilko days. (Wilko, meanwhile, had been absorbed into Ian Dury and the Blockheads.) Sadly, *Casebook* would also be the group's swansong release on Liberty.

'UA was a major label but with a small staff,' explained Lee. 'Apart from film scores, they only had a small rock'n'roll department – it was great, it was like being in a small independent company but under the umbrella of a big company, the best of both worlds. Then unfortunately the company was bought out, and I'm afraid poor Dr Feelgood were too small to be taken care of by a big company like EMI – they were looking after Cliff Richard and Sheena Easton ... a little band like Dr Feelgood soon got lost.' Considering the end of this relationship, not to mention the lowering *esprit de corps*, there was now an ominous sense that the winds of change might blow the Feelgoods apart completely.

On The Job, recorded the previous year at Manchester University, displayed Lee on formidable form, but it was far from one of their most vibrant, or essential, releases. 'It's hard to remember they were once the catalyst that sparked the imaginations of thousands of befuddled, guitar-totin' kids,' wrote journalist Steve Sutherland. 'On the Job' indeed ... Still boozers, still bandits, still the best but not quite so eager.'

Gypie, by all accounts, felt he was plateauing in the Feelgoods, but he had also been scorched by the road, flattened by the schedule and was in dire need of recuperation. The party line was that, in Lee's words, 'he got married and his wife didn't want him to go out on the road and, goodness me, all this business, you know the score?' 'Score' may well have been about right – as Pete Zear recalls, the guitarist had also been 'getting into the hard stuff', and his partner wanted him away from the temptations of the road. 'But I think Gypie was also fed up of going to colleges bashing out the same old stuff,' adds Zear. 'Gypie was a pure musician, a wonderful player. Lee wanted me to join after Gypie, which is something I couldn't do anyway, I wasn't good enough.'

Brilleaux would also tell the press Gypie had said he 'felt that playing R&B had run its course, as far as he was concerned'. But Sparko and, the following year, Figure would leave as well. Figure had actually been trying to leave for some time, but Lee would always cajole him into

staying. 'Every year, we'd go, "Oh come on, Fig, stay another year."
We'd coerce him and force him to stay,' admits Lee. When Figure
gave notice for the last time, agreeing to work out the year, Lee was
saddened but not surprised.

'It was getting to me, especially when we were out in the Far East,
Japan,' said Figure. 'I thought, no matter what the consequences, I've
got to spend more time at home. Lee and Chris weren't prepared to cut
back on the schedule to allow for that, because they were so much in
love with what they were doing – and I respect that. At the time, Lee
was only twenty-nine, how could he understand?'

Lee was more shocked when Sparko announced he was quitting.
'He was always the sort of bloke who was most likely to be outrageous
at any moment, didn't give a damn about anything,' said Lee. 'All of a
sudden he met a girl, fell in love, married her and she just went, "No
more going on the road."'

Lee would be more sympathetic in later years, describing his
bandmates' respective decisions as 'inevitable. It's a very hard slog
doing 220 gigs a year; if they're married or have children they're going
to be separated from their families. It gets to you after a while.' But
it seems at times that Brilleaux rather begrudged the influence of his
bandmates' partners. 'To see [Sparko] tamed was an awesome sight,'
said Lee. 'A demonstration of the power of woman over man, I can tell
you.' Tamed, or just exhausted? There's no doubt that the Feelgoods'
partners will have simply missed them, but they also worried about
them. It would be reductive to pretend the forthcoming split was
nothing to do with the obvious distress 'the road' was beginning to
cause. It's understandably preferable for the one being 'left' to blame
outside forces, even though this situation would arise three times in
relatively quick succession. There was no coincidence here. (Lee may
also have been projecting a bit of his own conflicted situation onto
what was happening with his bandmates – Shirley was not enjoying
being home alone all the time, to put it mildly.)

'I was just sick of being constantly on tour,' said Sparko. 'You couldn't
have any personal life. If someone said, "Do you want to do something
next week?" You'd say, "I don't know." Even if you had free time, the
phone would often just ring. You remember the old phones with the
dials? The ringing noise they made still haunts me.' Sparko had started
to feel like he was 'in the army, always being told where and when to
go'. Figure, on the other hand, felt the lifestyle was becoming like that
of 'a biscuit salesman'.

The weird, wired world of the Feelgoods was also causing some members to experience a bit of an identity crisis. They'd all projected their 'characters' for so long, reality and fantasy was starting to merge. Figure explains: 'I'd always been encouraged by the others to become "The Big Figure". The white suit and the ponytail, maybe the slightly aggressive attitude on the TV ... that wasn't really me. Lee was able to switch off. I saw him at home and he was always quite relaxed – but I remember coming back from tour still being The Big Figure. My wife would have a go at me after a couple of nights and go, "Oi. You're at home now, chill out!" You get caught up in it. It all got a bit much.

'It was purely my own decision,' continues Figure. 'I didn't take leaving lightly. I think Lee, at the same time, was hoping to bring me round again. I don't think he realised how seriously I took my decision. It was just unfortunate we were being worked so hard that we ran out of steam. What we needed was a three-month break to reflect and get ourselves together, but it was literally: back for two days, off somewhere else, back for a few days, off somewhere else. Then we've got an album out, then we've got a TV [show] in Germany ... it was just going on and on.

'If we had only had the presence of mind to say, "Look, the three of us are going to have a break for six weeks, we need to get our breath back." But because it was all haphazard and in the middle of work we sort of broke at different times.' Gypie was just the first to snap, and a press release duly winged its way to the *NME* who read between the lines – or just shared what they actually knew – noting Mayo had left '"for personal reasons" – read gone stone Canvey crazy ...'

After a round of auditions, Count Bishops guitarist Johnny 'Guitar' Crippen was recruited: a striking presence, a fellow blues nut and, most importantly, a powerful player and a writer to boot. The Feelgoods promptly picked up their tools and got straight back to work. 'It's a bit like a football team,' Chris Fenwick observed dispassionately. 'One leaves, another arrives, but as long as you keep the team standard up, and keep the spirit of the team moving forward, and for what we were after, making it a quality class act, that's what was important to us.'

There would be one more Feelgood album with Figure and Sparko – the Vic Maile-produced *Fast Women & Slow Horses* – and, as it would turn out, their only recording with Johnny Guitar. It would also be released on Chiswick Records, their contract with UA being no more, and the title was certainly appropriate. Never mind slow horses, these steeds were decelerating to a complete stop despite being whipped and spurred.

The resulting album, released in October 1982, was more relaxed than the usual Feelgood fare, proving vaguely Springsteen-esque at times, and Paul Strange at the ever loyal *Melody Maker* wrote that 'everything's on heat. Brilleaux's in there, shouting the odds, napalming hysterically with his harp.' The record features 'Monkey', a song written for the group by Squeeze, and some material Brilleaux had written in collaboration with Johnny Guitar ('Rat Race' and the country-inflected 'Bums Rush', reflecting Lee's enthusiasm for country musicians such as Johnny Paycheck) and classic covers such as 'Beautiful Delilah' by Chuck Berry.

'Educated Fool' would feature some noticeably Wilko Johnson-influenced guitar licks, and Johnny Guitar would provide songs including the artless single 'Crazy About Girls'. Lee delivers a killer harmonica solo, but the song is not their finest hour. There are brighter moments, but the album is far from their best and it seems to reflect the listless, conflicted mood, not to mention the fact that Sparko and Figure already have one foot out the door. By the time the record was released in October, they had long since gone. *Melody Maker* described the situation as a 'mass split sensation'. Lee and Chris were reeling but still, they immediately tried to patch everything straight back up again.

'The whole band collapsed at one point,' said Figure. 'Lee was left without anybody, Johnny Guitar brought his friend Pat McMullen [fellow Count Bishop] in on bass, and I recommended a drummer, Buzz Barwell.' Barwell seemed an appropriate choice. He'd played with Lew Lewis, Wreckless Eric and Wilko Johnson, while McMullen had worked with Screaming Lord Sutch – a fact that will have brought memories of the Wembley Rock'n'Roll Show flooding back. Lee insisted he was pleased with his new line-up. 'If I close my eyes, I can hardly tell the difference,' he said. 'Sometimes I wish they'd relax and go their own way but they won't hear of it.' It might have been easier on him if they had – Lee must have missed Sparko and Figure keenly.

What also proved to be a strain on Lee was the fact that, behind closed doors, things were more than a little turbulent. Mr and Mrs Brilleaux had sold their home on Canvey, and after a few months lodging at Feelgood House, had found a property in Hillside Crescent, a quiet road just over the water in Leigh on Sea. 'The house was more than Lee wanted to pay,' said Shirley, 'but we loved it. I wanted it immediately! We moved in the spring of 1982.'

This house would famously become known as 'The Proceeds'[47], that is, paid for by the proceeds raised by rock'n'roll. The name was suggested by Larry Wallis, who would become a regular house guest there, 'examining the virtues of Rémy Martin brandy with Lee, spending Christmas in the East Wing'.

'We lived there quite happily for maybe six months,' remembers Shirley, 'but we had a major falling out, and I ended up leaving and going back to the US. I don't even remember what we'd fought about – we fought all the time. I guess I was fed up being left at home while the band toured. They just never stopped working. Part of what I'd been unhappy about was the fact that when we'd got married, almost the next day Lee had to leave. I think I had unresolved anger issues over that! In retrospect what I should have done was live my life and get on with it, but I wanted what I wanted – I wanted him to be home more. I'm sure if he *had* been home more we would have killed each other.'

Gritting his teeth, Lee put his energies into promoting *Fast Women & Slow Horses*, and he was, initially, belligerently positive about it. 'It really shows on the album [that they all knew it was the last], everyone was trying very hard,' he said at the time. 'I spoke to London on the phone yesterday and apparently we've got the best reviews for an album we've ever had, since the early days.'

Later, however, Lee would admit to having 'mixed feelings' about the record, 'oscillating between hatred and passion'. It would surely have been hard not to associate this record with the upsetting period of estrangement from his wife, not to mention the loss of Figure and Sparko, but when speaking about it publicly, Lee remained discreet and concentrated on discussing the material.

'I hate some songs like "She's The One",' he said. 'I find it too pop, but I really love the songs I co-wrote with Johnny Guitar. I will always have a certain affection for this record, the last Vic Maile worked on with us before his death.' (Vic Maile died from cancer in 1989 at the age of forty-five.)

The reality of the situation was that, as Johnny Guitar observed, Lee was just unhappy. Everything seemed to be crumbling around him: both of Lee's precious marriages – to Shirley and to the Feelgoods – had hit a wall; his wife was in New Orleans with apparently no intention of returning; the friends Lee had worked with for more than a decade had gone; and he'd given himself no time to recover from the trauma of either loss. 'Lee was always great,' said Guitar. 'He always gave his all but he became a little ratty towards the end. It wasn't fun any more.' This short-lived Feelgood line-up saw out a UK tour throughout November and December before Lee called it quits.

'Things started to deteriorate. It wasn't working,' admitted Lee. 'So I just said, "Right, stop it. This is a bus going downhill with no driver, it's going to end in disaster. Just stop."'

Dr Feelgood was, as Lee put it, 'officially disbanded', and, for the first time, this seemingly unstoppable rock'n'roll juggernaut had ground to a halt. Chris Fenwick decided to clear his head and travel to India, but he was anxious about Lee, who was in a state of shock and needed a positive focus. 'When I come back,' Chris told Lee, 'I want you to have a new line-up.'

Lee Brilleaux in full flow during an interview.

DR.FEELGOOD

RECORDS

Christoffer Frances

As the 1980s wore on, Dr Feelgood became
known for its flexible line-up, however, Phil
Mitchell (bass) and Kevin Morris (drums)
are in the line-up to this very day. Guitarist
Gordon Russell, pictured here, auditioned to
replace Gypie Mayo after he left, and was
deemed brilliant but a little too young. Johnny
Guitar got the gig instead, but Russell's time in
the Feelgoods would come.

16. THE BAND THAT CAME IN FROM THE COLD

Musically this is the best band, it's very tight – of course, the original band had a magic ingredient ... but those days are gone and that's the end of it and we're living for today, as far as I'm concerned.

A defiant Lee Brilleaux on the subject of the new Dr Feelgood line-up

While 1982 had been, in many ways, something of an *annus horribilis*, 1983 would be the year Lee managed to put everything back together. After three months off, Lee was bored and he'd had plenty of time to consider the future. His initial intention was not to create a new Dr Feelgood, but to form 'The Lee Brilleaux Band' instead. Of course, as we now know, the tempestuous Dr Feelgood daemon would not go gentle into that good night.

Lee had been going to the Zero 6 club near Southend airport to check out musicians at the venue's weekly jams, and it was there he bumped into old schoolmate Phil Mitchell who was now playing bass with Mickey Jupp and Lew Lewis. By all accounts, Phil approached Lee and expressed that, if he ever wanted to get a new band together, he would love to work with him. Before long, Phil was called up to make good on his offer. Hard-drinking drummer Buzz Barwell was invited back into the fray, and finally Lee rang up a young guitarist who had auditioned after the departure of Gypie, losing out to Johnny Guitar. Gordon Russell had been working with Geno Washington (enjoying a renaissance thanks to the Dexy's Midnight Runners hit 'Geno' in 1980), his playing had impressed and Lee hadn't forgotten him. The addition of Russell would not only inject a real vitality into the group, it would introduce a strong new songwriter.

Lee would subsequently explain in an Australian TV interview, a nervous Russell by his side, that 'when I auditioned him, I felt he was a little bit too young', adding warmly and not a little paternally that 'when the job came up again, I got on the phone quick because I was frightened I might have lost him to somebody else. I just got him in the nick of time.'

As true as it was, Lee also wanted to build Russell's confidence and make him feel safer in a stressful situation. 'He was just a really sensitive guy,' said Russell. 'Thank God Lee was there during that interview. I was *so* shy … He really helped me, right from the beginning, but it was also, you know, "Come on, this is your life now, off you go!" He could handle himself in any situation. Even now, I often think, what would Lee have done?'

Once the new line-up was announced, Lee had to take on the inevitable tsunami of press. The media had plenty questions, the main one being along the lines of: 'Did you not consider throwing the towel in when Sparko and Figure left?' Lee was prepared, and admitted that he had, 'but have you seen what they pay down the dole office? It was very daunting putting a new band together, but I realised there were so many people who want to still play R&B, it wasn't that hard.'

The world loves a definitive line-up, however, and there would never be an original Feelgood reunion in Lee's lifetime. Dr Feelgood were now, to many people, 'Lee and whoever else', as one journalist rather bluntly put it.

'The early 1980s were pretty bad years for Dr Feelgood,' Lee would later concede. 'It was a combination of factors: there was bad morale, we lost the original rhythm section, it was quite demoralising to find new musicians, and the other thing was that musical fashion was completely at odds with our own way of looking at things. Most bands in that position would have quit, but we [himself and Chris] decided to carry on. We're just very persistent.'

Less straightforward was the mission of persuading Shirley to come back, but she would, eventually, return. 'I was so angry when I left, it took six to eight months of not being around him [to want] to try and make it work again,' she said. 'I went back for a number of reasons, but it was also the realisation that I couldn't hang out in New Orleans and drink and play for the rest of my life. Lee was calling me and asking me to come back. I missed him, I loved him.'

Lesser marriages might not have survived such a protracted break, but Shirley Brilleaux's return to Southend would actually mark the beginning of their happiest years together. 'I think we grew up a lot,' admits Shirley, who adds that, while she was originally irked by Lee's frequent absences, they would ironically prove to be the key to their relationship's longevity – his 'aggression' largely being released during the shows. Lee was inclined to agree. 'I think it's a positive,' he said. 'If you're there day in, day out, you start to take each other for granted. I think in my case it might be an advantage to my marriage – the fact I'm not there half the time.'

The Brilleauxs would flourish at The Proceeds, which was, incidentally, the perfect party house, playing host to many a gathering ranging from civilised to downright uproarious. But it was also the perfect family house, and one year after Shirley came back to Lee, they would have their first child, Kelly Elizabeth, in November 1984. This would temper the Brilleaux lifestyle, for Shirley at least, if not Lee. 'I cut way back because I had to, for the sake of my baby,' said Shirley. 'But it didn't slow Lee down, not that much. There was still all that going on, but I became more of a bystander than a participant.'

All the same, it wouldn't be long until Brilleaux started to embrace and develop other dimensions in his character, and the slow but steady process of turning sartorially into something of a 'country gent' was soon to begin, once the band started earning a little more wedge anyway. As Kelly would later explain, the 1980s was when Dr Feelgood really 'became like a job' for her father, but the other elements of his life were opening out, the colours heightening in direct proportion to the comparatively workaday reality, in some respects, of his career. Lee's interest in food would blossom to the extent that he started experimenting in the kitchen himself, scribbling notes and his own diagrams inside the cookery books he worked with, collecting wines and growing produce in the garden, the latter appealing to his thrifty streak.

Rather less thriftily, the famous Brilleaux suits would soon become more expensive, tailored by Soho's famous Mr Eddie of Berwick Street. To my mind, one can almost split the Lee Brilleaux story down the middle, or at least the story of his adult life: the first half consisting of, basically, full-on rock'n'roll pandemonium, and the second seeing the gourmandising gentleman Lee Brilleaux come to the fore, all *Telegraph* crosswords, well-cut suits, Bacchanalian dinner parties and boozy Yuletide festivities.

Larry Wallis remembers spending a particularly *Joyeux Noël* at The Proceeds munching on homemade pork pies (complete with chutneys made by Brilleaux himself), 'crying with laughter over *Squire Haggard's Journal* by Michael Green – his favourite book,' he told Will Birch. 'I referred to Lee as Squire Haggard – very English, fond of a decent brandy,' his preference being 'the Spanish brandy Cardenal Mendoza,' Lee's old friend Keith Smith told Will Birch. 'If you were dining at The Proceeds, you knew you were in for a very late night when Lee announced it was time for the Cardenal.' Indeed, a flask of the stuff would be kept on hand at all times.

Work-wise, the situation still wasn't quite right, and one thing was abundantly clear: they needed a new drummer. Gordon Russell's first show with Dr Feelgood was in Monte Carlo, and, as he remembers, 'The Big Figure came and played drums because Buzz couldn't do it.' The reason Buzz had to go, paradoxically, was because he had a drink problem.

'The trouble with Buzz,' explained Lee, 'was that he used to drink gin at ten o'clock in the morning. Now, nobody likes to drink more than me, but I did say, "Look, wait until six o'clock, just be sensible." He did it one time too many and I had to say, "I'm sorry, Buzz, but you can't be in the band any more." I sacked him.' Kevin Morris, a former Pigboy Charlie Band member (and schoolfriend) and now an in-demand drummer working with the likes of Sam and Dave, would be his replacement. Little did he realise he'd still be in the group more than thirty years later.

Lee wanted to rebuild Dr Feelgood, and this meant almost non-stop live work at a grass roots level. This was a personal mission for Lee and Chris, but from the point of view of the rest of the group, the promise of being a musician in constant work was irresistible. After a handful of rehearsals, they fuelled up and went for it, promoting *Fast Women & Slow Horses* with an almost entirely different band.

'We worked very hard and very professionally,' Lee told *Blues Bag*. 'We worked in Europe while times were dodgy in this country. We'd do seven nights a week in clubs out in Germany and Sweden, Spain. It wasn't my favourite sort of work but it kept us ticking over.'

The venues might not have been as big as they once were, but Lee was pragmatic, and, he insisted, that 'while my manager would prefer it if I played bigger venues and earned more money ... for the feeling of the music, it's better to play in a small house.' R&B was thriving in the more intimate nightspots, which suited Lee just fine, even if he did find himself having to work considerably harder to maintain his lifestyle. Still, when he wasn't having to put on a gracious front in interviews, it was sometimes a challenge to remain cheerful during the laborious 1980s.

'I don't have to tell you that four people in a band together, sitting in the same van for hours ... it's not always easy,' said Gordon Russell. 'Lee could be difficult at times. I saw the darker side, of course – he could explode. He'd get fed up with one of us, or all of us, or something else ... he'd take it out on us, but then he'd realise and be really sweet to you and apologise in his own way, and off you go and you're mates again.'

The gig would often be the turning point: the adrenaline, the gin, the crowd and, most importantly, the music allowing Lee to somehow 'reset' himself. As he'd always maintained, rock'n'roll was his release, a way of working out his anger. 'After the gig, he'd always be all right,' said Gordon. 'And then he'd go, "Tomorrow I'm going to have a really good lunch," and that would cheer him up too. He was just the happiest person alive sitting at the table having lunch. First glass of wine of the day … He'd always like to meet the chef too, he'd shake his hand and say, "Excellent meal, thank you so much." A big part of touring was lunch, basically.'

Copious amount of beer and many, many slap-up meals were, to be fair, starting to have an effect on Lee's once lithe physique. At over six feet tall, Brilleaux could get away with gourmandising for a little longer than his more diminutive associates, but while the early 1980s saw the weight pile on, Brilleaux couldn't care less. 'Oh, [we're] supposed to be young, handsome pop stars,' he sneered. 'We've never put across a glamorous image, that's not the appeal we've gone for – getting the little girls excited and stuff like that. So it doesn't matter how old I get, how fat I get, if my hair falls out or my teeth drop out, I don't think that's going to affect our popularity.' *Garçon*, the dessert trolley, if you'd be so kind.

Sheer love of food aside, the promise of tastebud-pleasing new discoveries would be instrumental in enlivening tour after tour. This, a good book, a radio and the promise of meeting some choice new characters were vital elements of Lee's road-tested psychological First Aid Kit, and they would become more important by the year. But when even they weren't enough, Lee would just think of Howlin' Wolf. Provocative stage act aside, Chester Burnett would inspire Lee on a deeper level when all else failed.

'I like to think his spirit … you know, if ever I feel a bit down,' Lee pondered. 'Or, "Oh, I don't really fancy playing tonight", I think, well, that's not how the Wolf would have handled it. The Wolf's a big man, he'd have gone out and done it.'

It must have occurred to Lee that when he and Chris saw Howlin' Wolf when they were still schoolboys, the man onstage was no longer at his peak, playing for smaller audiences in rundown pubs, and yet those shows proved to be a lifelong inspiration to them, Lee in particular. This must have been one of the reasons Lee's commitment was so enduring and so absolute; even if a promoter failed to publicise a show, resulting in only a handful of people turning up, Lee would never pull out. 'He dug deep and he never short-changed anybody,' said bass player Dave Bronze, who would work with Lee in later years. '[It] was extraordinary.'

After this intensive live stint, it was time for the new Dr Feelgood to record their first album together. The residential Chipping Norton Studios in Oxfordshire were booked, Mike Vernon was called in to produce (having worked well with the group on *Let It Roll*), and, in the early spring of 1984, the Feelgoods set to work on what would become the authoritative *Doctor's Orders*. This record would include a number of original compositions by Gordon Russell, who was hitting the ground running, but the guitarist noticed how shy, even now, Lee was when it came to writing material.

'Lee was very humble,' said Gordon. 'He used to say, "I'm not really a songwriter", but he used to write really good lyrics. A couple of the songs I got credit for, he really did have a few good ideas on how the melody should go. But then he'd go, "No, no, that's your song." He had ideas in his head but was too modest to put them out there. I saw some of those ideas come through and there are a few credits on albums with his name on, not loads, but I don't think it bothered him. He just was happy to be the singer, that's what I felt. Obviously he had to sing the songs and be comfortable with them; he knew how he wanted to hear things, but he didn't want to get in the way of anybody else's creativity.'

'Close But No Cigar' – written by the group with Larry Wallis – would be selected as the opening number, and the closing track, 'Dangerous' – featuring the ubiquitous mean women, dodgy dealings and city lights – was written by the same songwriting team. But in the main, *Doctor's Orders* would be light on original material; rather Lee would use it as an opportunity to pick an abundance of vintage covers including Louis Jordan's 'Saturday Night Fish Fry', the paranoid 'I Can't Be Satisfied', 'You Don't Love Me' and 'Neighbour, Neighbour' – a bundle of classics Lee had always wanted to sing.

The finished record would be the most polished Feelgood album yet. It was slower paced and had the overall feel of, basically, a strong, well-rehearsed pub band. To those who sniffed at the fact that the Feelgoods still played R&B, Lee had this to say: 'People don't talk about an orchestra and say, "Oh, are you still playing that fucking old Beethoven stuff?" Why should they say the same to us?'

Lee was proud of *Doctor's Orders*. It was, as he put it, 'very straightforward R&B, the best album [we've] done for about three or four years'. 'Straightforward' was a Brilleaux buzzword. The more straightforward things were – from the music to the meal to the logistics on the road – the happier he was. For better or worse, freewheeling creative chaos was not his style; Dr Feelgood was now delivering well-played and gleamingly well-produced blues, warm, comforting, familiar. What was increasingly intriguing, however, was Brilleaux's world behind the scenes.

'We'd go round to Lee's for these lunches,' remembers Will Birch. 'One Sunday, it was the most surreal thing. Shirley said, "We've got a guest, he's a bit shy, he won't come down." Suddenly the lounge door opened and Alex Chilton walked in. Alex Chilton of Big Star and the Boxtops in Lee Brilleaux's house on a Sunday afternoon in Leigh on Sea. Crazy stuff. He was a friend of Shirley's. I was a bit groupie-ish and asked him about Big Star, and then he walked out and I didn't see him again. Lee was saying, "I don't listen to that music, Uncle, it's poncy, effeminate …" It was a bit of an act he put on. He had that humour down, you had to take it with a pinch of salt.'

Unusual scenes would also occur at, or at least begin at, the Grand, Lee's preferred local pub. Pete Zear remembers: 'Dave Hatfield, who was originally in the Kursaal Flyers, he was into promoting what we would now call Americana. He brought over Flaco Jiménez, a Mexican-American squeezebox player, and his band. It was Tex-Mex music. They'd do strange songs, songs like "Roll Out The Barrel" – turns out it's a drinking song in San Antonio as well. Anyway, somebody had been putting these guys up while they were here.

'The guy they were staying with came into the Grand and said, "I've been drunk out of house and home, these guys have cleaned me out. I've never known anything like it." Lee's head popped up and he said, "Great. I'll have 'em round!" He got them round just on the basis of that. There was a little invited audience of about ten people in the front room in The Proceeds, and they played their music in his front room. It was magic. That's the kind of thing Lee would do.'

The Grand stood (and still stands, just about)[48] at the top of Grand Drive in Leigh on Sea, an impressive Victorian hostelry and a place that famously included Laurel and Hardy as guests of yore when the duo were appearing in Southend. By the 1980s, the slightly grubby Grand was not exactly a destination for Hollywood stars, but it was Lee's home from home, mere minutes from Hillside Crescent and a place one could generally find him, quietly sipping his pint and doing the *Times* or *Telegraph* crossword if he wasn't on tour, his daily timetable shaped by the opening and closing times.

The Grand would also be Lee's first port of call post-gig, no matter where he'd been in the world. Stopping off there before heading home no doubt gave him a chance to decompress, to enter a kind of mental anteroom (and have a few drinks, obviously) before becoming the 'other' Lee, family-man Lee. This behaviour isn't unusual. Bono's wife Ali Hewson actually books a week at a hotel for her husband to adjust post-tour before coming home to his family. There's a certain wisdom in it. Pete Townshend, on the other hand, used to come straight home and, during The Who's peak, his daughter recalled seeing her disorientated father sitting on his suitcase weeping in the hall as his equipment was wheeled past him by roadies.

One of Lee's drinking buddies at the Grand was Colin Crosby (dubbed 'Colin the Socialist' by Brilleaux, who was emphatically *not* a socialist). 'There were three different bars in the Grand,' explains Colin. 'There was the really dirty bar on the left; we used to call it "Gluesniffers". Your feet used to stick to the carpet.

'Then there was the front bar, which was a bit nicer, and then there was the back bar, where we used to go, which was charming. There was a little stage and people used to play music there on a Sunday. The bell would ring at two p.m., and there was always a race. Lee would buy a round and there'd be about four pints to drink in about fifteen minutes. He could certainly drink a lot.' (Lee did once tell a wide-eyed Feelgood auditionee in the early 1980s that he was 'an alcoholic', but by all accounts he didn't drink from the moment he woke up, it wasn't a compulsion, and it was rare to see him out of control. 'It was something he gave a lot of thought,' said Shirley.)

Lee, as his close personal showbiz chum Larry Wallis recalls, 'had a quiet way about him, and he enjoyed the Human Carnival wherever and whenever it was happening. Throughout our years of friendship, he often seemed to be enjoying a private joke. He did find the human race extremely amusing, and was a great one for dining and pubbing alone.' He had ample opportunity for character observation at the Grand. While, formerly, he would be the one being observed, here Lee could almost melt into the background, confident no one would bother him, and find out more about the people he was drinking alongside – solicitors, teachers, car mechanics, travellers. It was a welcome break from the music business and he would much rather ask them about their lives than crow about rock'n'roll.

Lee's experience at the Grand was more understated than that at the Jellicoe – apart from anything else, the Jellicoe and its regulars had witnessed the Feelgoods' ascent to fame. It was almost impossible to have a quiet drink there. The drinkers at the Grand just took Lee for who he was on face value – a courteous gentleman seeking alcoholic refreshment and a bit of space. 'People tended to leave Lee alone,' says Colin. 'There was a gypsy bloke who would always ask Lee for money, and Lee would slip him a few quid but he always got it back. He was always very pleasant to people, but he could get quite intense.'

Many Feelgood fans will know the following story, but Will Birch famously remembers seeing the Brilleaux temper in all its magnificence at the bar at the Grand in later years. This time, it was sheer incompetence that caused the eruption. Lee had, one afternoon, approached the bar and requested his usual gin and tonic, only to be informed that there was no ice, would that be a problem? This was, as far as Brilleaux was concerned, a big problem. Jugular vein pulsing, he called a cab, requested that the driver take him to the nearest Safeway, marched in and bought a bag of ice. Within minutes, he was back at the Grand. 'There's your fucking ice,' he bellowed at the bar man, slamming the bag down on with a crash. 'Now get me a gin and tonic.'

By August 1984, it was time for the itchy-footed Brilleaux to head back on the road and start preparing for a six-week tour of Europe to promote *Doctor's Orders*. Kissing his now pregnant wife goodbye on the steps of The Proceeds, Lee roared off in the van and Dr Feelgood travelled to Holland, Belgium, France and Germany before returning to the UK and capping things off with an appearance at a blues festival in Basildon, not far from home. Lee would, with any luck, be back at the Grand before they'd rung the last bell.

This tour would see the Feelgoods' return (well, Brilleaux's return) to the Mont De Marsan festival up in the Pyrenees, this time alongside new wave Liverpudlians Echo and the Bunnymen among others. Lest we forget, in 1977 Dr Feelgood topped the Mont de Marsan bill above The Clash, The Damned, The Jam and The Police. Things had, indubitably, changed quite a bit since then, although the festival was 'more civilised this year,' Lee noted approvingly. 'They've done it up 'andsome. All mod cons. They've got a chapel, an operating theatre, the lot.' Catering for the need to pray *and* for urgent medical attention – it sounds like quite a festival.

Allan Jones, after all these years, was as loyal as ever to the Feelgoods, and would travel with the band on the Dutch leg of the tour, reporting back to *Melody Maker* with photographer Tom Sheehan by his side. 'A decade ago,' he wrote, 'Dr Feelgood came roaring out of Canvey like an R&B hurricane. Ten years on, Lee Brilleaux is still causing maximum havoc in Europe.' And ten years on from this date in turn, Brilleaux would no longer be here at all. A cruelly short period of time by anyone's reckoning, but even ten years can seem like twenty, even thirty, if you cram them as full of adventures as this man did.

The 'havoc' Jones refers to on tour was about right. The drinking was well underway by the time the *Melody Maker* team met up with the band and, as well as the crushing hangovers and trademark Brilleaux rants (on this occasion reserved largely for 'frogs in caravans' clogging up the roads), Lee had also injured his back as a result of a 'disagreement' in the bar the night before. 'Must have pulled a muscle loading the gear in last night,' he lied, before admitting there was, 'as it happens, a scuffle that needed quelling.' (He only confesses to this after Fenwick dismisses his original claim as 'bollocks'.)

Holland had been Feelgood territory since day one, and in Brilleaux's eyes it was 'a damned civilised country. Nowhere's more than a hundred and fifty miles away, we can dash out, play a gig and be back in Amsterdam before closing time.' That said, a stroll through the leafy Vondelpark before the show riles Brilleaux once again as they find themselves picking their way through swathes of snoozing hippies who had crashed out on the grass. 'What this place needs is an artillery barrage to liven it up,' Brilleaux declared to Jones.

The euphoric crowd at that evening's show in the Vondelpark succeeded in lifting Lee's spirits while the Feelgoods simultaneously injected some much needed life into the surrounding area (read: woke up the hippies), but Jones was surprised when, after the gig, Lee testily chivvied everyone straight back into the van and started driving – very fast – to Calais.

This is, it must be said, a long journey, and one that has Jones wondering why they didn't just drive to the Hook of Holland and catch a ferry there. Lee wastes no time in explaining that not only will they avoid having to contend with the rucksacked German tourists at the bar, but that he and Chris have shares in Townsend Thorensen, whose ferries leave from Calais. 'Means we can get over for half price.' The idea of travelling in more comfort was, at this point at least, not something Lee was interested in, but, as he often pointed out, musicians who travel in 'limousines' and 'pose about' often forget those costs are coming right out of their pockets anyway. That was something he learned early on, and that attitude would certainly prepare him for the leaner times.

Next stop the unglamorous Basildon (Bas Vegas if you're local, or a comedian) for the aforementioned blues festival, and Lee is now weary and in need of succour. The Grand is so close he can almost touch it – it's within twenty minutes if the traffic's on his side. All in good time. Turning his attentions to the stage, Lee's face falls as he spots a local country musician tuning up. The signs are unpromising. 'If he starts playing that banjo I'm going to have to have a very large gin,' he growls to Jones who, understandably, takes the opportunity to ask why on earth Brilleaux continues to puts himself through it.

'Threat of bankruptcy, mostly,' Lee jokes. 'There's four million unemployed, I don't want to add to the numbers.'

There might have been a different way of doing it, but for Lee, it was Dr Feelgood or nothing – he and Chris had poured so much of their time and energy into it, and even if Lee had chosen to move forward with his original idea of 'The Lee Brilleaux Band', he would still have wanted to perform the same songs anyway. But from now on Dr Feelgood really was, in a way, 'The Lee Brilleaux Band', playing material from the Feelgood songbook.

The concept of the 'new' Dr Feelgood had long encountered criticism from purist fans and those still unwilling to accept a Feelgood without Figure and Sparko, let alone Wilko, but Lee remained unperturbed. 'That doesn't really irritate me. People have their own ideas about the group,' he said. 'If I were a member of the group I'd be annoyed, but the musicians who make up the Feelgoods today are mature enough not to be undermined.

'Dr Feelgood can't be only Lee Brilleaux, because I need the others and they need me. We are a team. The group is a quartet, and the philosophy that we always pushed remains as it always has, which is why Dr Feelgood still exists today.' Dr Feelgood was, as Shirley remembers it, 'his baby and his life. He couldn't conceive of doing anything else.'

Jokes about debt and the dole queue aside, ultimately the main motivating factor for Lee would be performing for people; he loved the idea of cheering them up, putting them in a better state of mind, allowing them to switch off from their own lives for an hour or two. It seems that Lee regarded the purveyance of live R&B as a profoundly transformative public service that existed for the good of people's mental health. It was *needed*. And as long as it was needed, he, and the Feelgoods, would be there. The onus was increasingly on the audience, and even if the travel was arduous, as with the act of giving a gift, the pleasure of entertaining was, for Lee, more than worth it. In the words of his mother Joan, 'it's what he lived for'.

Shirley Brilleaux on Lee's Sartorial Idiosyncracies

He'd carry his stuff in an old Millwall bag. He wasn't a Millwall supporter, but he knew the mere sight of it in this context would cause a reaction. 'People would cross the road. His friends would say, "Are you sure?" But he'd say, "I love the fact I'm carrying this to make fun of the people who *think* I'm carrying this because I'm a Millwall fan,"' says Shirley. 'I mean, I kind of got it, but it was so convoluted it gave me a headache to try and follow the reasoning. A lot of it really was Lee just fucking with people.'

And inside that Millwall bag? 'Twenty Rothmans, a flask of brandy – probably Cardenal Mendoza – and a Marine Band harmonica in the key of F.'

Lee on Retirement

Maybe when I retire from music I'll open a restaurant with home cooking for musicians. Give it a few more years yet. I wouldn't ever want to retire completely, maybe just cut it down to a hundred gigs a year from two hundred. I would miss terribly the opportunity to get up on stage and play. I want to do that for as long as possible.

Kelly Brilleaux on Joan

My grandmother loved my dad. She certainly thought he was the greatest thing that had ever happened to the world. She had pictures of him winning medals at school for reading, and she would always tell us, 'Your dad never wanted chocolate for Easter, he only wanted books. He didn't want toys or anything, just books.' We were like, 'OK … Well, we're not that cool, sorry.' Most people think their grandkids are way more perfect than their actual kids. This was the exception to the rule.

Shirley Brilleaux

Shirley Brilleaux

*Above: Family man Lee with toddler Kelly
on the beach at Costacabana near Almeria,
Spain. 'We spent many happy vacations
there over the years,' said Shirley. Below: Lee
with his mother Joan and baby Kelly, 1984.*

Top: Lee tearing it up.
Bottom: Gordon Russell-era Feelgood line-up.

17. THE TALENTED MR BRILLEAUX

I live in Leigh on Sea, a few miles from Canvey and Southend. There is something about that part of the world which has developed a lot of rock'n'roll and rhythm and blues. All the Essex girl jokes haven't put me off yet.

Lee Brilleaux

In 1985, amid a musical climate of Wham!, Five Star and Foreigner, not to mention the Band Aid charity single which, as you might imagine, Brilleaux had his opinions about,[49] Dr Feelgood grimly hoisted their way back into a position of greater stability on the live circuit. Lee was also encouraged to see that, despite the plastic, over-produced nature of most 1980s chart music, there were also groups such as ZZ Top coming out of Texas and playing hillbilly rock for the masses, converting a whole new generation to rootsy blues. The ripple effect would certainly be felt by the Feelgoods, at least at live shows. Brilleaux noted with pride that the average age of their audiences had dropped considerably, and, alongside the stalwart older fans, there was a small but significant percentage of people at the gigs who were clearly just starting their respective R&B journeys.

It must be said that when it came to new music, Lee was more open-minded than people might assume, and one of his favourite contemporary acts was Huey Lewis and the News – aka his old pals from the group Clover. 'Bit commercial but Lee liked them,' said Gordon Russell. 'The song, "I Want A New Drug", Lee really liked that.' Another artist Lee admired was David Bowie, picking out the 1975 *Young Americans* album as his 'favourite white soul album'. 'Lee was quite dogmatic,' Gordon adds. 'If he didn't like something, that was it, end of story. "Nope, don't like that, it's rubbish, get it off." But he wasn't completely shut off.' Will Birch recalls the amusing incongruity of hearing Lee singing along with The Bellamy Brothers' 'Let Your Love Flow'. 'He *loved* that song. That was quite strange, but he did have a broad appreciation of stuff.'

Plans were underway for a new release that would stand out in the latter Feelgood canon as authentic and exhilaratingly raw; interestingly,

Brilleaux himself would produce it. After years of taking a back seat in the studio, Lee would step up, break all the rules, and the result would be the scorching *Mad Man Blues*, a record that really sounded like them, like him – at times invoking that seductive Deep South juju that had attracted Lee to the blues in the first place.

Brilleaux's confidence in the studio had increased somewhat because he had recently been invited to produce some material by the French R&B band ART 314, a group very much in the Feelgood mould. 'I said I'd never really produced anybody before, but they said they didn't mind, and they would pay me to come to Bordeaux, so I said OK. It'll be a new experience for me. I've spent a lot of time in recording studios, obviously. I think I know what to do.'

The opportunity to 'go back to France and eat good food' – one of the reasons Brilleaux once jokingly (I think) gave for wanting to continue the band at all – probably sealed it, but he would subsequently transfer skills he never realised he had into *Mad Man Blues*. The process of working with ART 314 in this way showed him he could take control, follow his instincts and allow his ideas to come to the fore. This approach would pay dividends, artistically and personally if not commercially. For a start, the usual pressure of finding original material went out of the window.

'None of the songs are written by us,' said Lee. 'They're all classic blues songs. There's hardly any production on it, we just pressed the buttons on the recorder.' The songs Lee had chosen included the ageless 'Dimples', 'Dust My Broom', 'Rock Me Baby' and, of course, 'Mad Man Blues', a track suggested by Gordon Russell, opening with maniacal, distorted laughter courtesy of Brilleaux before they launch into the song, Lee's vocal wildly schizoid, snarling and shivering in turn.

Mad Man Blues, initially a mini-LP 'primarily intended to calm the impatience of fans,' as Lee put it, was recorded at Southend's then brand new Trackside Studios, just off Victoria Avenue, a five-minute drive from home. 'I horrified the engineer [Paul Page],' laughed Lee, in conversation with *Blues Bag*. 'He'd just opened this new 24-track studio and wanted us to use all his new toys. I walked in and said, "Nah, nah, nah. Take all these mics away."'

'On ['Mad Man Blues'] I sang through a little blown-up amplifier so that the voice sounded like it was cracking up, which resulted in him asking me not to mention his studio on the album credits ... [But] to me, that's how Dr Feelgood should sound.'

Summer was spent working on *Mad Man Blues*, but the road soon beckoned, and the Feelgoods were off again until the end of the year, the mini-album being released that October. The European tour would not be without incident, and a fair amount of blood would be spilled – some of it Lee's. One of the shows would be at the Tavastia Club in Helsinki, a venue the Feelgoods always played when in Finland. During this visit, a potential catastrophe would threaten to undermine the stoicism and professionalism that the band was famous for, and rather more besides. The incident was, as club manager Juhani Merimaa described it, 'a critical event, as the group was on its way [back] up'.

As soon as the Feelgoods had started their set, Lee became aware of a group of drunken fans at the front of the stage. Good-natured but out of their respective trees, they were holding their pints up to the singer like offerings to a rock'n'roll oracle, slopping their glasses around and, in one especially inebriated fan's case, repeatedly splashing Lee's suit. It was tantamount to a child ill-advisedly prodding a tiger with a stick. Sometimes Lee could treat instances like this with humour, even working them into the show, but tonight he was not in the mood. 'Brilleaux lost his temper and placed his boot smack in the middle of his face,' recalls Juhani. 'The guy just fell straight to the floor.' The injured fan had to be carried out of the venue for medical attention.

'After the gig, Brilleaux was very concerned,' continues Merimaa. 'I told him [the fan's] nose was at least a bit broken. He asked about the consequences: whether he would lose his passport and whether there would be any legal [proceedings]. Luckily the guy was a fan and was apparently content with having tasted the boot of his hero. He was cool about it. I hope his nose is all right.'

Later that year, as London tarted itself up for another Christmas, the Feelgoods played their old haunt, Dingwalls in Camden. 'Lee was wearing one of his lovely suits,' remembers Gordon, 'His "powder-blue suit". He'd slipped over just before he went onstage and he cut his knee on some glass. We were playing the gig and Chris came up and said, "Do you want to carry on?" He said, "I'm fine."'

The rest of the group hadn't realised he had fallen over, and, up until this point, hadn't noticed the blood pouring out of Brilleaux's knee, his light-coloured trouser leg turning a dark red alarmingly quickly. 'You're looking at your instrument, looking at the audience, you don't really look at the singer's legs,' said Russell. 'He really did hurt himself. Chris took him to hospital afterwards and he was told to take it really easy.

'The next time I saw him, he's got a walking stick – and he really enjoyed this, it was a very smart cane. We went to Belgium to do a New Year's Eve gig, and he had the cane with him onstage and of course, he was being Lee Brilleaux, taking no care at all about his leg. He just did his show and I think it made it even worse. But he would just not give in.'

The Feelgoods were lacking much in the way of financial support at this stage in their career. Lee admitted that, while they had plenty of contacts at record labels, they 'weren't Duran Duran' and therefore weren't of interest. Will Birch, however, a figure who had always had the Feelgoods' back, had been doing some production work for Stiff Records, the label Lee himself had given his support to in their early years.

'I said to Dave Robinson, "Have you seen the Feelgoods lately? They're really good." Stiff were going through a bad patch; they'd had Jona Lewie's "Stop The Cavalry", Tracey Ullman, the Belle Stars, but they didn't have a rock band on their roster at that point,' explained Will. 'Dave needed to feed the machine. He called Chris and offered the Feelgoods a deal. Then Robbo said, "And you're going to produce it." Right.'

For Lee, the development was 'wonderful news' – not only was he looking forward to working with his old friend Will in the studio, but the fact that Stiff were keen to work with the band meant a lot. 'Everyone had heard of Stiff Records,' said Will, 'and he was totally flattered by the intention. "What, they want me?" He was knocked out.'

As usual, there wasn't an abundance of original material on hand, and, as Will recalls, 'Lee was not particularly inspired in that area at that time in his life.' Will, on the other hand, had remained very much plugged in to what was happening in the pop world and was writing songs that, he hoped, would work for the Feelgoods. 'I shamelessly pushed [my songs] forward.'

Birch also selected some songs to cover (including John Hiatt's 'I'm A Real Man' and 'Where Is The Next One?' and Johnny Cash's 'Get Rhythm') and he would, somehow, convince Brilleaux to try a softer, more modern approach with a view to get the band back in the charts. 'I wasn't interested in making an R&B album,' said Will. 'They'd already made fifteen of those and they were going to make another fifteen – let's try and make a pop record. That was my take on it.'

Will's songs were especially pop oriented, 'Don't Wait Up' boasting a piano lick reminiscent of Carole King's 'It's Too Late' and a slinky pop sound that was far from Brilleaux's comfort zone. ('It was my attempt to be commercial,' said Birch, adding, 'it got on Radio 1.') In addition to the numbers Will had presented, Gordon Russell provided 'Play Dirty' and the energetic 'Come Over Here' while Larry Wallis offered up the pacy, 'Gloria'-esque 'I Love You, So You're Mine'. (As Larry recalls, if the titles made Lee laugh, that would often be the tipping point). Dave Robinson suggested 'You've Got My Number' by The Undertones, an idea which Lee was not sold on, although as usual he obligingly agreed to it.

'When [Robinson] first suggested 'You've Got My Number', I thought he was crazy,' admitted Lee shortly after the album's release in August 1986. 'I couldn't see what he meant. But then I listened to it a couple of times and said, "Yeah, why not?" On this album, we have gone out of our way to do stuff which isn't just old blues numbers, in fact I don't think we do any real classic blues at all. We thought, we'll try an experiment.'

The results of that experiment were smooth, largely light-hearted and 'very eighties', as Lee would say with a wince. Fellow Stiff artists The Mint Juleps were wheeled in to provide backing vocals, and the ambition to 'go pop' was achieved, although it would all sit rather awkwardly with Brilleaux. In direct contrast to *Mad Man Blues*, Lee was not following his heart. 'The overriding view was that if somebody is prepared to stick up a budget, a producer and some material they thought we should do, we felt obligated to go along with it,' said Kevin Morris.

'We found ourselves recording material that was not your typical Dr Feelgood R&B. Sometimes it was augmented by other musicians while we were there, or even after we had left, session people and horns and singers and keyboards,' continues Morris. 'Lee definitely felt uncomfortable because he wasn't sure whether he should be doing it; in fact we were all unsure. With this album, and *Classic*, the one that came after, we found ourselves in some very strange places.'

Sessions commenced at Trackside, and this time the 'new toys' at the studio would be utilised to within an inch of their lives. Dr Feelgood were at their best when they were themselves – tough and lean – but the album that would be *Brilleaux* would be a big, full-fat production number. (The working title was *Southenders*, inspired by the TV soap *EastEnders*, courtesy of Dave Robinson.)

'Lee very sincerely put himself into the project, and where one or two of the songs were a bit of a challenge for him – 'Don't Wait Up' being one of them – he did try,' said Will. 'We'd go in at about midday and record until about eight p.m., get about three tracks down, then we'd go out for dinner. Lee was mad for going out to eat. "Fancy another curry?" We'd had about five or six curries on consecutive evenings and it was starting to make me feel really odd.'

Lee was cautiously optimistic about his new working relationship with Stiff, and Dave Robinson had proudly proclaimed that 'Lee is going to be my new ambassador' – and let's face it, if you could choose an ambassador, Lee would be at the top of your wish list if you had any sense. However, as sessions progressed, it emerged that Stiff were 'going bankrupt,' said Lee. 'We thought, here we go again.' Fortunately, the ailing label would be rescued by Trevor Horn and Jill Sinclair's label ZTT – 'The money Frankie Goes to Hollywood were bringing in was keeping Dr Feelgood going,' observed Kevin Morris.

Stiff launched a high-profile poster campaign for *Brilleaux* which featured the album's eye-catching (and very Stiff) cover – a close-up head-and-shoulder shot of Lee in round sunglasses, hair slicked back and harmonica jammed into his mouth, looking to all intents and purposes as if his mouth *was* a harmonica – a play no doubt on the phrase 'mouth organ' and dreamed up by Dave Robinson. There was just one problem.

'I had always been convinced he had a very big mouth, snarling around the place,' mused Robinson. 'But it turned out we couldn't get a normal-sized harmonica into his mouth. I could, but he couldn't. We had to root around and get a small one. Didn't *quite* come off. Nowadays we'd have done it digitally.'

The image, plastered across town, was certainly eye-catching, but the problem was that the cover, and the album title, gave the impression that Dr Feelgood now really *was* just Lee (something Brilleaux would always strongly contest whenever referred to as 'the Doctor'), and that the rest of the group had been demoted to session musician status.

'I really regret that it [came over] as a pseudo-solo album,' said Lee. 'It wasn't my idea.' All in all, from the cover and the title to the material itself, little about *Brilleaux* seemed to represent the heart of Dr Feelgood. 'It has some great songs on there, it's produced very well, the performances are good,' said Lee. ' The trouble is: it doesn't sound like Dr Feelgood. It doesn't sound like me singing. Who's that guy? And I don't think doing "You've Got My Number" was a good thing. It didn't suit Dr Feelgood.' To add insult to injury, *Brilleaux* failed to garner the commercial success they'd been shooting for anyway.

'The record was only a hit in Scandinavia,' said Dave Robinson. 'Here we didn't quite get it going, but we made the album, and it was like a thank you to Lee for all the effort he'd put into supporting

Stiff.' And so, *Brilleaux* came and went, as Kevin Morris confirms, 'we kept our integrity live', and several *Brilleaux* tracks would work well onstage. 'The song "Get Rhythm",' said Brilleaux. 'At first you'd think, Dr Feelgood doing a Johnny Cash song? Not really. But it works brilliantly. The song "Come Over Here", written by Gordon, that's a real stoater. Those two are the ones I'd pick out [as highlights].'

The band toured *Brilleaux* largely in the Nordic territories, and this meant another trip to Finland. Lee was becoming increasingly over-wrought, and it didn't help that the weather was rarely on their side as they made the gruelling journeys from show to show. A bit of on-the-road hardship had been bearable, even fun, in his twenties, but, loth as Lee was to complain, it wasn't quite as much of a wheeze now he was in his thirties.

'One day we had a huge journey to do by car,' remembers Gordon. 'Lee went, "I tell you what, I'm going to pay for this myself and fly us to the gig." We got to the airport, and Finland, as you know, is famous for having a bit of snow. The flights got cancelled and they put us in this really uncomfortable little bus. It was horrendous.'

The band arrived at the venue, aching and broken of spirit, shortly before they were due onstage. The road crew, on the other hand, had arrived two hours earlier and had been in an increasing state of panic regarding the whereabouts of the group. By the time the band hit the stage, 'Lee was pretty wrecked,' said Gordon. 'He was so tired and so fed up that he'd spent all that money, and he was so drunk that he was just going for it. It was really funny, he was taking every song to the limit and over-exaggerating all the words, glaring at the audience, it was just such a funny night.'

The mid-1980s may have been a chequered period for the band, but a Lee Brilleaux performance was still a sight to behold, and it was often when things went awry that he would come into his own – no fuss, no hesitation, just a majestic display of improvisation. During the December of 1986, the Feelgoods played the packed-out Queen's Hotel in Westcliff. It was an edgy gig, there was trouble in the audience, and at one point the power suddenly went off completely.

Will Birch was in the audience. 'PA went down, place went black,' he said. This was tantamount to dead air on the radio. The venue was crammed with drunk and, in some cases, lairy Feelgood fans; the situation was charged with all manner of incendiary possibilities. But within seconds, the voice of Lee Brilleaux rang out through the muggy darkness. 'He just went: "Drum solo!"' continues Birch. 'Kevin starts a drum solo. The power came back on after about two minutes, Brilleaux goes, '"No Mo Do Yakamo", one, two, three, four!' and they just went straight into it. He was totally in command of that building. His showmanship and stagecraft was incredible.'

At home, Brilleaux was proving to be a devoted father to his spirited little girl Kelly – now two – and while he was away for two thirds of the year, when he was home, he was a hands-on, affectionate parent who rarely left her side. And yes, he did take Kelly to the Grand. 'There was a playground there,' said Kelly. 'It was a way of giving my mum some time off. How great that he was able to do that. There'd be other kids there too, I spent a ton of time there. I had at least three birthday parties at the Grand.'

Lee also relaxed by spending more and more time cooking, finding quality ingredients from local purveyors of comestibles, trying out recipes and ideas sparked by dishes – street food in particular – he'd tried while abroad. 'Musicians become interested in their stomachs,' said Lee, largely because it is so hard to eat well on tour. But cooking would become a creative, almost therapeutic practice for him, and he'd miss the opportunity to whip up three-course meals – complete with a hand-written menu taped to the door – while he was away.

'Sometimes I come up with quite a good meal, I'm quite pleased with myself,' Lee said in an interview with Radio Stockholm. 'Other times it's a disaster. But I think cooking, and eating, is very important – you must eat well on the road. It's a hard job you're doing and it's important not to eat too much rubbish. My favourite food is the home cooking of a country. That sometimes is the most difficult to find; when you go to a restaurant they try to make it international, and you end up eating steak as usual. What I'd really like to do is eat the cooking that people eat in their own homes.

'I took a vacation in New Orleans and I learned a lot about cooking there. I went into some kitchens with people I know and they showed me how to make the special brown roux that you need to make that Creole cookery. I think my wife likes it; when I'm at home it saves her the trouble.'

And when Lee was home he liked to stay home. Visits to Soho's Coach and Horses and the much missed Colony Room were diversions when he happened to be in town, but hanging around in a cheesy nightclub waiting to be recognised was never his style. 'I wouldn't go to Stringfellows,' he sniffed. 'I'd rather go to … I dunno, a dog meeting or something like that.'

Lee's penchant for inventing humorous yarns would be stimulated by having a bright little daughter to entertain, and one series he would come up with would be 'the Moggy The Cat stories,' said Shirley. 'And they were clearly modelled on the Feelgoods. Moggy is the singer, K-Cat pounded the drums, their agent Nigel Kerr was Niggles the Cat … Whenever he was about to leave to go on tour, he would go up to our children's bedroom and sit there and tell stories about what Moggy the Cat did on tour, where he went, which Michelin-starred restaurant he'd go to for dinner …' And to ensure his kids didn't miss Moggy the Cat too much when he was away, he wrote them down in a spiral-bound notebook, complete with illustrations, for them to look through. 'The way he wrote it, and the alliteration, was amazing.'

'After we had our kids [their son Nicholas arriving in 1988], there was this span of six to eight years that were really wonderful,' adds Shirley. 'We had our ups and downs, of course, but it was a good time, and, like everyone, we didn't realise how short life can actually be.'

After another Brilleaux Christmas with friends and family at The Proceeds, and another dry January (he'd still go to the Grand, mind, but he'd order orange juice instead), the Feelgoods were back on the road by February 1987, travelling out to Spain and then Sweden, kicking off another heavy year of shows. Meanwhile, back at Stiff HQ, Dave Robinson was already making plans for the next Feelgood album and, hopefully, a hit single.

'Dave Robinson, once again, came up with another idea,' said Brilleaux. 'He said, "You should get Dave Edmunds to make a single with you," and he said, "This is going to sound crazy" – and it did – "it's going to be 'See You Later Alligator'!" The old Bill Haley record. I thought, the man has gone completely round the bend.

'But he paid to fly us back from Stockholm and interrupt a tour for twenty-four hours to make this cut, and then to fly us back to Paris to resume our tour. I thought, anyone who's prepared to spend all this money on air tickets and hiring Dave Edmunds must have something to back it up.'

Brilleaux's initial instinct was, as always, correct, but still, they went ahead with it, joining Edmunds at Sarm Studios in West London (courtesy of their ZTT connection) and making a '1980s version of a 1950s record,' explained Brilleaux, brash synths (yes, synths, brash ones – Lee's nemesis in musical form) and all. 'I'm very pleased with it,' Lee would declare, a claim that is hard to believe on listening to the single and considering his feelings about 1980s pop stylings. To make matters worse, once again this compromise would not provide the band with the success they or Stiff were hoping for.

Sessions to make the new Feelgood album were booked at Chipping Norton Studios, this time with the esteemed producer and arranger Pip Williams – providing, among other new tracks, 'Hunting, Shooting, Fishing', a co-write with Gordon Russell. The next Feelgood album would be titled *Classic*, the most finessed release in their catalogue, and, as Lee sadly would later concede, 'the only Dr Feelgood LP I rather regret having recorded'.

The band was always great, Lee's voice and harp playing faultless, stronger than ever indeed, and *Classic* is a perfectly fine 1980s soft rock release – all very well if you like that sort of thing. But this was Dr Feelgood. *Dr Feelgood.* There was a sense they were coming unstuck.

'We do what we want – if people don't like it, too bad.' This attitude had once been in the bones of the band; it was what made them inspirational, but now the group were allowing themselves to be moulded by outside forces for the sake of a hit that Lee, arguably, probably wasn't too bothered about anyway. It's no wonder he was becoming increasingly unsettled – he was not being true to himself (except when he was on stage, when he could do exactly what he liked). You can see it in his eyes, in the uneasy cartoon play-acting of the 'See You Later, Alligator' music video, and certainly in a live TV version of 'I Wanna Make Love To You' – his vocal on the record is tremulous and expressive (he is miming on the TV appearance, of course) but as he performs for the cameras, Lee just looks like a cheetah on a leash, desperate to suddenly fly off at his usual breakneck pace.

'Oh, fuck all this pop music, let's just play rhythm and blues!' The words of Wilko Johnson from all those years ago may well have been ringing in Lee's ears (not that he would have admitted it if they were), not least because EMI were also putting out *Case History* – a storming Feelgood compilation from the glory years to the present day – just as the band were working on *Classic*. Talk about rubbing it in. Or was the universe just trying to ram a message home?

'We were taken out of our comfort zone quite deliberately,' said Kevin Morris. 'They were trying to make us more radio friendly. Pip Williams had come straight in off the back of Status Quo's "In The Army Now"; they'd had a massive hit and I think Robbo (Dave Robinson) thought that the way the Quo had been tidied up, the same could be done with Dr Feelgood.'

Lee had been put through the wringer on *Classic*. While generally ill at ease during sessions, Brilleaux was usually a one-take wonder anyway, and that suited him just fine. Pip Williams, however, was not going to let him get away with that on his watch. 'He made him record a line at a time,' recalls Morris, 'made a cassette and then said, "Now go away, learn it and come back and just sing it." He found a way of getting him to articulate the music which wasn't just getting up there and giving it all that. He had to *sing*, it was more tuneful.'

The album, released in the September of 1987, would feature the foursome looking debonair, making eyes at the camera, Brilleaux in a gleaming lilac whistle. They look as shiny and unnatural as the record in the sleeve, a handsome bunch of once rough diamonds, smoothed and buffed almost beyond recognition. Despite the album title, a classic this was not.

Brilleaux's take on it was breezy but unambiguous. '[It was] good fun doing it and very interesting to work with a producer who spent *forty-eight hours* on one track,' he said to *Blues Bag*. 'It's an experiment I've no need to repeat. If we get the chance to make another studio album I'm determined it's going to be a raw Dr Feelgood LP.'

If nothing else, the experience had ensured that Lee would be assuming more artistic control in the future, and this was just as well, because before long the Feelgoods would receive the news that Stiff and Jill Sinclair had fallen out, ZTT had withdrawn all support, and Stiff were going broke. 'We were back on the street.' They had no choice but to go it alone.

This, in a way, was a more positive development for the band than they might have at first imagined. They'd been granted the freedom to start their next chapter, strictly on their own terms. As Brilleaux later said, 'If you don't know what do to next, go back to your roots and have a think about it.' It was time to follow his own advice.

Lee Brilleaux on Wilko Johnson

I've got no hard feelings against him for something that happened long ago. I don't go through my life worrying about that, it's finished. At the time I could have killed him, but now I don't care. Life's been good to me anyway.

Will Birch

They were playing the Douglas Lido on the Isle of Man, a bikers' convention. I used to do the merch stall for Chris, selling the CDs and T-shirts – I can't believe I did all this. Anyway, that night at the Lido was the night the promoter came in with the rider, and there was a pint of Gordon's gin and Lee got three pint glasses almost half full of ice, and he decanted the entire bottle over those glasses, so they were each about two thirds full with neat gin. Maybe a slice of lemon. Then he floated about an inch of tonic on top and they were carried onto the drum riser on a tray. By halfway through the set, he'd drunk them.

They were doing 'Rock Me Baby', and there were two or three bikers at the edge of the stage shaking up cans of lager. I could see what was going to happen, whether they were Feelgood fans or not, I don't know, but they were spraying Lee with beer. Now a lot of performers would get a bit touchy about that – 'my stage, my set, what do you think you're doing?' Lee was brilliant. He just stood there with his arms out under the stage lights and it was like a waterfall coming over him, he was beckoning them to do it more, it was running all down his suit. They weren't being aggressive, but Freddie Mercury wouldn't have stood for it.

Shirley Brilleaux

THE POTATO BARN, LIMEHOUSE FARM, GALBY
NR LEICESTER
7/6/86

MAD MAN BLUES

{ LOOKING BACK
NO MO DO
WIND-UP

TORE DOWN
DUST MY BROOM
FEELS SO GOOD
SHE DOES IT RIGHT

{ YOU DON'T LOVE ME
ROLL ME BABY

SLOW DOWN
ROXETTE

{ HIT GIT + SPLIT
BACK IN THE NIGHT
MILK + ALCOHOL

SHOTGUN BLUES

{ SHE'S IN THE MIDDLE
RIOT IN CELL BLOCK #9 }

{ DOWN AT THE DR'S
ROUTE 66

Left: A merry night at The Proceeds.
Above: A 1986 set list, penned by drummer
Kevin Morris. (Lee had given him the task of
writing down the set list before every show.)

Family shots. From top left, clockwise: Lee and son Nicholas on the bayou, Louisiana; 'Collie' and Joan; the Brilleaux family at home in The Proceeds (note Lee's treasured collection of maps on the wall behind him); with Kelly and Nicholas in the bay window at The Proceeds; on the bayou with Kelly; providing some early driving lessons on the Dodgems; Lee and Shirley's wedding anniversary in Almeria, Spain.

18. BRILLEAUX'S LAST STAND

I've always felt out of my time. Frankly I think I'm in the wrong century. I hate all forms of modernism, but I suspect I would have been uncomfortable at any time.

Lee Brilleaux

After some discussions with Chris, it was decided that the Feelgoods could, and should, take full control of Dr Feelgood's output and start their own label. It would be called Grand Records, for obvious reasons, and, as Lee explained, 'the idea is to obtain the rights from the original record companies of all our old records and to lease them back, to re-press them in disc and CD form, and reissue them with the original artwork. Our aim is to have our entire Feelgood catalogue out on our label. I just like the idea of knowing that all our old records – after all, they took a long time to record – [are] available. It's sad when you go to a store and ask for a record and they tell you it's been deleted.'

Another change was on the cards in terms of live work. It was finally time to start streamlining the notorious Feelgood touring schedule, to a certain extent at least. 'We've cut down to two hundred and twenty shows [a year],' said Lee. (This may still sound like an insane amount of work – largely because it is – but bear in mind they were previously doing 280.) 'We'll get it down to about a hundred and fifty. I think that's a comfortable amount, and you can enjoy every single one without thinking, another day, another gig. That way we'll keep Dr Feelgood going for a good many years.'

One surefire reason Lee wanted to spend a little less time on the road was because his family was growing. His son Nicholas had arrived in January 1988, and it was increasingly hard to be away, 'because I know I might not be seeing them for three or four weeks,' he said. 'I make sure I spend all day with them. Some fathers work in a factory, by the time they come home they're tired, the kids have gone to bed, they only see their children maybe half an hour a day. At least I get more time to spend with my family. I think that's important.' These past few years had at last put Lee in the position Figure had been in a decade previously. 'When Lee became a family man,' said Figure, 'he took me to one side and said, "Now I thoroughly understand why you left the band when you did."'

'He'd take us to the beach and to Old Leigh,' said Kelly. 'And when we were very young he took us to Peter Pan's Playground [now Adventure Island] in Southend. It was hilarious. Being a kid I'd want to do stuff over and over, so he'd walk through there with me about four or five times in a day, which is ridiculous. We went on the Helter Skelter only one time because he banged up his elbow. He had to sit on the mat and put me on his lap before we went down and it went a bit wrong.

'I think it's so sweet and funny that I saw this side. There was this dichotomy between his crazy, wild onstage persona, and then his real life persona. As I remember, he certainly had a temper but he was big on manners. If anyone wrote him a letter, he would always write back. He'd explain it to me: "These people have written me letters because they want to talk to me so I'm going to write back on a postcard." That's got to be really exciting for a fan. When I went on his memorial walk in 2014,[50] there were so many fans telling me, "I wrote your dad a letter and he sent me a postcard back. I still have it."'

It was around the time of Nicholas's birth, according to Shirley, that Lee underwent something of a metamorphosis. Already rather old-fashioned, eccentric and older than his years ('it's the mileage,' he'd insist), the latest development was, in Dean Kennedy's opinion, 'weird. Lee seemed to change overnight. He just decided, "A man of my age should be like this."' He was thirty-five.

'It all started when they were earning money again,' continues Dean. 'One minute he was wearing Doc Martens and Levis and the next it was hand-made suede brogues or Chukka boots,[51] things he'd laugh at people for wearing ten years previously. He'd read books on Keith Floyd, and the restaurants got posher. He started to go to places like the Coach and Horses, where that playwright would go [Jeffrey Bernard] and the blokes who make *Private Eye*. He started getting the Barbour jacket, the Cavalry Twills ...' Indeed, on browsing the Barbours one afternoon, Lee was informed by the sales assistant that they were 'good for catching grouse'. Brilleaux gently explained that 'you don't get many grouse in Southend'. Not that that put him off, you understand.

'He was acting like an elderly country gentleman,' adds Fred Barker. 'Bit like Ray Winstone – what's the tweeds about, Ray? You were born in the East End, now you're a country gent? Lee went the same way ... sitting around in the Grand being a bit of a country squire. Couldn't work him out but it wasn't for me to work out. Be what you want to be. And he was always being the way he wanted to be.' Since childhood, Lee had always seemed significantly older than his physical years; now it seemed he was creating a period of distinguished old age for himself, a stage of life he would never actually see.

Another alteration to the Feelgood line-up was on the horizon, and for the most devastating of reasons – guitarist Gordon Russell was soon to leave the band after the loss of his daughter from cot death syndrome, a tragedy that would send shockwaves through the group. The Feelgoods would hold a well-attended charity show in the child's honour and, after spending almost the first three months of 1989 on tour, Brilleaux looked up Steve Walwyn, a guitarist who had played on the same bill as the Feelgoods a number of times with R&B group The DTs. 'Basically,' as Lee put it, 'we nicked him.'

'We also played as Steve Marriott's backing band,' explains Walwyn. 'We played one gig with the Feelgoods, and I remember when we finished, Lee came up and said, "You've done your job, mate, you can get the gear in the van and get off home – and very wise, if I might say so." That became a catchphrase for years: "very wise, if I might say so". Because everyone else in the band kind of knew me I got the call, went down for an audition on Canvey and got the job straight away.

'One thing that I think endeared me to Lee was that afterwards we went to the Lobster Smack and Lee was impressed that I bought the first round. "Can't be bad, he can play the guitar and he buys a round. He's in!"'

As Steve Walwyn sat at home and feverishly practised along to Feelgood records, the band headed straight back out to tour Greece and Spain, bringing Gypie Mayo with them to fill in on guitar. While everyone would have understood if they'd just pulled the shows, another reason Lee was insistent on getting back out there was that his father had recently passed away. 'Rather than just stay at home grieving, he wanted to get over it and be on the road,' said Mayo.

Hard work, as Lee well knew, always provided a useful diversion from heartache, and the man always put forward a stoic front anyway, but this tour would be especially distracting because Gypie was in such a state. 'Twice he nearly missed the plane,' said Lee, in the book *From*

Roxette to Ramona. 'Three times he drank so much brandy he couldn't stand up. We had to throw a bucket of water at him to make him work.'

It was a period of great anxiety for the rest of the band, and one of the Spanish shows was, truly, the nadir. The Feelgood set-up is a spartan one: no second guitar, no keyboards; in short nothing to hide behind if things go wrong. 'It had to be abandoned after a few numbers,' remembers Larry Wallis. '[Gypie] was incapable of standing up unaided by a roadie kneeling behind him. The crowd rioted, smashed up the amps, the band was lucky to escape with their lives.'

Lee had long been saddened by Gypie's apparent lethargy, 'messing around in Southend', taking his gift for granted, but he was, at this point in his life, out of control, and Brilleaux had to let him go. 'He is a lovely man, the finest musician I have ever worked with,' said Lee. 'But he's totally disorganised and unreliable. He needs someone to guard him all day long to make sure he don't fall or hurt himself. It's a tragedy but it's impossible to work with someone like that.'[52]

Gordon Russell would return to cover some of the Feelgoods' French dates, but before long Walwyn would be a permanent fixture. One of his first shows with the group was in June 1989 at the Town and Country Club in Kentish Town, North London, 'which I didn't realise beforehand was going to be recorded, and televised,' said Walwyn, the results of this recording making up the 1990 release *Live In London*.

'Lee was very, very nervous about it,' adds Walwyn. 'Big crowd, one of my first gigs, he was more nervous than me! I think it shows on the record. Everything's played really fast.' It was a set of high-energy crowd-pleasers including 'She Does It Right' and 'Baby Jane', and *Live In London* proved to be the ultimate way to introduce the guitarist who, at the time of writing, is still in the Feelgood line-up to this day. (Lee, incidentally, was proud of *Live In London* on a personal level because, 'very unusually,' he said, 'my vocal performance is almost word perfect'. So there.)

'Bit nerve-wracking,' admitted Lee later that year, 'but now it's as if Steve's been playing with the band for ten years. Gordon was very fluid in his playing. I think Steve's probably a bit more aggressive. They're both interesting stylists, and they both fitted in perfectly with Dr Feelgood.'

As for the release of *Live In London* – 'not a very imaginative title, I know' – it was significant not only in that it was Walwyn's Feelgood debut, but it was also the first new recording to be released on Grand Records. 'We're going to remix [the tracks] ourselves without doing anything horrible to them,' said Lee (evidently still traumatised by the group's Stiff releases). 'Just tidy them up a bit, put a bit of echo here and there.'

The promotional tour, despite Lee's insistence that they were cutting back, still made for little time off throughout 1990. Those close to the group were becoming increasingly worried they were overdoing it, and Lee had to admit he was becoming 'mentally bogged down' by the strain. 'The music – that's the easiest bit,' he said. 'It's the travelling. My arms feel like they are getting longer because the suitcase is getting heavier as I'm getting older. Hanging around airports, airplanes being cancelled ...'

Birch was hired in to help with admin at Grand Records while the band worked, Steve Walwyn quickly learning that the elements that made the rigours of a full-on Feelgood tour tolerable were, according to Lee, good food and drink, plenty of time to explore, an English newspaper (Lee read one as often as he could wherever he was in the world) and, as always, a few well-timed practical jokes.

'One prank springs to mind which will illustrate his humour,' says Walwyn. 'We were playing a gig in Spain, and Alvin Lee, the guitarist with Ten Years After, was due to play there a week later. The dressing room had been whitewashed, no graffiti anywhere. We were talking about Alvin and I said, "You realise that's not his real name?" Lee said, "What is it then?" I said, "Well, he doesn't like people to know, but it's Graham Barnes."

'At the top of one of the walls was an electrical junction box. Lee got up on a chair with a black marker, and he wrote on this junction box in very small letters: "Graham Barnes!", with an exclamation mark. You had to go right up to it to read it, almost get up on the chair, but when Alvin came to do the gig the following week, he'd have seen it. To even think of doing that was typical of Lee.' Poor old Graham. I mean Alvin.

Somehow Lee managed to snatch some time with his family in 1990 between flying to Russia, Spain, Holland and seemingly everywhere in between, and certainly Kelly's fondest memories are of the frequent dinner parties her parents used to host. She was always treated as a little adult – as Lee had been by his own parents – and 'doing grown-up stuff' like joining in at parties and listening to music with her dad are memories she holds dear.

'My dad would play music for us – I remember him coming home one night pretty drunk. I came downstairs and he was playing "Yakety Yak". He had a really fine turntable which we obviously were not allowed to touch, but if he was up late and my mum had gone to bed, I did a lot of sneaking downstairs – any time anything was going on I had to be a part of it – and he would play stuff for me which was really cool.'

Kelly and Nick were allowed to listen to CDs (Squeeze's *Singles 45's And Under* was a favourite), but not Lee's vinyl, and definitely not Dr Feelgood; or at least, not when their father was around to hear it. 'We *loved* listening to my dad's stuff,' said Kelly. 'But he hated us playing it when he was there, which I can understand. If he got home and we were listening to Dr Feelgood, he was like, "No! No, no, no, no. Can't listen to that."' Oddly enough (and undoubtedly when Lee was out), Shirley put on a Feelgood CD for the kids one afternoon, and Nick, still a toddler at the time, 'stood in the middle of the floor and shook his head really fast and hard with his hands out, just like his dad,' said Shirley. 'Nick had obviously never seen the Feelgoods play; it was just a natural reaction to the music. It was the image of his dad, it was scary.'

Christmases at The Proceeds were always 'way over the top', according to Kelly. 'It's a very Brilleaux thing to overdo celebrations. We'd spend a lot of time with the Fenwicks, and my dad used it as an opportunity to cook a crazy meal and have a lot of people over.' There'd be dancing in the living room to some of the greatest music ever made – everything from classical music ('if you can believe that,' said Shirley) to soul, and 'Roadrunner' by Junior Walker and the All Stars, still the record he loved and related to the most, would invariably make an appearance before the end of the night. Then there'd be the jokes, the anecdotes (probably when the children had gone to bed), and he'd whip up hot buttered rums for anyone suffering from a seasonal cold. The all-important port – for Santa's benefit, naturally – would be bought in and Lee would start preparing the feast 'weeks in advance', says Shirley.

'Harrison's was Lee's butcher of choice. He loved that place. He would order the rib of beef or whatever we were going to eat for Christmas dinner, go to all the different grocers, order casks of beer – it was quite a big to-do. I remember him having a whole Stilton delivered, it was massive. We had food all over the house and he would make pickles and chutneys to go with it; he used apples from the tree in the garden.'

Even when they weren't marking an especially festive occasion, Lee would create special menus – complete with wine and cheese courses – whether for one of their all-night dinner parties (it wasn't unusual for guests of the Brilleauxs to stumble down the front steps of The

Proceeds just as the milkman was approaching) or just for when Shirley was coming home from Southend Hospital, where she now worked as a nurse. Many a time Shirley would return for lunch to be greeted by a menu tacked to the front door, ornately decorated and proclaiming the goodies Lee had been preparing for them: rack of lamb, pears in red wine, *gougères*, jugged hare, cassoulet …[53]In terms of touring, 1991 would be a slightly lighter year again – apart from anything else it had been a while since Brilleaux had been in the studio[54] and fans were hankering for new Feelgood material. Time was set aside for sessions during the spring, and Will Birch was, once more, primed to work with the group as producer. The next album would be, at Brilleaux's insistence, closer to the band's roots.

Before they could concentrate on recording, it appeared that the suitcases were coming out again. The good news: Dr Feelgood were going to Japan, where they were always treated like kings. The not so good news: they would be supporting the Wilko Johnson Band. Chris Fenwick had gingerly approached the subject with Lee, adding, with a wince, that they were also booked on the same flights. Rather than explode at the apparent indignity of the situation, Lee, according to Will Birch, slyly replied that he would upgrade to first class, 'get stuck into the champagne' and then turn to raise a glass to his former sparring partner down the aisle before saying, 'Oh, sorry, Wilko, you don't, do you?'

In the opinion of at least some of the collective, on both sides, this seemed 'an ideal time for them to just sort this out', said Kevin Morris, but the Japanese promoters, realising the potential for bust-ups a little too late, then set about keeping the two groups apart as best they could.

Brilleaux and Johnson *could* have connected with each other if they'd really tried, but they were both stubborn and if they weren't forced together, it just wasn't going to happen. Lee, interestingly enough, did slink into the wings to watch Wilko's set. 'Savvi [Salvatore Ramundo, Wilko's drummer] claimed he was standing there looking at me in a poignant manner,' said Wilko with a laugh of disbelief. 'I don't know.'

'Very interesting scenario, us and them on the same bill,' Lee later said, with characteristic understatement, during an interview with Johnnie Walker.' He was excellent,' he added. 'Very, very good, great band.' Maybe one of rock'n'roll's great feuds was starting to heal after all.

Phil Mitchell: 'Take Lee out of the line-up and that would finish things.'
Lee Brilleaux: 'No! Nobody's indispensable. There's ways around these things.'
Kevin Morris: We'll get Lee Remick in.
Lee: Yeah. Well, it'd be better for you, wouldn't it?
(interview for Central Television show *First Night*, 1991)

Dr Feelgood recorded new album *Primo* at Greenhouse Studios in London in 1990 and, as promised, this record would represent a return of sorts to their R&B roots, albeit with a clean, modern twist. It was the band's first studio album in four years, and anticipation amid Feelgood fans was high. 'We're not trying to do anything clever, it's just rock'n'roll,' insisted Lee, adding meaningfully, 'it's definitely nothing like *Classic.'*

Among the tracks chosen, there would be the jubilant Nick Lowe number 'Heart Of The City', a nod to Stiff Records, being as it was the B-side to the label's first release in 1976 (Lowe's 'So It Goes'). There would also be Mickey Jupp's 'Standing At The Crossroads Again', The Doors' 'Been Down So Long' ... 'Then there are a couple of songs we wrote with Will Birch,' said Lee. 'Down By The Jetty Blues' would be one of them, an 'anthem for our old home town of Canvey Island.'[55]

During the making of *Primo*, there would be some shuffling in the Feelgood ranks: Phil Mitchell would vacate the bass chair, and he would be replaced by the bassist and producer Dave Bronze after The Inmates' Ben Donnelly filled in. Bronze was already acquainted with Lee and Kevin – 'when you're a muso in Essex, you kind of know everybody anyway' – but a chance encounter while browsing the racks in Leigh on Sea record shop Fives would lead to Bronze's engagement, and he'd remain in the group for the next three years.

'Kevin came in and said, "Are you busy?" "Not terribly," remembers Bronze. 'They were in the middle of making *Primo*, there was an issue, and they needed a bass player. "Can you come and do it? Couple of days, won't take long." One evening after the sessions we went down to the local pub, and Lee said, "We're going to France at the weekend, fancy coming with us?" "Yeah, all right!" The following Friday a van came and picked me up, and suddenly I was in the Feelgoods! Nobody ever said, "Oh, by the way, do you want to join the band?"'

Primo would be released in 1991, and was promoted by the usual live dates and radio sessions, including one for LBC which features a stunning vocal performance of 'Down By The Jetty Blues'. Lee was using the studio's old-fashioned crystal bullet mic which gave his voice a cracked, distorted quality – he admitted he liked it so much he was tempted to walk off with it. Before the live session had started, the DJ, after interviewing Lee, said that the band's rehearsal had been the loudest they'd ever had on the station. 'Really?' said Lee, genuinely incredulous. 'I thought we were being quite quiet.'

'The new bass player, Dave Bronze, he's great,' said Lee. 'We're very lucky to have him. How long he'll stay I don't know, because someone else might steal him. But for the time being we've got him and I think he's enjoying himself. We do like to have fun, you see … there's more to life than just work.'

And with the 1980s firmly behind them, Brilleaux was pleased to note that the pendulum had swung back. The new decade had ushered in a resurgence of interest in 'real' music. From Nirvana to The Stone Roses to Iron Maiden, the guitar band was once again *de rigeur* and back in the charts (well, alongside Vanilla Ice and Right Said Fred), and Dr Feelgood themselves were 'on a bit of a crest at the minute. I'm thoroughly enjoying it.' As for their position as perennial purveyors of R&B, 'nobody else really does what we do,' said Lee. 'We're specialists.'

As content as Lee appeared in interviews, those close to him were aware that something was amiss. During sessions for *Primo*, Lee was noticeably under the weather. Normally robust, he was picking up every cold going and also becoming short-tempered over 'trivial matters when things weren't exactly slotting into place,' said Will. 'It was a character trait no one had experienced before.'

'He'd been unwell,' adds Kevin. 'We were playing in Paris, and our friend Joanne, who is a nurse, said to Lee she was concerned that he was very red in the face. She was concerned about his blood pressure. He said, "I'm all right." She said, "I'm sure he's not all right." But nothing more was said.' Lee had already commented on the increasing 'mental strain' he was experiencing, but, as was his way, he'd continued to push himself instead of taking time off when he needed it. Now, it appeared, his body was starting to complain as well.

Once the band were back in the UK, Lee dropped into the Grand Records office on Canvey for a chat. He was agitated, and, as Chris Fenwick recalled to Feelgood biographer Tony Moon, he 'waved the troublemaker flag' much to Chris's astonishment. Lee had always been the one who could take the lifestyle, the schedule, the drinking and, to a point, the travelling, but something had changed.

Sitting Lee down, Chris looked his friend in the eye and asked him if he wanted to stop. 'You seem a bit pissed off with it all,' said Chris. Lee simply replied, 'I like it more than I don't.'

Still, an agreement was made that Lee would work through 1992 before taking a sabbatical. 'He was going to have a year off, completely,' said Will Birch. 'Of course, ironically, that was when he got the illness. It was terrible.'

A page from the 'reduced' but still rather punishing Feelgood schedule (kindly provided by Dr Feelgood secretary Ann Adley).

Lee Brilleaux's Top Twelve Blues 'n' Rock 'n' Roll Sides.

TITLE	ARTIST
1) Road Runner	JNR. WALKER + THE ALLSTARS
2) Hoochie Coochie Man	MUDDY WATERS
3) Dust my Blues	ELMORE JAMES AND HIS BROOM DUSTERS
4) E.Z. Rider Blues	TAJ MAHAL
5) Blues With a Feeling	LITTLE WALTER
6) Evil	HOWLING WOLF
7) Don't You Just Know it	HUEY 'PIANO' SMITH & THE CLOWNS
8) Bony Maronie	LARRY WILLIAMS
9) Who Do You Love?	BO DIDDLEY
10) The Night Life	B.B. KING
11) I'll play the Blues for you	ALBERT KING
12) She Moves Me	JOHNNY GUITAR WATSON

It goes without saying that this is not an exhaustive selection: any of the above (with the possible exception of Road Runner) could be interchanged substituted by different songs by the same artists. There are also dreadful sad omissions from obvious artists like JOHN LEE HOOKER and CHUCK BERRY to less well-known such as SMOKY HOGG (or CLIFTON CHENIE) Anyway, the above dirty dozen would keep me satisfied in C.D. Heaven – for a while at least.

LB.
AUG. 93.

Lee's 'Top Twelve Blues 'n' Rock 'n' Roll Sides',
'Roadrunner' taking the top spot, naturally
(kindly provided by Ann Adley).

19. THE LONG GOODBYE

He promised Shirley he'd give up when he was forty. I thought, he never will ... But of course he did – because he had to. Strange really, isn't it?

Joan Collinson

In December 1991, artist Anthony Farrell began painting a portrait of Lee at his studio, just off Leigh Broadway. 'I got to know Lee in the Grand,' he explains. 'I thought I'd like to paint him but I never ask people directly. It's more embarrassing if they say no, so I go through third parties. Anyway he was all for it.' For two hours a week, Brilleaux would sit for Farrell, discuss art, talk about his children with great pride, and plan trips with Farrell to exhibitions to the Royal Academy (usually via the Colony Room in Soho).

'Lee was funny,' said Farrell. 'He had a very mild manner, but sometimes he'd get up to go to the loo, and you'd hear him trip over something – "FUCK!" – and then he'd be back, all courteous. He used to really make me laugh. This was when he was well, of course. If he couldn't make one of our appointments, I'd get these formal little notes offering alternative dates – and then you'd see him onstage, who is that guy? He was still OK then.' While Lee was ostensibly still 'OK', the portrait, which was completed in July 1992, displays the florid complexion Kevin Morris's friend had noted on the previous year in Paris. Whether Lee's reddening features were just caused by the broken blood vessels of a lifetime's drinking at this stage, it's hard to say.[56]

What was unusual, however, was the small and apparently insignificant lump on the side of Lee's neck which, for a while, he chose to ignore. A few months down the line, he was 'suffering from flu symptoms', said Kevin Morris. 'He just couldn't shift them.' After one show, he came off stage feeling decidedly ill, only to find he had a temperature of over a hundred.

Still, there were plans for yet another album. It was time to lay down a fistful of originals after the cover-heavy *Primo*; Steve Walwyn had written several new compositions, including the ebullient 'Tell Me No Lies' and 'Fool For You', while Dave Bronze was writing strong material with Kevin Morris.

Lee, in his sleeve notes for upcoming album *The Feelgood Factor*, explained in his customary way (elaborately formal but completely tongue-in-cheek) that they'd been discussing the new record while on the road – or rather 'on a ferry between mainland Scotland and the Orkney Islands. I seem to recall being relatively sober but cruelly tormented by a vicious hangover. The latter was significantly alleviated by a judicious intake of the barley waters prevalent in those parts, but more particularly by the collective enthusiasm for the project in hand; it's not often that the Muse and the Mammon sit well together.' And, during said discussions, it was stipulated that, as Lee would later write, 'the songs would be straightforward and they would be recorded straightforwardly and that they would be played and sung by members of Dr Feelgood without the unnecessary augmentations of a plethora of session musicians, backing singers and guest appearances.'

After rehearsing upstairs at the Grand, the band began recording in February 1993 at the residential Monnow Valley Studio in Wales. Lee and Kevin would cook and, of course, 'it was close to the Punch House, curiously enough', adds Steve. All the requisite comforts were taken care of.

The mystical 'Wolfman Calling', co-written by Bronze and Morris, stands out on the otherwise high-spirited *The Feelgood Factor* (co-produced by Bronze and Monnow's Dave Charles). Obviously the track paid tribute to Lee's lifelong passion for Howlin' Wolf, and musically gave a nod to 'Smokestack Lightning' as well as the riff in Pink Floyd's 'Money'. Under the circumstances that were soon to come to light, 'Wolfman Calling' would prove to be a strangely poignant song.

It was during sessions for *The Feelgood Factor* that Lee had become quietly concerned about his health. 'I had been feeling rather poorly,' he later explained, 'but I just put this down to encroaching years.' However, in addition to his general malaise, his lymph glands had become swollen and he was starting to lose weight. While the rest of the group worked, Lee drove to London to see a doctor.

'Everyone knew there was something up,' said Bronze. 'Lee was definitely in trouble, there was something not right. He was getting short-tempered, he was obviously in distress.'

The lump on Lee's neck was removed and biopsied, and the results revealed that Brilleaux was far from just 'under the weather'; he was suffering from Hodgkin's lymphoma, a cancer of the lymph glands which would, in this case, spread to the liver and spleen. 'He came back the next day,' said Kevin Morris. 'We went for a drink and he told me then that he had something quite serious, and that as soon as we'd finished in the studio, he'd be going into hospital.' When Lee then delivered the news to the band, they were in shock, but he stoically continued to work. Once the announcement was out of the way, he didn't speak of it again.

'When it was time to do the vocals we had to put him through the mill a bit,' said Dave Bronze. 'I remember thinking, how hard can I push this? To his credit, he was right there. He definitely wanted that record finished properly. When he gave us the news, it was devastating for all of us, but he carried on. He was a consummate professional, in his own lawless way.' Once sessions were complete, he was admitted to London's Middlesex Hospital the very next day for treatment. 'We just cancelled all of our work,' said Kevin.

The doctors informed Lee that he would be receiving very severe doses of chemotherapy, warning him that it could either kill the cancer, or it would kill him outright. He was kept in on reverse barrier; all visitors having to wear masks to eliminate any chance of him picking up an infection while his immune system was compromised. The ordeal brought with it, as Lee told Malcolm Wilkinson, 'all the usual unpleasant side effects of going bald, feeling violently sick etc. This was compounded by the necessity of the drugs being extremely strong, i.e. enough to kill a horse. I have lost nearly three stones in weight.'

Larry Wallis was among those who visited. On asking in advance whether he wanted anything brought in from the outside world, Larry was instructed to smuggle in 'a big cream cake, a newspaper, and a single malt. I said to him, "Are you going to be all right?" He said, "The jury's still out on that, old boy. Don't quite know yet."' Colin Crosby would also come to see Lee regularly, surreptitiously drawing the curtains around Lee's bed and unpacking takeaway boxes of curry from Brick Lane, plates and all, for them to enjoy together. Perhaps unsurprisingly, considering who we're talking about here, Brilleaux's love of a good meal seemed to have shown little signs of diminishing; the arrival of a curry and a beer was a rare and much needed sign of familiarity and normality during a time in which Lee was having to endure being in a very unfamiliar place, in every sense.

Kevin Morris would visit once a week, and before long 'had to steel myself to the fact that it was Lee, because it didn't look like Lee any more. He'd wasted away to the point that he just looked like ET. And he was heavily dosed on morphine, so we'd have quite surreal conversations.'

In the meantime, Chris Fenwick, his brother Chalkie, Dean Kennedy and their associates had set to work on a project that would give them a focus during this agonising time. Together they were redeveloping the old Oysterfleet building on Canvey where the old jug band used to play almost thirty years previously, and they were turning it into what would become the Dr Feelgood Music Bar. Once Lee was well enough to leave hospital, he was unable to work, but he could, and would, get involved with the venue himself, 'channelling some of my excess energies into [it]', he said. It was the ideal distraction for Lee, a man who was not accustomed to kicking back at the best of times. But now he had no choice.

'The chemotherapy kind of knocked me for six actually,' said Lee. 'It was pretty strenuous, and I'm sure many other people have suffered it and know what I'm talking about. Unfortunately, it's left me unfit to go back on the road, so I've been concentrating my efforts on the new album and this music bar, and just relaxing and generally quite enjoying being off the road, in one way.' He still insisted he and the band would be making a follow-up to *The Feelgood Factor* 'if the doctor allows'. But when it came to kissing the travelling side of his life goodbye, as he told Radio 2's Paul Jones, 'after twenty years of living out of the suitcase, it's quite nice to hang my hat up'. He was making light of the situation, of course. He wasn't hanging up his hat out of choice.

Back at The Proceeds after his treatment was complete, Lee rested up, surrounding himself with books and records to divert him. Andrew Lauder had put together a box of blues albums for him and had them sent to the house. 'I got a really nice letter back saying, "Well, that's the one upside of this bloody illness … I've got bags of time to play these records."'

Lee's strength began to return and he started to regain a little weight. 'He'd nearly died,' admits Kevin. 'But all through the summer, he was just taking walks and relaxing, and his hair grew back.'

'Obviously only time can tell of the success or otherwise of the treatment,' Lee wrote to Malcolm Wilkinson in a letter he kindly shared with me for this book. 'In the meantime, I am determined to enjoy my life, eat, drink, be merry, all that kind of stuff. Enough of that,' he concluded, before turning his attention to the old days. 'Like you, I have the fondest of memories of Canvey and the early days of the Feelgoods; I would go so far as to say our adventures comprised the happiest days of my life.'

On the subject of Wilko, Lee assured Malcolm that while the 'poison' which had grown in the band had been upsetting, he hoped that 'you remember me well enough to know I am not a vindictive or malicious man, and any beef I had with Wilko is long since gone'. As with everyone who receives a brush with death, Lee, just like Wilko would twenty years later, now viewed the past with a greater sense of perspective, although Lee would not be receiving the same miraculous reprieve that was granted to Wilko.[57]

In terms of the eating, drinking and being merry Lee had talked about, he would certainly hold good to his word. He travelled with Shirley to Barcelona, linking up with former Feelgood tour manager Jerome Martinez one last time, visited his favourite local restaurant Los Caracoles and, during the summer of 1993, he took the family to Disney World. 'Then we drove to Louisiana to see my grandparents,' said Nicholas Brilleaux, who 'surprises [himself]' with how much he recalls. 'I remember going to Spain and riding on his lap in the car – so I was driving the car. And one day he took me to London. It was just the two of us, and he took me to an exhibit at the Naval Museum in Greenwich. I was *obsessed* with pirates and ships, so he'd always take me out to see boats. He gave me a ship in a bottle which I still have.'

Kevin remembers Lee doing 'a little tour of his favourite spots', which included the Carved Angel in Dartmouth, the Sow and Pigs in Hertfordshire, not to mention Soho's Coach and Horses and the French

House, which is where Nick Lowe would see him for the last time. 'He looked like a Medieval English professor at some red-brick university, swathed in tweeds and finishing *The Times* crossword, which he put away very hurriedly when I arrived. He was pretty focused that day on things he wasn't focused on before. He was always very elegant, but towards the end there was this great knowingness.' Whether this was a 'knowingness' of a more mystical nature, one can only guess. Lee was not known to be a spiritually inclined man, although, as Kevin Morris recalls, Lee surprised him one day by divulging that he'd been going to Saint Clement's Church in Leigh for regular chats with the pastor there during recent months.

Of course, he could still be spotted at the Grand – thin but still immaculately dressed (his Soho tailor Mr Eddie having taken in his suits for free) – at the Billet and the Dr Feelgood Music Bar. There he would spend time with Sparko, among others, who noted the oddly circular nature of what was happening: the fact that they were now at the site where they used to busk outside as teenagers.

'We'd start talking about the jug band days,' said Sparko. 'I said, "We should do a jug band one night." He said, "We'd need to make an album." Often people in these situations start making all these plans. Nothing came of it, unfortunately.' Lee had also talked about writing a cookbook, a *Brilleaux Guide* (like his beloved Michelin guides) and even an autobiography. 'It was very sad he didn't have that time left,' said Shirley. Maybe he'd have gone on to be a successful restaurant critic (Pete Zear insists he'd have made a great James Whale-style late-night television presenter). There's no doubt Brilleaux packed a great deal of living into his forty-one years but there was still so much potential waiting to be fulfilled. As for whether Lee's lifestyle had played any part in bringing on his illness, 'that's hard to say. He was doing what he loved,' said Shirley. 'I can't picture him having done it any other way.'

'When I look at the movies I've got and see the state he was in by the end of the evening, why he had to throw so much into it, I don't know,' said Joan. 'I mean, he'd be dripping with perspiration. It was incredible – enough to kill anybody.

'It strikes me now whether things would have been different if we'd stayed in Ealing … but he had a lovely life, he went around the world, absolutely everywhere.' Well, almost everywhere. There was one place Lee had still hoped to visit. 'He really wanted to see South Africa,' adds Joan. 'But he couldn't because of apartheid, so he never did get back to see the land of his birth.'

Sparko, on first hearing of Lee's condition, had initially dropped round to The Proceeds to see how he was. Lee had gone for a stroll, but Shirley was in. 'We were sitting in the kitchen talking when we heard the front door open,' said Sparko. 'Suds called, "There's somebody here to see you," and the voice that came back … I was shocked. It sounded, well, it didn't sound like Lee any more. He was quite gruff normally, but his voice had gone a lot higher.'

Life was changing – for Lee, for his family, for Chris, who was more like a brother than a friend – but, as Shirley observed, the more the reality dawned that time was short, the more 'outrageous' he became, especially in terms of dressing up. It was something he had always loved, not least because it gave him an opportunity to indulge in a little make-believe and confuse people in turn. The way he dressed was also something he had control over, even when he felt he had little control over what was happening to his body.

'Oh yeah,' said Shirley. 'He went off the deep end with some of that stuff towards the end. After he got sick, he was like, "Fuck it, I'm getting a smoking jacket." He also had a smoking cap with a little tassel, velvet smoking slippers, a monocle … I think Chris was quite horrified, he didn't know what to make of it. When I offered those items up for display [for the Dr Feelgood exhibition in 2014], Chris was like, "Er, no, I don't think so. We'll just take the waistcoat and the harp, that'll be fine!"'

'I remember him dressing up as Dracula on Hallowe'en,' adds Nicholas. 'It was quite good, he did a really good job with his costume.' But for the children's birthdays Lee would be in touchingly smart dress, and as for Christmas, well, it was the smoking jacket all the way. Lee always went magnificently overboard at this time of year, as we know, but he was determined to give his family and the Fenwicks 'the best Christmas yet', even though it would be heartbreakingly bittersweet. Lee was frail – the outfit ('what outfit?' as he was known to deadpan) perhaps a deliberate distraction from his now dramatically changed appearance – and his prognosis indicated he would not be seeing another. This was not the only thing on Lee's mind. He was quietly bereft at the thought that he might never perform again, unless something was organised quickly.

Over the festive period, Lee took Chris aside and told him he wanted to play two shows at the Dr Feelgood Music Bar, on his home turf of Canvey and with the latest line-up of the Feelgoods. Chris was dubious, and asked him to consider waiting a while. 'You might feel a bit better,' he said. 'Yeah,' replied Lee. 'And I might feel a bit worse. I want to do the shows.'

DR. FEELGOOD MUSIC BAR

21 KNIGHTSWICK ROAD, CANVEY ISLAND, ESSEX.
TEL: 0268 682318

OCTOBER

FRI 1 ELVIS DaCOSTA AND HIS IMPOSTERS

SAT 2 THE BIG GROOVE
STAX - MOTOWN - BLUE BEAT

MON 4 MUSICIANS WORKSHOP
THE BIG CANVEY BLUES JAM

WED 6 THE ELECTRIC EXPERIENCE PLAYING HENDRIX AND FREE ECT

FRI 8 THE BIG GROOVE
SOUL - SKA - ATLANTIC

SAT 9 BLUE GRASS ACID ROCK

SUN 10 NORTHERN SOUL
DJ. CHAD FROM THE ZOMBIE CLUB LONDON

MON 11 MUSICIANS WORKSHOP

WED 13 THE BULLET BLUES BAND
PLUS ENGLAND V HOLLAND ON T.V.

FRI 15 THE BIG GROOVE
REGGAE - MOTOWN - JAZZ

SAT 16 THE INMATES INC DIRTY WATER + THE WAY

SUN 17 GUEST D-J THE DOCTOR FROM DOCTOR AND THE MEDICS

MON 18 MITCH AND THE ATOMS MUSICIANS WORKSHOP SPECIAL

WED 20 AGAINST THE GRAIN SOUTHERN ROCK IN TOP GEAR

FRI 22 THE BIG GROOVE
ANTHING THAT GROOVE'S

SAT 23 LOVE AFFAIR THE 60' HIT MAKERS OF EVERLASTING LOVE

SUN 24 THE SULTANS OF PING GUEST D-J. NAILLO'FLAERTY FROM

MON 25 MUSICIANS WORKSHOP

WED 27 CADILLAC 50' - 60' ROCK - ROLL

FRI 29 THE BIG GROOVE
SOUL - DUB - STAX

SAT 30 THE ABDABS ONE OF BRITAIN'S FINEST BLUES BAND

ALL ADMISSION "FREE"
OPEN ALL DAY FRIDAY and SATURDAY
A CHILDRENS ROOM SAT and SUN LUNCH TIME

ADMIT ONE	DR. FEELGOOD

Appearing at the
Dr. Feelgood Music Bar
Canvey Island

TUESDAY 25th JAN. '94
DOORS 7pm

No.

No.

£7.50

No.

Shirley Brilleaux

*Lee Brilleaux in his favourite place (other than
the Grand) – the kitchen in The Proceeds.*

The dates were booked – 24 and 25 January 1994 – and the band members were notified. 'That was astonishing,' said Dave Bronze. 'I get a call from Whitey one day. "Bronzey, can you meet me and Lee down at the Billet?" Now, Lee was very ill at this stage, and it showed. I went down there and he said, "I want to do a live album at the Feelgood Bar, and I want you to take care of the technical side of it." I said, "Are you sure?" "Yeah. I've thought about it." It was just an extraordinary commitment. A live Feelgood show takes a lot out of anybody, but when you're on your last legs, as it turns out he was …'

By New Year, Chris was still unsure. He was worried it would make Lee feel even worse, but Lee refused to cancel. He was determined, even if his loved ones were perturbed. 'He wanted so badly to do it,' said Shirley.

And so, on a freezing night on Canvey Island, the faithful walked into the Feelgood Bar to witness what would turn out to be the first of two final Lee Brilleaux performances. The ever loyal Chris had arranged a minder – 'cousin Gary' – who would assist Lee with getting on and off the stage. Chris: 'I told Gary to stand by his side and if anyone starts coming on, get rid of them. Don't wear gloves, be quick because I don't want him cornered. I was trying to protect him.'

In support there would be, on one night Barrie Masters from Eddie and the Hot Rods, and on the other, Bill Hurley from the Inmates. 'They did a little opening slot,' explained Kevin, 'and if Lee couldn't carry on, they'd come and jam a few songs and take it to the end. He was fine though, he hung in there. He was very brave.'

Among the songs Lee had chosen to perform were 'Heart Of The City', 'Roadrunner' (surprisingly, a song the band had never played before), 'Tanqueray' (a little nod to his great love of gin), 'Down At The Doctors' (Lee demands sixteen bars of piano – and gets it this time) and the swampy 'Wolfman Calling'. Lee and the band gave a spine-tingling performance of this song, which now took on a deeper meaning – perhaps the Wolf himself was now calling Brilleaux away for some harp battles on another plane.

'I really don't know how he managed to sing like that,' said Sparko. However, while he'd had to remain seated throughout the shows, Lee gave a powerful, resonant vocal performance that belied his physical fragility. He had always referred to 'the spark' that would give him a transfiguring strength, light him up and lift him out of whatever mood he might have been in before stepping onto the stage, as if there was a kind of magic that poured through him, radiating from somewhere deep within and transmitting through every pore. Listening to the recordings of Brilleaux's last ever shows, the 'spark' has clearly not let him down. That and 'sheer will', said Shirley.

'He should never have done those shows really, but still,' mused Lee's mother Joan. 'He was so pleased he did it. Little Nick came home and said, "I was really proud of my daddy."'

Bronze had been recording the shows and, after he and Morris went through the tapes to select the best tracks, set about mixing what would become *Down At The Doctors* – the title a wry joke, and one that only Brilleaux could really make. The artwork was a play on the cover of *Sneakin' Suspicion*: there was Lee, spivvily sparking up a cigarette under his sheepskin once more, looking startlingly elderly but still with a naughty twinkle in his eye, his band behind him, looking on. 'He'd come back to life quite amazingly, but he still looked very different,' said Kevin. 'The picture on the sleeve was the only one that could be used.'

Thus Lee was granted his wish of one more album after *The Feelgood Factor*. *Down At The Doctors* came out shortly after Lee had passed away, 'but he had heard it and he'd seen the artwork,' said Kevin. His desire to perform again after so many months away from his beloved stage was also fulfilled, but it came at a price and he suffered a decline immediately afterwards, becoming 'depressed,' said Shirley.

'He knew he had a poor prognosis, but I don't think he realised how short his remaining time was. In the weeks after the shows, he was very low and getting weaker. In retrospect, it took a lot out of him to do that, and I don't know if having done it, he suddenly realised he wouldn't be doing it again.'

'He got ill again,' said Kevin. 'He got a cold, just felt rough. Nothing in particular, but he knew it was the same thing coming back. I went round there one day for a cup of tea and he said, "They've said I've got to go back into hospital for chemo. But I don't want to." I said, "Well, don't then." He just couldn't face another session.'

Lee would, instead, be cared for by the Southend Community Extended Nursing Team, who offered hospice care in his own home, and many of his friends stayed in the house to support the family as Lee started slipping away. But even towards the very end, there were still glimpses of the real Lee as he rambled and murmured, morphined up to the hilt. Colin 'The Socialist' Crosby remembers that 'when he was dying, he suddenly said, "What's for dinner?! I haven't seen the menu yet!"'

Lee Brilleaux died on 7 April 1994 at his home in Hillside Crescent, with Shirley by his side and his family around him. 'You never get over it,' said Joan Collinson. 'He was the only child I'd got. I'm so glad [Arthur] died before Lee did. He would have been absolutely heartbroken. But if there's one thing I console myself with about his early death, he really did have a magical life.'

Lee's funeral would take place on 15 April 1994 at Saint Clement's Church in Leigh on Sea. Emotions were running very high that day – Chris Fenwick had written a heartfelt eulogy to his closest friend, his then wife Beverley reading it at the ceremony as Chris was too grief-stricken to deliver it himself, and Wilko Johnson, seated at the back of the church with his (now late) wife Irene and pianist John Denton, was 'visibly upset', as Kevin Morris recalls. During the service some well chosen pieces of music were played, including Boccherini's Guitar Concerto ('He was amused by the castanets,' explains Kevin, 'he always chuckled when they came in') and 'Roadrunner' by Junior Walker and the All Stars. It was at this point that Wilko, according to John Denton, 'dissolved into tears. He was inconsolable. Up until that point he'd just been staring ahead. It was difficult. He was never very touchy-feely, I didn't know whether to hug him – fortunately Irene was there to do that. I think he just realised all those years had been wasted for this nonsense feud.'

Sadly, Lee had hoped to see Wilko before he died, but Wilko was in conflict about going over to see him. He too wanted to finally put the past behind them but 'we'd not seen each other for years ... and I really wanted one of them to come and get me and take me there to see him, I didn't want to just go round. So I never did see him.'

'It was ridiculous, really,' said Malcolm. 'Because Lee and Wilko were great friends and had so much in common, that you would have thought that that would overcome any other problems. It was so final, he should have done it. I should have tried harder to get him to go because I knew he would regret it. But there we are, I'm not good at persuading someone as strong-willed as Wilko.'

After the service, and a ceremony at Southend Crematorium for close family, the funeral party migrated to Canvey Island for the wake at the Feelgood Bar. 'I'd never been there before,' said Wilko. 'It was a really nice club and there were some great pictures of Lee and all of us.' Musicians took to the stage, raised their pints and played songs in honour of the man they were all there to celebrate. Chris Fenwick approached Wilko and asked if he'd like to get up and play a number. 'I got up and I realised it was me, Sparko and Figure [on the stage]. We played "Back In The Night", and, of course, there was an empty space in the middle. Fucking hell, it was a fantastic feeling, not a sad feeling. Lee's absence really just showed how strong his presence had been.'

And that presence was still making itself felt, and assertively too. His final resting place certainly appeared to have been decided by the man himself, according to Shirley. 'When Lee had passed away, I was so distraught by the whole thing. He'd been cremated and I could not – and I tried – I could not bring myself to go and pick up his remains. I was traumatised by the entire experience, and it freaked me out … the thought of having his ashes, I couldn't get my head around it. Thankfully Dave Bronze and [his partner] Julie went to get them for me. But I didn't know what I was going to do with them.

'Shortly before I left for the States, I was clearing the house, still living there – that alone was a horrible experience. I was cleaning out the cupboard under the stairs where there were boxes of Lee's old papers, blues magazines, bits and pieces – frankly I didn't even realise most of that stuff was there. I was going through it and I found a map, much like the "Map of the World", with "X marks the spot" on this little island in the Estuary between Canvey and Benfleet where he used to play as a kid. I was like, "That's where his ashes need to be scattered." It was like Lee was saying, "Here! This is where I want it, please, right here." It was like an epiphany.

'Our friends Nick and Erica Finegan had helped me enormously, and Nick was working on the lifeboats out of Southend at that time. I said to Nick, "Would it be possible for you to take the ashes out and scatter them over the little area in this map?" He was supposed to do that the day before we left for the US. But the tide was not where it needed to be. He said, "I'm going to have to do it after you've gone." I couldn't control the tides and I was in no condition to even try and think my way around that.

'Nick did it and he called me afterwards. He said, "And I threw a pack of Rothmans and a harp into the water." Apparently he got a call to rescue someone so it was cut short. But I did feel like that was where Lee needed to be.'

Chris Fenwick

For a man that appeared to have no great show business ambition, Lee was truly amazing at what he did. I guess he didn't have to have ambition, because his show performance was so natural to him that it gave him the long career that he had. Our professional partnership lasted for over twenty-five years, until Lee died. The personal relationship between us was always good, and we had great trust in one another. Lee actually had a very cool head through all the madness, and kept intact a very good lawyer's brain.

While the early years of Dr Feelgood were very exciting and a great rollercoaster ride – and quite frankly a lot of the time passed in a completely drunken and stoned haze – our focus was always on doing our best at making each gig as good as possible. Lee's persona on stage was something that slowly developed over the years, and his command over his musicians and the audience was truly magic. He had the ability to wind an audience up within the first few numbers, then take things down to a cruise position, and then ram it home at the end, getting the whole building into a complete rock'n'roll frenzy. It wasn't unusual to do three or four encores every night. In fact, as management, it was always difficult to shut the show down.

People often ask me what is my favourite period as manager of Dr Feelgood. After a lot of thought, I've decided it was the 1980s, when Lee became a man on the stage as opposed to being a boy. He came out of the earlier rock'n'roll frenzy, and developed into an experienced, well-crafted, sincere performer, who would have audiences eating out of his hand at every show.

Lee always had time for fans. He was truly loved and respected worldwide.

The first Lee Brilleaux memorial concert would take place at the Feelgood Bar on what would have been Lee's forty-second birthday, just one month after his passing, and the event would become an annual tradition for the next two decades, attracting fans from all over the world and artists who knew and loved Lee, playing for charity (initially SCENT and then the Fairhavens cancer charity) and paying tribute. Twenty years after Lee Brilleaux moved on, this comparatively underrated figure remains respected, practically worshipped by some, and certainly still looked to as a barometer of *savoir-faire*.

At the time of writing, there's a campaign to rename Southend Airport 'Lee Brilleaux Airport', as with Liverpool's John Lennon Airport, while the artist Scott King has proposed a plan for a majestic 300ft golden statue of Brilleaux to stand by the Kursaal, like the Colossus of Southend. The suggested height may have been tongue in cheek, but it's indicative of how highly Brilleaux is regarded. The legendarily modest Lee would surely have been touched and embarrassed in turn.

But aside from the charisma and charm, the voice and the stance, the style, the wanderlust and the wisdom, almost everything Lee did was shot through with a profound love of people; he was fascinated by them, amused by them, he felt his *raison d'être* was to entertain them and he saw the value and importance of being able to give them a good time. 'People of all ages, all different types, bourgeois, working class … as far as we're concerned that's all bollocks, people are people,' said Lee. 'And there's nothing better than people. The rest don't mean a thing.'

Lee Brilleaux. Old soul. Bright spark. And quite the gentleman, as it happens.

A giant Lee Brilleaux towers over Southend like an Estuarine Colossus, the Kursaal to his right. ('The Triumph of De-Regeneration – Lee Brilleaux 1952–1994', Scott King, 2012. Courtesy Herald St, London/Focal Point Gallery, Southend)

FINAL WORDS

Shirley Brilleaux
He was a really hard act to follow and I miss him very much.

Nicholas Brilleaux
I'm really lucky that there are so many fans and there's so much stuff out there. It seems like every few months or a couple of times a year there's a new clip of my dad that I'd never seen. The fact that I lost him when I was six years old, and I still get to experience him through these random videos or just meeting people, it's wonderful. It's certainly a blessing.

Dean Kennedy
When Lee died, to me, Dr Feelgood died. It took me ten years to get over it. I still haven't really got over losing Lee.

Lew Lewis
Mostly I remember Lee as a good-times mate. He found – and had – a good time, and he took his friends there too.

Big Figure
His heart and soul was in black blues and rhythm and blues music, and I think he would like to be remembered for being able to further the cause of rhythm and blues and rock'n'roll.

Sid Griffin
Towards the end, Lee had been told by his doctor he was allowed one pint of Guinness per night, so Lee would have a pint of Guinness and nurse it. It was sad watching the great man hold the same pint for two hours … he couldn't have a cigarette either. I was whining, 'I don't know why I do this, nothing's really going to happen.' This guy tapped me on the shoulder and pulled me around. It was Lee, and he was literally in my face. He said, and I mean loudly, 'You don't stop doing what you're doing, you don't complain about what you're doing, you have talent, you have good songs and the fact you're not making a million dollars is just too bad. But you don't quit playing music.' People are looking round. 'That's the life you've chosen.' He really gave me a lecture for about a minute and a half. By the

end of it, I had a lump in my throat. This skinny Ichabod Crane figure who'd been such a vibrant young man, prodding my shoulder as he spoke. He wasn't just saying it to be a nice guy.

I wished I'd thanked him for that moment and that I'd told him how much I admired and just loved him. But I didn't think like that then. He gave me the greatest speech ever and I've never forgotten it. When he died, he left me forty harmonicas. I pull them out and look at them the way a small boy fondles his marble collection.

On the Continuation of Dr Feelgood

'With Brilleaux, his band died as well,' came the official statement. 'Dr Feelgood will be disbanded.' Kevin Morris had also said, in an interview with Radio 1 shortly after Lee's death, that that was the end of the band, but of course, this would not be the case. Lee had, on more than one occasion, insisted to the rest of the group that 'no one is indispensable', and when he was in hospital, he repeated the mantra. 'He said, "You guys can't stop just because of me. You guys have got families, you've got to carry on,"' remembers Dave Bronze. ' The impact of that didn't really make sense at the time. My remark at the time was that it would be like the Rolling Stones carrying on without Mick Jagger. It wouldn't work. But it did work, they're still working, that's great.

'I find it strange sometimes that we carried on without Lee,' adds Kevin. 'I didn't think we'd be able to. Quite a few people in the business had said it was something that should be considered, plus some ex-members were asking Chris what was going to happen to the name. Chris said to me, "If anyone's going to do anything with it, it's got to be the guys who were with Lee at the end." So I said, "All right, well, we'll try it out."' The band reformed a year after Lee's death with Kevin Morris, Steve Walwyn, Phil Mitchell and Pete Gage on vocals. Gage stepped down in 1999, replaced by Robert Kane. 'And here we still are.'

Lee Brilleaux onstage in France, early 1990s.

Patrick Higgins

ACKNOWLEDGEMENTS

The author extends love and thanks to the following individuals: Dylan Howe, Sean and Jo Street for their incredible support and encouragement. Alison Rae and Polygon Books for taking on this project with such genuine enthusiasm. Everyone I spoke to for their faith, encouragement and fascinating contributions: very special thanks to the wonderful Shirley Brilleaux, Kelly Brilleaux, Nicholas Brilleaux – this book is for you. Wilko Johnson for being my first interview for this project and for being so generous with archive material, Chris Fenwick, John B Sparkes, John 'Big Figure' Martin, Phil 'Harry' Ashcroft (for also being extremely generous with archive material), Dean Kennedy, Larry Wallis, Steve Walwyn, Ann Adley, Geoff Shaw, Fred Barker, Kevin Morris, Dave Bronze, Gordon Russell, Jools Holland, Lew Lewis, Will Birch, John Denton, Hugh Cumberland, David Marx, Anthony Farrell, Jerome Martinez, Malcolm Wilkinson, Maggie Newman (RIP), Dave Robinson, Sid Griffin, Louder Than Words, Metal Culture, Steph Stevenson, Colette Bailey, Sean McLoughlin, Michaela Freeman and Idea13, Allan Jones, Every Record Tells A Story, Scott King, Richard Balls, Neil Biscoe, Pete Zear, Stephen Foster, Tim Hinkley, Patrick Higgins, Adrian Boot, Rob Beddington and Sarah Bates, Jo Kendall and Ed Mitchell at *The Blues Magazine*, Colin Crosby, Simon Benham and all at *Unbound* who helped effect a smooth transition, Richard England at Cadiz Music and Caroline Richards for allowing me to see Joan Collinson's wonderful outtakes from *Oil City Confidential*. I would also like to thank Ruth Hazel and Focal Point Gallery, Jemma Street, Paul Lagden, Jonathan Maitland, Nick Owen, Lorraine Warren, Christopher Somerville, Steven Hastings, Daryl Easlea, Peter Knock, Bernard Fassone, Ian and Zoe Sanders, Al Johnson, Christoffer Frances, Gabi Schwanke, Billy Reeves, BBC London, BBC Essex, Steve Tolton, Al Reid, David Farren, Paul Forrester, Alan Joseph, David Bullock, Angela Smith, Keith Levene, Kathy Di Tondo, Nigel Roberts, Lee Watkins, Dave Burke, Zoe Randall, Clare Kimber, Mark Lancaster, Gavin Martin, Wayne Williams, Dave Collins, Ian Pile, Mark Beasley, Kelly Buckley, *Southend Echo*, Liz Vater, Graham Burnett, Pete Mann, everyone who helped, guided, connected or spread the word, and everyone who supported the project when it was originally to be published via Unbound. I am unable to access the names of those who pledged but please know your enthusiasm and support is much appreciated. You proved there was a real and actually quite overwhelming demand for a book about Lee Brilleaux. You are rock'n'roll gentlemen and 'goddesses', all.

BIBLIOGRAPHY AND SECONDARY SOURCE MATERIAL

Film
Oil City Confidential, directed by Julien Temple (Cadiz Music)

Books
Down by the Jetty, Tony Moon (Grand Records)
From Roxette to Ramona: Dr Feelgood and Wilko Johnson on Record,
   Roland Jost, Teppo Nättilä and Rauno Mäkinen
No Sleep till Canvey Island, Will Birch (Virgin Books)
Wilko Johnson: Looking Back at Me, Wilko Johnson and Zoë Howe
   (Cadiz Music)
Apathy for the Devil, Nick Kent (Da Capo Press)
Be Stiff: The Stiff Records Story, Richard Balls (Soundcheck Books)

Articles
'Dr Feelgood at Dingwalls', live review by Mick Farren, *New Musical Express*,
   December 1974
'The Breeding of Dr Feelgood', essay by Hugo Williams
'Dr Feelgood, Kokomo, Chilli Willi: eat your heart out, Arthur Howes', Nick
   Kent, *New Musical Express*, 18 January 1975
'Oil City meets the Riviera – and wins', Tony Tyler, *New Musical Express*,
   23 August 1975
'The almost collected thoughts of Dr Feelgood', interview with Jonh Ingham,
   Sounds, 18 October 1975
'Everyday life in rural California', Cal Worthington for *ZigZag*, July 1976
'Brilleaux Agonistes', Neil Spencer, *New Musical Express*, 14 June 1975
'Dr Lee', interview with Lee Brilleaux, *Rock & Folk* magazine, August 1975
'Dr. Feelgood: Hammersmith Odeon, London', review by Charles Shaar
   Murray, *New Musical Express*, 15 November 1975
'Lee Brilleaux', interview, *Rock & Folk* magazine, 1976
'The goods on the Feelgoods: did Wilko fall or was he pushed?',
   Nick Kent, *New Musical Express*, 4 June 1977
'A day in the life of a bunch of Stiffs', Allan Jones, *Melody Maker*,
   6 August 1977
'Life with too much salt on your chips', Roy Carr, *New Musical Express*
Lee Brilleaux interview with Radio Forth, with thanks to Chris Frances

Lee Brilleaux interview with Radio Mafia, with thanks to Chris Frances

Lee Brilleaux interview with Radio Bellevue, Lyon, with thanks to
Chris Frances

Lee Brilleaux interview with Paul Jones, BBC Radio 2, featured on *Looking
Back* compilation box set

Lee Brilleaux interview with Johnnie Walker, BBC Radio 2

Lee Brilleaux interview with Stephen Foster, BBC Radio Suffolk, featured on
Looking Back compilation box set

'Private Practice', Allan Jones, *Melody Maker*, June 1978

'Friday Night MacFever', Allan Jones, *Melody Maker*, October 1978

'MUSIC OOR', Martijn Stoffer, 1979

'Jukebox', Bruno Librati, 1980 (sourced from DrFeelgood.Fr)

'New Feelgoods know the ropes', Don Snowden, *LA Times*, December 1980

David Hepworth interview, *Smash Hits*, 21 February 1980

'Up Scheitzstrasse with Dr Feelgood', Paul Du Noyer, *New Musical Express*,
1981

Lee Brilleaux interview, *South Bank Show*, 1981 (exact date unknown)

Lee Brilleaux interview, Rock's Backpages, Ian Ravendale, 1981

'Meanwhile, back at the Feelgoods', *Charles Shaar Murray,* New Musical
Express, 2 January 1982

'An officer and a gentleman', Allan Jones, *Melody Maker*, 15 September 1984

'Dr Feelgood and the Canvey Delta', Christopher Somerville

Lee Brilleaux interview, *Blues Bag Fanzine* no. 3, March 1990

Lee Brilleaux interview, *Rock Spirit*, 1991, sourced from Dr Feelgood France

Ian Fawkes, *Feelin' Good*, newsletters 5 (October 1996) and 12 (July 1998)

'Mecca!', Will Birch, *Mojo*, November 1993

'An officer and a gentleman: Will Birch remembers Lee Brilleaux', *Uncut*,
1994

'Joan's Feelgood memories of her son Lee', Joan Collinson interview, *Thurrock
Gazette*, 22 November 2010

'*Down By The Jetty* 40th anniversary feature', Zoë Howe, *The Blues Magazine*

rocksbackpages.com

drfeelgood.org

drfeelgood.fr

drfeelgood.de (with thanks to Gabi Schwanke)

NOTES

Prologue

1. Ealing was a great place for rhythm and blues – if he could just have hung on for a few more years, he'd have been old enough to take advantage of the Ealing Club (a haunt of The Who and The Rolling Stones) and the licentious blues hotspot that was Eel Pie Island. But this would not be the Island to feature in Brilleaux's story. His destiny lay at the other end of the Thames.

Chapter 1

2. Also attended by future pub rock cohort Brinsley Schwarz's Ian Gomm.

3. The use of clothes as a tool, as costume, armour, or just to create an effect, would serve him throughout his life. He would choose the character he wanted to inhabit onstage and 'move into it … adopt a stance', as he put it. One reason he loved wearing suits as an adult in everyday life was because he knew that, as his widow Shirley recalls him explaining, 'People want to be rude but they think: better not, he's wearing a suit.'

4. Lee's schoolboy ne'er-do-well-ism was a little more sophisticated. On a new school noticeboard in the playground, Lee wrote 'PHALLUS' in large letters, much to the amusement of his cohorts. 'This uptight little teacher came over,' remembers Phil. 'He caught him, but Lee was denying it. The teacher said, "Do you do geography or biology?" We said, "Geography." His line was that we couldn't know this word unless we did biology. Still, we were given overalls and had to paint this noticeboard.' The other side of Lee's character, however, displayed an unusual level of empathy. 'I remember him saying he found these balls of fluff under his mum's bed,' says Phil. 'He said, "I felt sorry for them, so I put them in a little box." There was a real contrast between this sensitive soul who felt sorry for the fluff under the bed, and this sarcastic wild man who could cut people dead with his words.'

Chapter 2

5. Lee was the only youngster amid a close-knit clutch of adults, and he was spared little detail in subjects that were adult in nature; on asking his mother about his only-child status, Joan explained to Lee that she had had a miscarriage, and what that had entailed. 'She told him in quite a lot of detail for a teenage son,' remembers Phil. 'She didn't pull any punches.'

6. Chris used the name 'Fenwick' as there was already a Chris White on Equity's books.

7.	As Lee put it: 'Group transport's very important. Gives you an image when you turn up at a gig straight away, don't it? Before you play a note.' And no one can deny the Pigboy Charlie ambulance will have made an impression.

Chapter 3

8.	Putting one in mind of the Howlin' Wolf song 'Commit A Crime'.

9.	Lee's driving skills came in handy for Wilko, who didn't drive and still doesn't to this day. Wilko and Lee spent a lot of time 'driving around in shades posing' and trying to pick up girls in Lee's Ford Consul. Lee would also give Wilko, and others, lifts when required, although he had to put the kibosh on one situation that he felt was getting 'a bit fucking Laurentian' (à la DH 'fucking' Lawrence, needless to say); Lee would obligingly drive Wilko to meet a fellow schoolteacher with whom he was having a liaison, but one afternoon, as they approached the water tower in Benfleet where one of these clandestine meetings was to occur, a thunderstorm broke overhead, presenting something of a pathetic fallacy. Wilko was thrilled, but this was the last straw for Lee, who'd already gritted his teeth on one too many car journeys as Wilko expounded poetically upon his illicit romance in the passenger seat. 'Jolly good,' muses Wilko. 'But yeah, Lee thought it was a bit too Laurentian. And he was exactly right!'

10.	Interestingly enough, Lee's daughter Kelly Brilleaux is herself a lawyer, so there was obviously some legally inclined Collinson DNA that carried into the subsequent generation.

11.	Mickey Jupp, known by many as 'the white Chuck Berry', was already a local star, having fronted 1960s Southend group The Orioles and Legend. No home should be without Legend's so-called *Red Boot* album.

12.	This happened to the Feelgoods quite a lot, although there is also a school of thought that Heinz was afraid of losing his job at the newspaper if he was seen to be moonlighting. Either way, his behaviour was rather furtive whenever they came round to rehearse or pick him up in the van.

13.	Also on the bill was Detroit proto-punk band MC5 – seeing MC5 was a life-changing experience for Wilko, and in homage he wanted to perform subsequent gigs with gold face paint, Wayne Kramer style, with the rest of the group wearing silver make-up. Lee and Sparko surprisingly played ball for a bit, but Figure flatly refused and the idea was soon abandoned.

Chapter 4

14.	Mojo being a powerful hoodoo spell. Very New Orleans, 'eaux yes indeed.

Chapter 5

15.	Lawnmowers present something of a theme here when it comes to entertaining the Feelgoods.

Chapter 6

16. During the interview with Joan Collinson for *Oil City Confidential*, the producer George Hencken made the interesting point that a skill for writing song lyrics often lies in being able to think in 'slogans' rather than the free prose style that came naturally to Lee.

17. Lee listened to a lot of reggae, and especially loved the soulful voice of Toots Hibbert. 'Once you've listened to [reggae],' he said to skankin' Neil Spencer (preaching to the converted), 'your ideas about rhythm are never going to be the same.'

18. Recorded live at Dingwalls, Camden Lock, recorded on the Pye Mobile Recording Unit, 8 July 1974. This track also features members of Brinsley Schwarz, with whom the Feelgoods performed on a number of occasions.

19. Wilko Johnson explains the lack of a photographer credit on *Down By The Jetty*: 'We agreed what he would get for it. Later, he decided he wanted ten times as much. Chris said, "Have your fucking money, but your name ain't going on that sleeve."'

Chapter 7

20. *Down By The Jetty* was 'not off the turntable' during a certain New York loft party later that year, attended by members of Blondie, Television, the Ramones and the New York Dolls. 'This isn't folklore,' said Chris Fenwick. 'It definitely went down, and they were all driving into their careers at that point.'

21. Managed by the infamous Jake Riviera, who had conceived the idea for the tour in conjunction with Chris Fenwick, and would swiftly be employed as the Feelgoods' tour manager.

22. Strummer had his own pub rock band, The 101ers, and he, like many future new wave 'pioneers' would be taking plenty of notes from the likes of Dr Feelgood, the Hot Rods, and Kilburn and the High Roads. Another figure who managed to amalgamate both Lee Brilleaux and Wilko Johnson into his persona is Paul Weller; it certainly worked for him.

23. Chris Salewicz was present at the Led Zeppelin party and observed that 'they seemed as big as Led Zeppelin. Generally with "the entertainment", people don't pay much attention, but people were standing, rapt, just watching them.' Word was that this appearance was something of a showcase for Atlantic boss Ahmet Ertegün to check out the Feelgoods and give them their chance in the US, but they would move forward with CBS instead.

24. Even during the Keith Morris photo shoot for the *Malpractice* album artwork, which included shots of the group outside various local Canvey Island high street establishments, (such as Discount Furnishings, 191 High

Street, and Phil Moss's barber shop on Maurice Road, as featured on the cover), the towering Lee, in his mirror shades and white suit, allowed for one costume change before cutting proceedings short because he had 'some business to attend to'.

Chapter 8

25. One could draw a connection with Ealing Studios film *The Man in the White Suit*; the titular outfit, conversely, never becoming dirty at all.

Chapter 9

26. The reason behind this sobriquet has been subject to some mythologising, but the real story is that Shirley used to work at the Dog and Suds diner in her hometown of Hammond, Louisiana, serving hotdogs and foaming tankards of root beer. 'I was nicknamed Suds, and it stuck. Everybody called me Suds. I called me Suds.'

Chapter 10

27. Lee Brilleaux, come 1977, would be heard dismissing The Clash as 'a bleedin' skiffle group on speed', although to be fair, one could say that wasn't something that had particularly held back the Feelgoods, who would often refer to themselves as 'skifflers', and they were no slouches when it came to amphetamine consumption either. Lee wasn't threatened by punk; far from it – he was interested in it, and was also quietly proud of his own position as one of the movement's galvanising forefathers. '[Dr Feelgood] played a large part, or was perceived to have done, which is almost the same thing,' Lee would tell Paul Jones. However, he felt punk 'broke its promises, like any revolution' and ran out of energy all too quickly.

28. Joan Collinson once remarked that Lee 'wanted to bring New Orleans to Canvey', so it's neatly serendipitous that he would indeed bring New Orleans native Shirley Alford to Oil City, even if she wasn't too keen on the place at first.

29. The following story nicely illustrates Lee's kindness towards fans. Lee was always more than happy to speak to Feelgood fanatics, but before shows, if he wanted a bit of peace, Lee would go to the pub on the third block along from the venue – that way the band could always find him, but he was less likely to be mobbed. However, the pub on the third block along could sometimes be quite a long way away. One evening Lee realised he was a little further from the gig than he'd initially intended, and time was moving on. Due to an absence of cabs, Lee decided to catch a bus – but it was a bus filled with excited Feelgood fans on their way to the show. Rather than spending the journey hiding behind his paper, he chatted to them all and even paid their fares.

Chapter 11

30. From the poem 'Maud Muller' by John Greenleaf Whittier.

31. 'Sneakin' Suspicion', 'Paradise', 'Time And The Devil', 'All My Love' and 'Walking On The Edge'. Covers selected for the record were 'Lights Out' (written by Seth David and Mac 'Dr John' Rebennack), Willie Dixon's 'You'll Be Mine', 'Nothin' Shakin' But The Leaves On The Trees', the menacing 'Hey Mama, Keep Your Big Mouth Shut' and the contentious 'Lucky Seven' by Lew Lewis.

Chapter 12

32. Wilko explains that things could have been different. 'This guy I knew said, "I've been talking to Lee Brilleaux." This was about a year after I'd gone. He's going, "He'd have you back in that band. I've fixed up a meeting with you and Lee in the Ship [in Soho] tomorrow." I was thinking, wow, yeah! It was close enough to do it and I knew what I'd got wasn't as good as that. But, well, I'd just met someone, I spent the night with her and I never went to the meeting. We never did meet again.' Even in the late 1980s, Lee, on being asked as to whether he had ever seen Wilko again (living, as they did, less than a mile from each other), said, '[I] hardly clap eyes on the man. I sometimes bump into his missus in Southend, that's the closest we get.'

33. 'Jonesy' was definitely a Feelgood kind of guy: when he wrote to *Melody Maker* seeking employment, his letter of application concluded: '*Melody Maker* needs a bullet up its arse. I'm the gun – pull the trigger.' And so they did, and it would be far less painful than it sounds.

34. Shirley took some bar work at Bardot's, a pivotal Canvey landmark on the roadmap of Dr Feelgood's trajectory. Also known for its fights. 'Buckets of claret', in Lee's words, were often spilt there in the name of a top night out.

35. 'Basher' was a nickname given to Lowe by the Feelgoods in tribute to his penchant for 'bashing things out' in the studio.

36. And talking of conservatism, just a few short years down the line – despite having been brought up in a staunch Labour household – Lee would be voting Tory, hailing Margaret Thatcher as 'the best thing since sliced bread', said Shirley, who did not share his political stance to say the least. 'I found that shocking. I could never figure it out.' Maybe it was connected to Lee's view of Dr Feelgood as a 'business'. As we know, there's no business like show business. Two parts business to one part show.

Chapter 13

37. On the subject of threads, the Brilleaux stage look had expanded considerably, so to speak, from the white suit/white jacket look. Lee had jackets made for him by a seamstress in Westcliff-on-Sea, one of which

boasted a loud palm-tree pattern. On the other hand, the white suit, Feelgood fans will be dismayed to learn, is no more. It would be disposed of when, Shirley Brilleaux informs, 'it became too disgusting to hang on to'.

38. Cockney rhyming slang for Yanks, as I'm sure many of you already know.

39. Mandrax, quaaludes, sedatives. You get the picture.

40. If Steve's Cabs weren't available, a slurred call would be received by the chirpy operators at Trio. After a few close shaves with the police on Canvey, it was prudent not to drive oneself home, even if it was just around the corner. Shirley remembers an evening when the police spotted Chris, Lee and Shirley weaving their way back to Rainbow Road in Chris's car. Lee rushed Chris inside and immediately started pouring drinks in him, in a bid to fox the police and make out that the alcohol in his system was merely from the hurried succession of beverages he'd just downed – as one does – after getting inside. 'I mean, the police were at the door, and the door was open,' Shirley says. 'They were like, "Come out here ..."'

Chapter 14

41. A title possibly inspired by *The Dice Man* by Luke Rhinehart (pen name of George Cockroft), a book the Feelgoods loved and were inspired by, often rolling the dice to make a decision and see where it took them.

42. Clash tour manager and raconteur Johnny Green gets yet another nod, in 'Take A Tip', although this mention is perhaps not the most flattering kind. 'Oh Christ,' groans Lee as 'Johnny' approaches the imaginary bar. 'How many more times do I have to listen to this bloke burble?' We are also treated to Lee's oddly convincing 'lady voice' in his imitation of a predatory groupie. 'Bend Your Ear' is, as Lee put it, 'very unusual'.

43. Shirley's first foray would be making pots of chicken liver pâté, working from a Delia Smith recipe, albeit using what can only be described as 'Feelgood measures' when it came to the more interesting ingredients (brandy, for example). 'I'd made this pâté and I thought, that's good. But if a little of this is good, then more is better, right?' She was clearly the woman for Lee.

Chapter 15

44. The Feelgoods had also covered Rush's 'Love Hound' on *A Case Of The Shakes* – and Lee would also buy and treasure a portrait of the bluesman painted by none other than Malcolm Wilkinson, Lee being the first person Wilkinson had ever sold a painting to.

45. The video was directed by Charles David Whiting, Adam Ant's stylist for the 'Stand And Deliver' music video and artwork in 1981.

46. Barney Bubbles was the radical British graphic artist often employed by Stiff Records and very much associated with the UK new wave scene. He also directed music videos, including 'Ghost Town' by The Specials. Paul

Gorman's *Reasons to Be Cheerful – The Life and Work of Barney Bubbles* is a recommended tome.

47. In a bizarre coincidence, when I first moved to Leigh on Sea myself, it turned out the flat we'd chosen to rent was next door to The Proceeds. (I didn't know about The Proceeds at the time, so the sign outside hadn't caught my eye, nor would I have understood the reference if it had.) One afternoon Wilko came round to visit – we weren't sure what his reaction would be, but when we told him about the synchronicity, his response was initially heartening. 'Oh!' he said. 'Well, that makes me very happy.' 'Why?' I asked. 'Because my house is much nicer than his.'

Chapter 16

48. The Grand, now derelict, is awaiting refurbishment at the hands of *TOWIE* star Mike Norcross at the time of writing, although works have been delayed due to a virulent bout of Japanese knotweed. Many former Grand drinkers have migrated to The Broker on Leigh Road, which hosts an excellent pub quiz, by the way.

Chapter 17

49. 'Ideally, I'd be pleased to sing for a humanitarian cause,' said Brilleaux. 'But I believe that those who [do that] can be condescending and few are sincere; it's easy advertising.'

Chapter 18

50. After Brilleaux's untimely death in 1994, Chris Fenwick organised yearly memorial walks and charity shows on Canvey Island, raising funds for the Southend Community Extended Nursing Team, who cared for Lee when he was ill, and the local Fairhavens cancer charity (2014 was the last year the memorial event was held).

51. From New & Lingwood of Jermyn Street, in case you were wondering. And on the subject of 'foot furniture', Lee would surely have approved that the shoemakers Jeffery West have made a series of reassuringly expensive 'Brilleaux' shoes and boots – all with slim, squared-off toes and righteous heels.

52. Gypie Mayo died from cancer on 23 October 2013.

53. Lee's love of the French peasant dish cassoulet, a hearty stew containing beans and sausages, grew to the point that he formed The Royal Belton Hills Cassoulet Club, Belton Hills being situated by Marine Parade overlooking Old Leigh. (I think Lee might have added the 'Royal' himself, presumably enjoying the juxtaposition of the idea of being a toff but chowing down on cassoulet – a 'poor people's food', as he described it.)

54. With the Feelgoods, that is – he'd make an appearance playing slide guitar and providing backing vocals on the 1991 release *Escape From Oil City* by the Canvey Island All Stars – a group made up of local musicians featuring

the likes of Dean and Warren Kennedy, Paul Gray from Eddie and the Hot Rods, Ian Gibbons, The Damned's Roman Jugg, Phil Mitchell and Larry Wallis. The CIAS are still going, with a flexible line-up (including Lew Lewis and Pete Zear), to this day.

55. 'One foot in the water, one foot on the pier' – the lyrics of 'Down By The Jetty Blues' are a little prescient; with hindsight they seem almost indicative of someone who is stepping between two worlds and is soon to move on, which, it would sadly transpire, he was.

Chapter 19

56. 'I started a second portrait in 1993 after he was diagnosed with cancer – his idea,' says Farrell. 'I don't show it. I would have been happy to not carry on but he insisted. It was very painful. He last posed on the tenth of March 1994 and he died on April the seventh.'

57. Shortly before Christmas 2012, Wilko was diagnosed with pancreatic cancer, and, having refused chemotherapy (wisely, as it turned out), he was given eight months to live. After a farewell tour during which Wilko felt no ill effects (other than the increasing size of 'Terry the Tumour', as Wilko called it), he had his case reviewed, underwent major surgery and was declared 'cancer-free' in 2014.

With Compliments

from

Dr. FEELGOOD

CANVEY ISLAND
ESSEX.

Telephone: (0268) 694888